METALSMITHING

for jewelry makers

For dear Barbara—"What laughs"

First edition for North America and the Philippines published in 2014 by Barron's Educational Series, Inc.

Copyright © RotoVision SA, Sheridan House, 114 Western Road, Hove, East Sussex BN3 1DD, England

All inquiries should be addressed to:
Barron's Educational Series, Inc.
250 Wireless Boulevard, Hauppauge, New York 11788
www.barronseduc.com

ISBN: 978-0-7641-6584-9

Library of Congress Control No.: 2013941059

Printed in China

9 8 7 6 5 4 3 2 1

Commissioning editor: Isheeta Mustafi
Editor: Angela Koo
Assistant editor: Tamsin Richardson
Art director: Emily Portnoi
Art editor: Jennifer Osborne
Cover design: Emily Portnoi
Design and layout: Emma Atkinson and Jennifer Osborne
Photography: Michael Wicks
Picture research: Heidi Adnum
Images of tools: Cookson Gold
Technical adviser: Courtney Gray
www.courtneygrayarts.com

Image credits
Front cover
Row 1 (L-R): Recycled gold and natural opal ring by Christine Mighion; Anodized titanium bangle, by Vanessa Williams; Silver clay pendant, by Esmeralda Woestenenk
Row 2: Aquamarine and palladium white gold ring, by Lilia Nash; Gold cuff, by Doron Merav; Silver clay earrings, by Anna Siivonen
Row 3: Silver laser-cut bracelet, by Sakurako Shimizu; Silver pendant with diamond, by Michelle Chang; Moissanite and gold stacking rings, by Tamara McFarland
Row 4: Roll-printed silver ring, by Maria Apostolou; Silver earrings, by Esmeralda Woestenenk; Titanium and silver earrings, by Marina Lampropoulou

Back cover
Row 1 (L-R): Patinated bronze ring, by Stephanie Maslow-Blackman; Palladium and gold ring set with moissanite, by Tamara McFarland; Silver and topaz necklace, by Elan Lee-Vance
Row 2: Gold and diamond necklace, by Michelle Chang; Silver round wire ring, by Cynthia Nge; Silver and diamond ring, by Michelle Chang
Row 3: Patinated silver earrings, by Anna Siivonen; Gold ring, by Doron Merav

METALSMITHING

for jewelry makers

traditional and contemporary techniques for inspirational results

JINKS McGRATH

BARRON'S

CONTENTS

Clockwise from top right:
Steel brooch, by Iris Saar Isaacs; Gold ring, by Niessing; Gold and diamond ring, by Niessing; Silver necklaces set with a variety of stones, by Kirsten Muenster.

SECTION 2
TECHNIQUES

SECTION 3
GOING PRO AND RESOURCES

INTRODUCTION

In the mid-seventies, the opportunities for studying metalworking and jewelry were few and far between. I was lucky enough to be living just around the corner from one of the few colleges offering part-time courses, and the occasional full-time one, which I was able to take advantage of. There were also very few books on the subject at that time, the main one being what we referred to as our "Bible"—Oppi Untracht's *Jewelry: Concepts and Technology*—for which I and the two other full-time students were eternally grateful. For the sheer volume of information as well as his enormous attention to detail, Oppi, for me, remains the top man.

However, during the last decade or so there has been an explosion of different courses and hundreds of different books covering every aspect of the art and craft of metalsmithing and jewelry. Students now have fantastic choices when it comes to learning and reading.

I cannot begin to claim that I have covered even half of these subjects in this book, but I hope that what is here will be of some use, both to budding jewelry makers as well as those wanting more information to further their career. I hope, too, that this book will inspire those who simply enjoy being creative and working with their hands. Making jewelry is a hugely rewarding discipline and lives up well to the old saying, "Practice, practice, and more practice makes perfect!"

This page: Silver double ring, by Jinks McGrath.

Opposite: Gold necklace, by Jinks McGrath.

SECTION 1
TOOLS AND METALS

1. TOOLS

This section provides details on all of the essential hand tools, electrical machinery, chemicals, and other equipment that you are likely to need as a professional metalworker. Some are everyday items that can be purchased in a local hardware store; others will be available from specialist suppliers. Naturally, tools vary in price —from a few dollars for a good steel rule, up to a lifetime investment for more complex machines.

Of course, you will not need to possess all of these items initially, but you should aim to equip yourself with the basics, and to familiarize yourself with the rest, so that you can acquire them as necessary as you progress along your journey.

Previous pages: Various metalsmithing tools.

Opposite and above: A selection of the different tools to be found in a jewelry workshop.

DRAWING, MEASURING, AND MARKING TOOLS

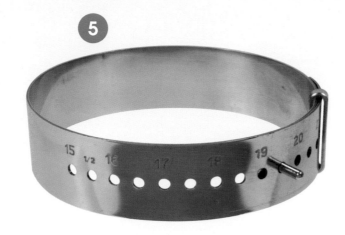

1. **Steel rule:** This shows both inches and millimeters, and is useful when you need a straight edge.

2. **Set square:** The set square can be used to mark a parallel straight line by holding one edge against a straight side of a sheet of metal.

3. **Digital vernier:** The calipers of this vernier open to measure both the inside or outside dimensions of a piece, given in the digital display in either metric or imperial. (The inside measurement is taken using the smaller top jaws.)

4. **Ring sizer:** This tapered stick features ring size markings. The size of a ring is established by sliding it down to the closest-fitting marking.

5. **Bracelet sizer:** This measures hand or bracelet size. It is placed on the wrist and adjusted using the movable pin to achieve the correct size (in centimeters).

6. **x10 loupe:** A workshop essential, this is held close to the eye to inspect older settings, look closely at stones, etc.

7. **Ring sizer:** This collection of graduated rings is used to establish a ring size by finding the ring that fits best. Sizes are marked on top of each ring, in both full and half sizes.

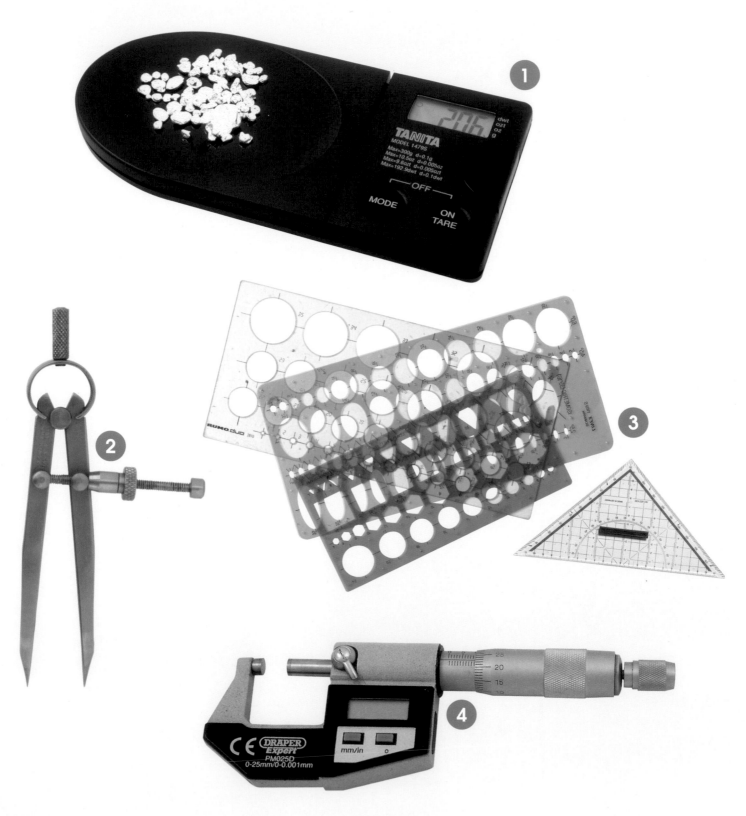

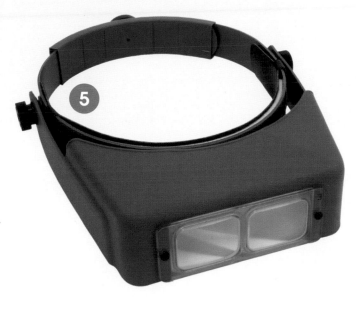

1. **Pocket scales:** Choose your pocket scales carefully. It is useful if they show weights up to two decimal points so that stones and small pieces can be weighed accurately. (Those shown here measure weights in both grams and ounces.)

2. **Dividers:** Dividers provide a very accurate way of measuring distance. They are also used for drawing a straight line when one side is held against a straight edge.

3. **Oval, round, triangular, square templates:** These are used for drawing directly on metal using either a sharp pencil or a scribe.

4. **Micrometer:** This measuring tool shows both inches and millimeters. The piece being measured is placed in the gap and the handle is turned until the gap is closed around it. The end is then fastened to find the measurement, which is read from the handle.

5. **Optivisor:** An optivisor is worn on the head; the visor is pulled down over the eyes. These have good magnification, and are best if they also include a light.

6. **Marking punch:** The point of this punch is placed directly on the spot where a hole is to be drilled. The top of the punch is then hit once sharply with a ball-peen hammer to leave a little indent.

7. **Scribe:** The sharp metal point of a scribe is used to draw directly on metal.

8. **Letter punches:** These punches come with a full alphabet and, as with a marking punch, they are held directly above the work and struck firmly on top with a ball-peen hammer—or a mallet, for a lighter touch.

CUTTING TOOLS

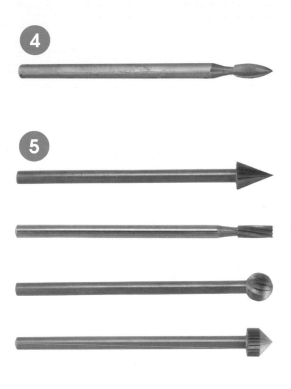

1. **Piercing saw:** This is an adjustable piercing saw, which means that any broken blades (if they are not too short) can be reused. The blade is fastened first in the top fixing, then pushed against the jeweler's pin so that the bottom of the blade can be fixed under tension.

2. **Chenier cutter:** A length of "chenier" (or tubing) is placed in the V slot of this tool and the required length fixed by the flat end, which is shortened or lengthened to suit. A piercing saw is then used to cut the chenier, guided by a slot that it cuts into.

3. **Craft knife:** This useful tool is used to cut away any excess glue when fixing anything. Always work with the blade away from you, never toward your fingers.

4. **Diamond-cutting tool:** Diamond-cutting tools generally come in a set of ten or more, and are fixed in the flexible shaft of the pendant motor. These different shapes give access to curves and hollows. Use them carefully as they will remove metal quite vigorously.

5. **Burrs:** These burrs are used with the pendant motor. They usually come in a small stand containing at least 12 separate burrs, and are used specifically to open settings of faceted stones. They have sharp cutting edges, so they should be stored carefully.

6. **Saw blades:** Blades to fit in a piercing saw come in little bundles of 12. The finest cut is achieved with a 06, and the largest with a +6. Very fine blades are used to cut very thin metal, and the coarsest ones are used for thicker metal of 10 gauge or under (3 mm and over).

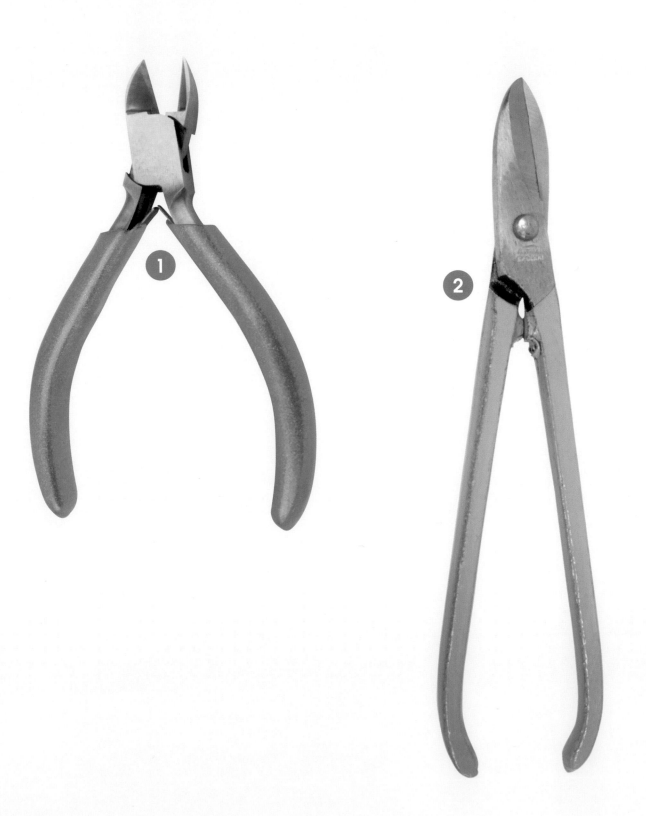

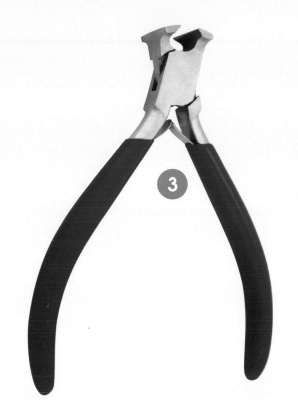

1. **Side cutters:** These are used to cut as close as possible to the edge of something—for example, wire.

2. **Tin snips:** Tin snips are used to cut thinner metal, no more than around 19 gauge (1 mm) thick. They will leave a slightly raised edge that will need to be filed down. They are useful for cutting up strips of solder.

3. **Top cutters:** Once strips of solder have been cut using tin snips, top cutters are used to cut these strips into tiny squares (called "paillons").

4. **Circle cutters:** Before using this tool, all the cutters are removed, then a sheet of metal (no more than 22 gauge /0.7 mm) is placed horizontally into the block. A circle punch is placed into its slot and given a few sharp blows until it has cut right through the metal.

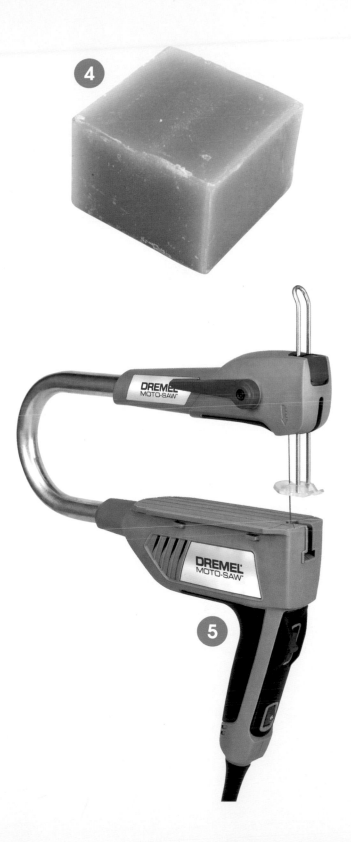

1. **Coping saw:** This type of saw has a larger frame than a piercing saw—approximately 4³/₄ x 7¹/₂ in (12 x 19 cm)—and is fastened with levers. The blades are thicker and have larger teeth. They are used for cutting plastics, wood, and waxes.

2. **Guillotine:** This should be fastened securely to the bench before use and there should be a pin lock fitted to ensure that the blade cannot be moved until required. A line is drawn or scribed on the metal, which is then lined up with the start of the blade when it is raised. It should be held firmly in one hand with the line clearly visible; the blade is then slowly drawn down along the line, with the metal being pushed along in the same direction until the complete line is cut. The blade should always be stored in the flat position. Be careful—they are sharp and heavy.

3. **Skin:** This is cut to fit below a jeweler's bench to catch all of the chips and filings created while working.

4. **Beeswax:** If you run a saw blade through a block of beeswax it will ease the beginning of a cut. Equally, if a few drops of beeswax are melted onto a strip of wire, it will make pulling the wire through the drawplate ten times easier.

5. **Scroll saw (fretsaw):** A scroll saw has an electric motor, which drives a vertical blade up and down to cut through metal. A piece of metal is held by hand on the flat steel table of the saw and carefully guided along the line that is being cut. These machines are small enough to have in the workshop, but need very special care when being used, especially with metals over 13 gauge (2 mm thick).

HEATING AND SOLDERING TOOLS

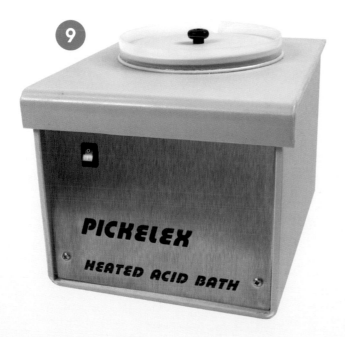

1. **Soldering block:** These blocks are used to support work when soldering or annealing.

2. **Charcoal block:** As charcoal blocks are a lot more expensive than a soldering block, these are only used sparingly. They reflect heat better, and therefore, are useful when reticulating or melting little balls.

3. **Flat soldering block:** This is just a little larger than the normal block, so it is useful for annealing long lengths of wire.

4. **Borax:** This cone is dipped in water and ground in a borax dish to make a milky paste called "flux." It must be painted on and through all joins prior to soldering.

5. **Dish for borax:** This dish is used for grinding a borax cone. Little paillons of solder can also be dropped into the flux produced so that they are coated before being applied to a soldering area.

6. **Revolving soldering tray:** Soldering blocks are placed on a soldering tray so that they can be turned during the soldering process. This makes it easy to see if all the solder has run.

7. **Aurflux/Auroflux:** This is a liquid flux, used in a similar way to borax, but without the need for grinding. It is applied with a paintbrush.

8. **Binding wire:** Reels of this wire come in different thicknesses; it is used for holding pieces together while soldering.

9. **Heated pickle tank:** This contains a plastic container that is filled with water. A small glass container with pickle solution in it is placed within the bath, and the heat is then controlled by a thermostat.

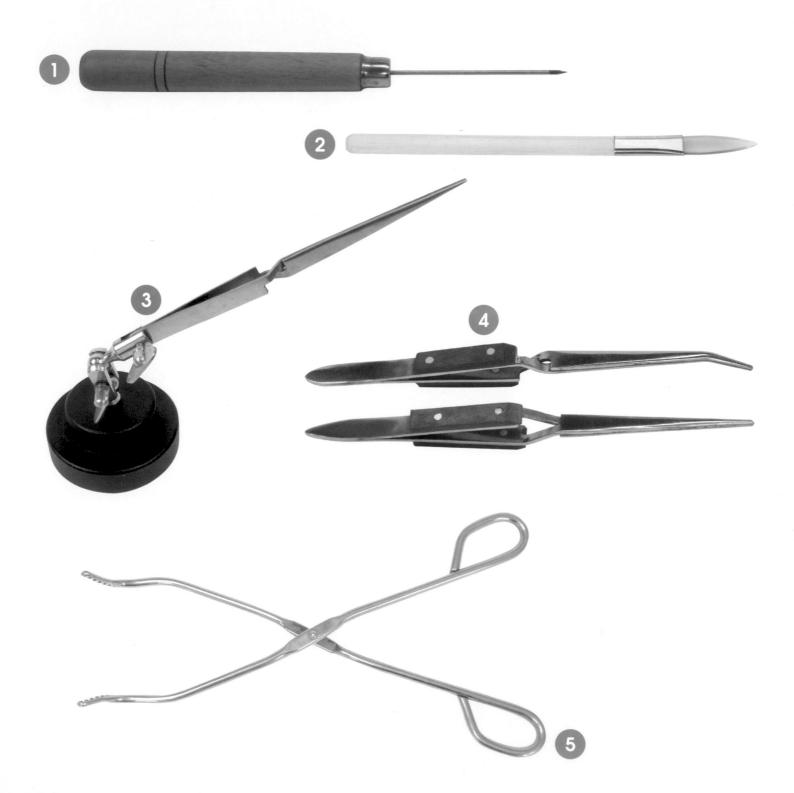

1. **Titanium soldering pick/probe:** This is used while soldering to move any little paillons of solder that are not in the right place back to where they should be, and to gently smooth out the solder as it runs around a join.

2. **Flux brush:** A little brush with a fine point is the best to use when applying flux and paillons of solder. Hold the solder right at the tip and then gently brush it on the area required.

3. **Third arm:** This is a flexible joint into which soldering tweezers are fitted. The tweezers then hold one piece of metal steady while it is being soldered to another.

4. **Insulated tweezers:** These tweezers are handheld or steadied on a block themselves, and hold one piece of metal which is to be joined to another.

5. **Brass tweezers:** These are used for taking pieces in and out of the pickle solution.

6. **Rouge powder:** A small amount of rouge powder can be mixed with water and applied with a paintbrush to a previously soldered area that may be vulnerable on a subsequent solder. Make sure it does not spread to an area that does need soldering, and only use it when necessary.

7. **Thermo-Gel:** This thick paste can be applied over a solder join that you do not want to be heated again. It will flake off after each solder, so will need reapplying.

8. **Stainless steel tweezers:** These are used to take pieces in and out of the pickle solution, to move paillons of solder when heating, picking up tiny pieces of wire or balls, placing cloisonné wire for enameling, and taking pieces in and out of acids when etching.

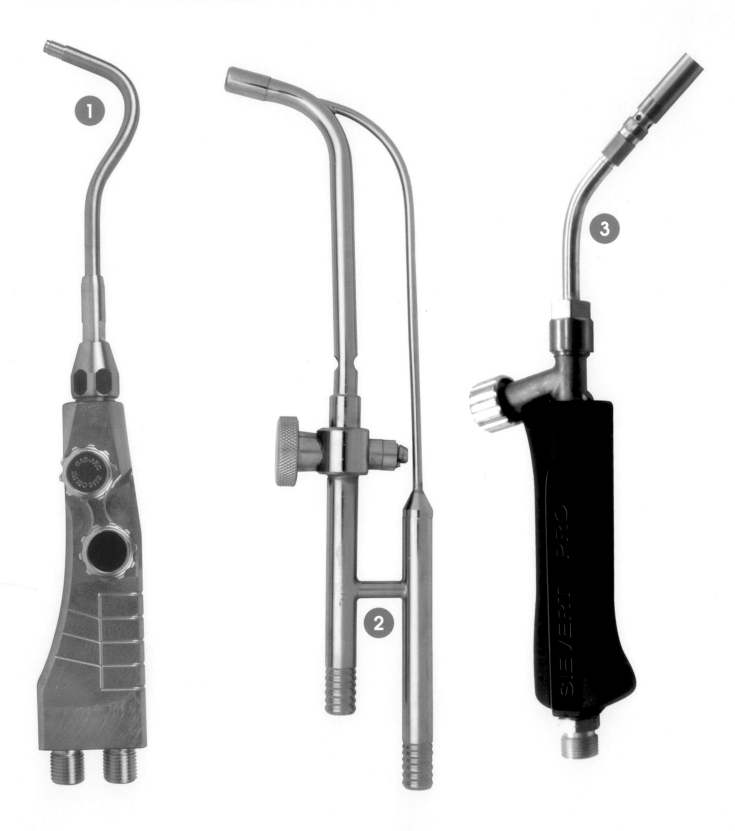

1. **Oxypropane torch:** This torch will give a very high heat if required (enough to solder platinum). It is fixed to both an oxygen cylinder and a propane one.

2. **Mouth-blown torch:** This torch has two tubes. One is connected to a propane gas cylinder with a regulator. The other tube is blown into to introduce some oxygen, which then mixes with the gas to produce the flame.

3. **Propane gas torch:** This only needs to be fixed to a propane cylinder, and different sized heads can be fixed to the torch base. The largest head is hot enough to melt gold, but not hot enough to solder platinum.

4. **Blow torch:** This "crème brûlée" torch has a very small flame and is only really useful for soldering small pieces. It is not suitable for annealing anything larger than around 3 in (8 cm) square.

5. **Solder:** Silver solder comes in strips of hard, medium, and easy. Gold solder comes in little rectangles and the grade is imprinted on them. It is useful to thin solder down through the rolling mill before using, and always scribe "hard," "medium," or "easy" on the end of a silver solder strip so that you know what it is.

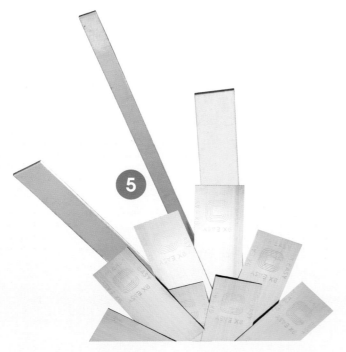

BENDING, SHAPING, AND STRETCHING TOOLS

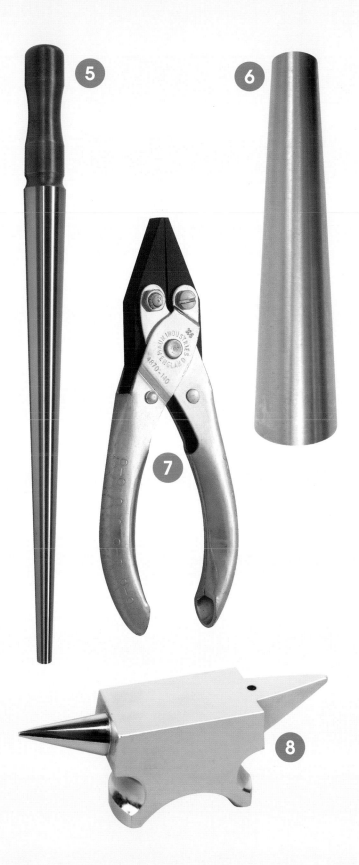

1. **Round-nose pliers:** Used to make loops and small "S" shapes by pulling wire around the nose. If the wire is held tightly between the tips they will leave marks on the outside of the bend.

2. **Snipe-nose pliers:** Used to grip something close to an edge, or to make a sharp bend close in.

3. **Half-round pliers:** Used to make curves and bends, with the curved side held on the inside of the curve being made, and the flat side on the outside. This prevents any marking.

4. **Flat-nose pliers:** Used to make a right angle. These are also used to close up a join in a jump ring or a ring with a side-to-side action.

5. **Collet mandrel:** After making a collet for a stone, it can be shaped on a round, oval, or square mandrel. These allow you to shape the various shapes that cannot be achieved using a ring mandrel.

6. **Bracelet mandrel:** Bracelet shapes can be formed on this mandrel. Always make sure that whatever hammer you are using, that it hits only the work and not the mandrel. If a mandrel has a lot of hammer marks on it they will transfer to any subsequent work.

7. **Parallel-action pliers:** These pliers are really useful when holding anything with parallel edges. They are quite heavy-duty, so they are strong enough to hold larger pieces.

8. **Small anvil:** This is a very useful little tool that can be used to shape curves around the nose, or to hammer little pieces flat.

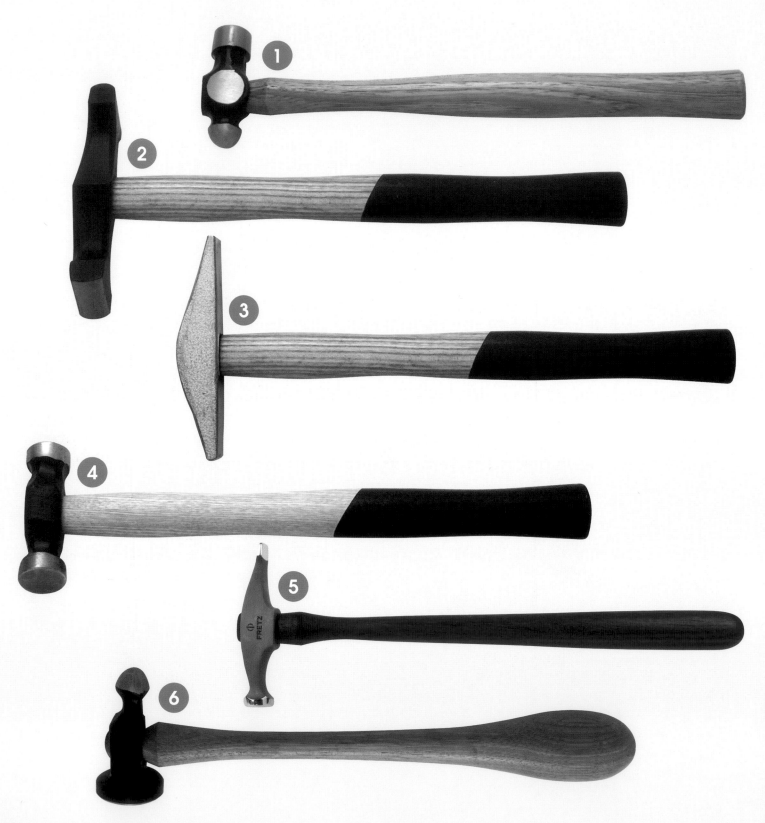

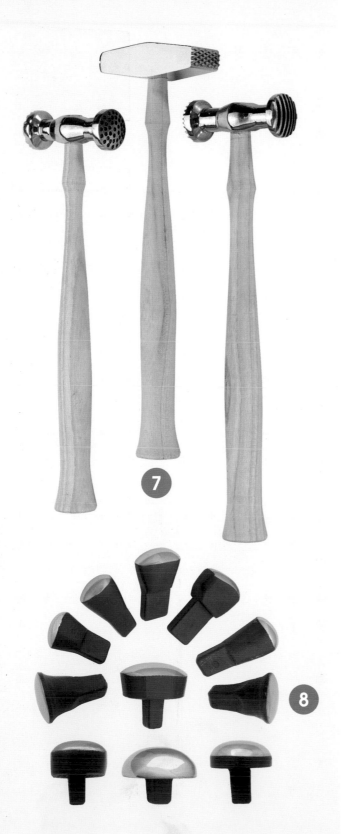

1. **Ball-peen (ball-pein) hammer:** A good all-purpose tool. The round end is used to make indents or add texture, but will spread metal a little. The flat head can be used to strike punches, chisels, or even a small steel plate when flattening metal between two surfaces.

2. **Raising hammer:** Used to stretch metal. This has two curved ends, one slightly more curved than the other, with ends shaped so that they do not mark the metal. Metal is stretched in front of and behind where the hammer strikes.

3. **Wedge hammer:** Used when making anticlastic (saddle-shaped) curves. It can also be used to make indented lines and to stretch metal directly in line with the strike when forging.

4. **Planishing hammer:** Its flat ends, slightly rounded off at the edges, are used with a slightly stroking action over a whole piece to smooth out marks made by other hammers. It should be kept clean and polished.

5. **Jeweler's hammer:** A small, lightweight hammer for anything needing a light touch. The polished flat end is used for making small rivets, flattening wire or sheet, or with a punch to set a cabochon stone. The wedge end is used to create linear patterns.

6. **Chasing hammer:** The larger flat end is used to make short "bouncing" strikes on a chasing tool as it is drawn across metal to mark a line. The round end makes indents.

7. **Marking/texture hammers:** These are used to create different textures on annealed metals.

8. **Metal stakes:** These are held in a heavy-duty vise and used as a support when shaping metal with either a mallet or a hammer.

1. **Drill bits:** Sizes range from very tiny ($1/64$ in or 0.5 mm) up to $3/16$ in (5 mm). Most can be fitted into either a hand drill or a benchtop electric drill. Fasten the drill into the chuck right up to the start of the twist. Always keep the drill perpendicular to the work.

2. **Swage block:** This is used to curve pieces of metal evenly. The metal is pushed down into one of the curves of the block using a former (see p. 45).

3. **Nylon mallet:** Mallets are used to shape metal without leaving any lasting imprint. The work should be held on a firm background.

4. **Hide mallet:** This is used in the same way as a nylon mallet.

5. **Blocking mallet:** The rounded end is used to compress metal into a wooden block with curved depressions.

6. **Wooden bossing mallet:** The narrow end is used to shape metal in a wooden block with depressions in it; the wider end is for shaping metal over a domed stake.

7. **Large wooden mallet:** Available in different woods. A mallet made of lignum vitae is heavier than a box wood or ash mallet, and is used on heavier pieces of metal.

8. **Rolling mill:** Available in a variety of sizes, with various rollers, which can decrease the thickness of sheet metal, roll out melted-up ingots, decrease the dimensions of square wire, and make D-section wire from round.

9. **Doming block with punches/formers:** Metal circles are placed in depressions of a similar size and the rounded end of the matching punch is used to push the metal down.

1. **Drawplate:** Used to reduce the diameter of wire. The drawplate is held in a vise with safe jaws. Different profiles can also be made from a round wire drawn down into, for example, a D-section or square hole. One end of a piece of wire is filed down so that it will fit into one of the holes from behind. It is then pulled through using a pair of pliers with a serrated edge.

2. **Third arm stake:** This stake is held in the vise in the center. This allows the required arm to be held out from the side of the vise.

3. **Steel plate:** This has many uses. Primarily, as it is flat, work that needs to be flat can be placed on it. A smaller flat plate can then be placed on top and a mallet used to strike it. A metal plate is also used with a sheet of wet/dry abrasive paper when rubbing down a flat surface.

4. **Sandbag:** Used to support any work that might get scratched if it is held on the jeweler's pin. It is also used to support engraving and provides a semi-firm platform when shaping soft pieces.

5. **Oval mandrel:** This gives the correct shape to an oval bracelet. It is usual to make a bracelet round first, and then shape it down around the mandrel until it is oval.

6. **Vise:** This should be fixed solidly to a bench or a wall. It is important that it does not move when pressure is put on it. A vise can be purchased with safe jaws, or copper or aluminum can be soldered over existing serrated jaws to prevent work from being marked.

7. **Floor-standing wood block:** This is a heavy block of wood made from part of a tree trunk. Indentations are chiseled out of the top to form shallow or deep, round or oval hollows.

ENGRAVING TOOLS

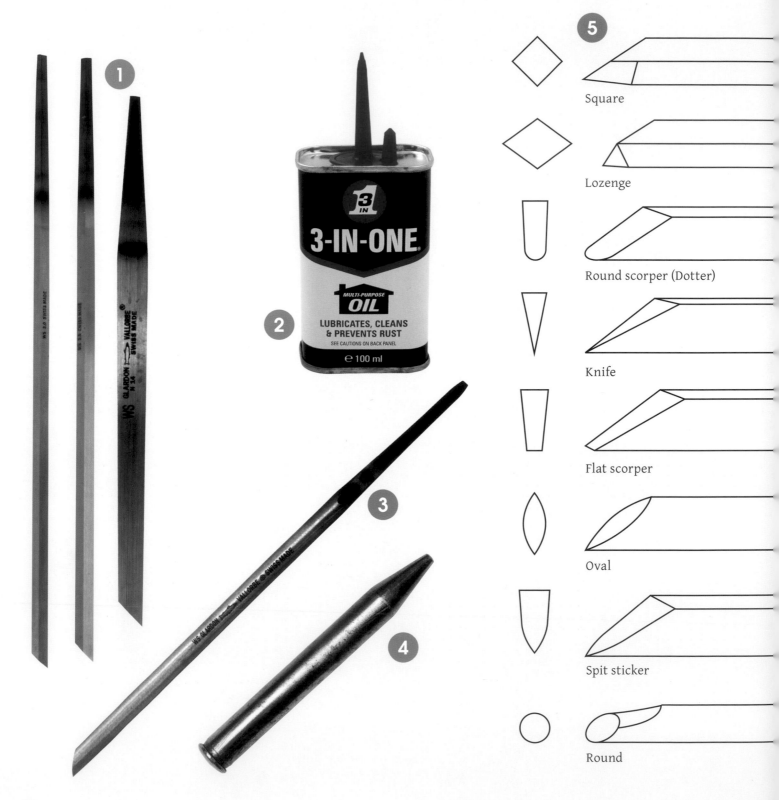

1

2

3-IN-ONE

3

4

5

Square

Lozenge

Round scorper (Dotter)

Knife

Flat scorper

Oval

Spit sticker

Round

1. **Gravers/scorpers:** The basic engraving tools. The tang (base end) is fitted into the handle (no. 9) and, as the ends are sharp, it is a good idea to use a cork on the ends when storing them. See also no. 5.

2. **Oil:** This is used on sharpening stones to allow free and smooth movement when sharpening the ends of the gravers.

3. **Bull stick:** This has to be shaped as described on p. 238. It is used to shave away the inside edges of stone settings.

4. **Onglette:** This graver is often used to neaten up the edge of a stone setting. Its profile allows only the bottom pointed edge to touch the metal, which protects the stone from scratches.

5. **Gravers/scorpers:** These are available with different profiles, which can be used for different thicknesses of lines and curves when engraving.

6. **Carborundum stone:** This stone has two usable sides—one coarser than the other. It is used with oil to sharpen hand engraving tools.

7. **Arkansas stone:** This is a much finer stone. It is used after the carborundum stone to create a smooth finish.

8. **Clamp for engraving:** Used to hold a small piece of metal while engraving, which opens out to size and then has little pins to hold the work steady, in the holes.

9. **Wooden handles:** These are used on the end of engraving tools and should fit neatly in the palm of the hand. Some have a flat side to ensure that they do not roll off the bench.

FINISHING AND POLISHING TOOLS

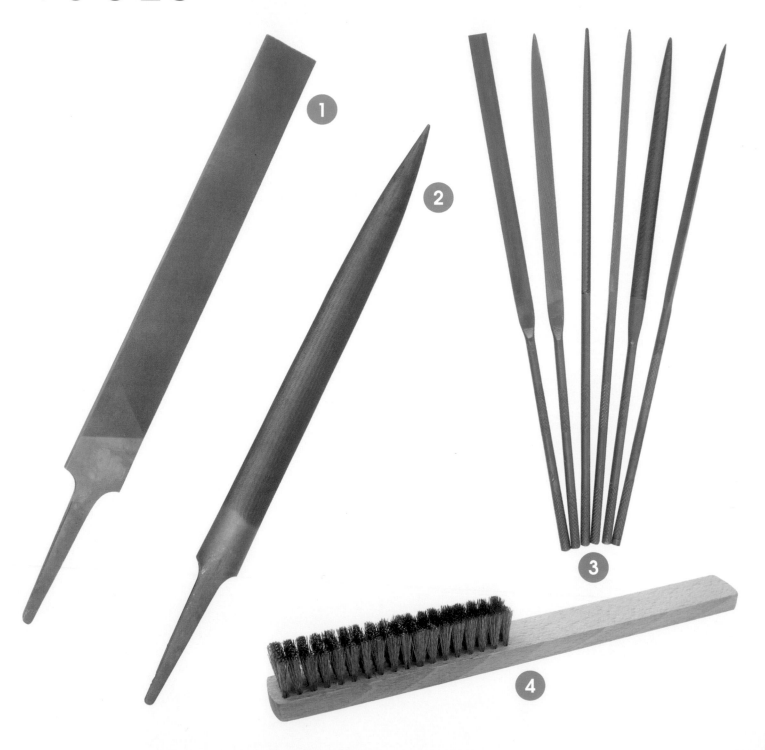

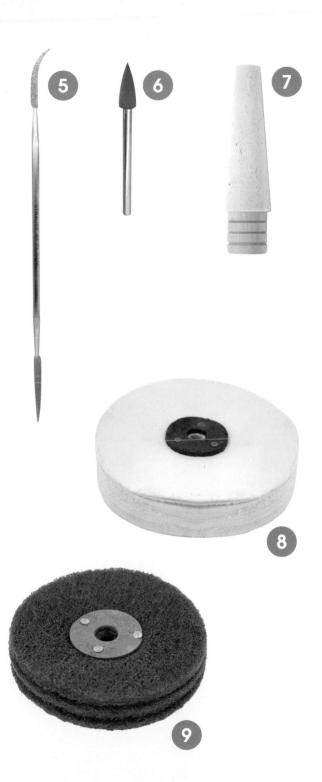

1. **Large flat file:** You will need more than one large flat file. If possible get a wide, coarse one and a slightly smaller one with a finer cut.

2. **Large oval file:** This can have quite a fine cut. It is used to smooth out the inside of a curve.

3. **Needle files:** A set will include a flat, oval, knife, triangular, square, and half round/flat small file. These are used for close or smooth filing.

4. **Brass brush:** Used with liquid soap and water to clean and shine work after it has been pickled.

5. **Riffler file:** This curved file is used to clean up scratches and solder from the inside of curved pieces. Use it sparingly because marks made by the file will have to be removed using graded wet/dry papers.

6. **Silicone point:** Roughly equivalent to a grade 300/400 wet/dry paper, this is used with the pendant motor to smooth the inside of a ring or other curved piece.

7. **Felt ring cone:** This cone is screwed onto one arm of the polishing motor and, when charged with polish, is used to shine up the inside of a ring. Make sure to hold the ring carefully as the cone needs to go right through it.

8. **Muslin polishing mop:** This mop is fixed onto one arm of the polishing motor and is used in conjunction with a medium polish. It may need to be trimmed around the circumference before use. To prevent fraying, scorch the edges using the small flame of a lighter. (This should be done before it is screwed onto the arm.)

9. **Coarse fiber mop:** This mop is fixed onto the polishing motor to give a nice, matte finish.

1. **Small brass brush:** This is held in the pendant motor and used with liquid soap to give a matte finish.

2. **Steel brush:** For use with the pendant motor, this will create a roughed-up surface on metal.

3. **Abrasive cone:** This too is used with the pendant motor and is a coarse cone reserved to remove larger lumps of unwanted solder.

4. **Rubber polishing mop:** For use with the pendant motor, these come in different colors and grades. They will polish in hard-to-reach places without the need for any polish.

5. **Lambswool mop:** Also for use with the pendant motor. This mop is used with rouge polish. For a smoother finish, the rouge polish should be dipped in turpentine before charging the mop.

6. **Polishing strings:** These are hung from a hook on the workbench and are used to clean difficult areas, such as joins and borders. The strings should have lighter fuel dripped along them before the required polish is rubbed on.

7. **Finger guard:** This is a useful little protector to wear on your index finger when polishing.

8. **Glass brush:** Used to clean the surface of metal so that water runs evenly over it. It ensures that a surface is clean and free from grease. It may be used with liquid soap and should always be used while wearing rubber gloves.

9. **Stainless steel media for barrel polisher:** These little stainless shapes are placed into the barrel of a polisher with a soapy medium and water. The different shapes ensure that all parts of the work are "burnished."

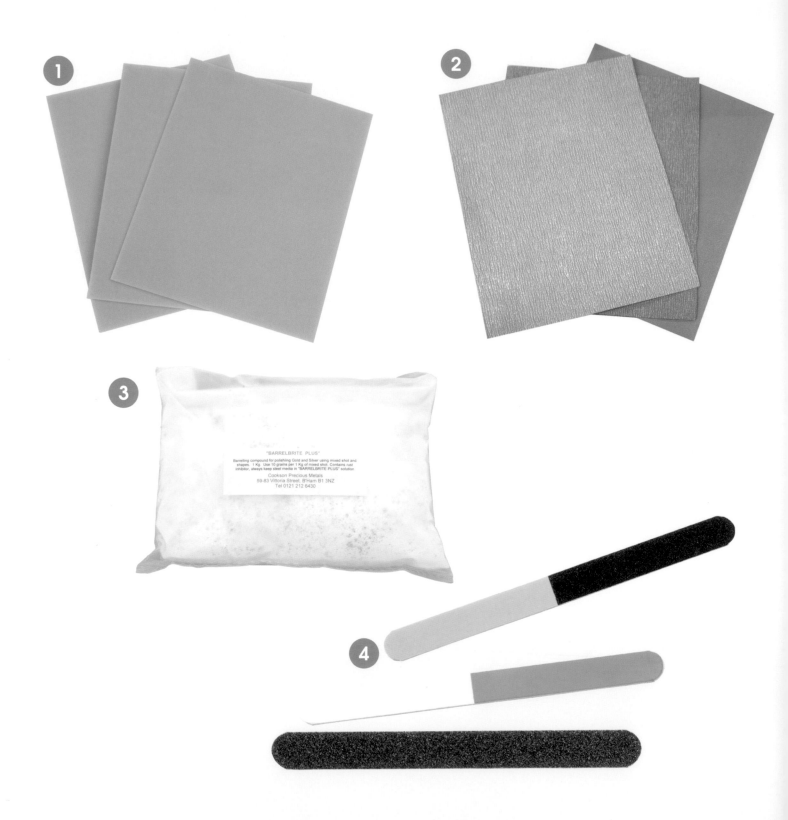

"BARRELBRITE PLUS"

Barrelling compound for polishing Gold and Silver using mixed shot and
shapes. 1 Kg. Use 10 grams per 1 Kg of mixed shot. Contains rust
inhibitor, always keep steel media in "BARRELBRITE PLUS" solution

Cookson Precious Metals
59-83 Vittoria Street, B'Ham B1 3NZ
Tel 0121 212 6430

1. **Fine abrasive cloths:** These come in different grades (the coarsest used first) and are very flexible. Pieces can be cut off from the sheet and used with either a finger or wrapped around a shaped file or equivalent.

2. **Wet/dry papers:** These are used similarly to the polishing cloths except that they can be used either wet or dry, and therefore, are very useful for cleaning up enamels. They can be wrapped around shaped wooden sticks to allow for a more vigorous polishing.

3. **Medium for tumbler:** A full tablespoon of medium with about 2 pints (roughly 1 liter) of water should be enough to create a good cleaning lather in the barrel polisher.

4. **Flexifiles:** A useful addition to your finishing tools, these are medium soft files, not dissimilar to a disposable nail file. They come either in gray—the coarsest—or four different colors (from coarsest to smoothest: dark gray, pink, white, and smooth pale gray).

5. **Polishes:** These are used with mops, either on the polishing machine or the pendant motor. Hyfin is a medium polish, and the green (vert) and rouge are fine polishes that are used to produce the final shine.

6. **Tripoli:** This is the coarsest of all the polishes and is usually used with a brush mop. It will remove light scratches, but not deep ones—that has to be done with a file.

SETTING TOOLS

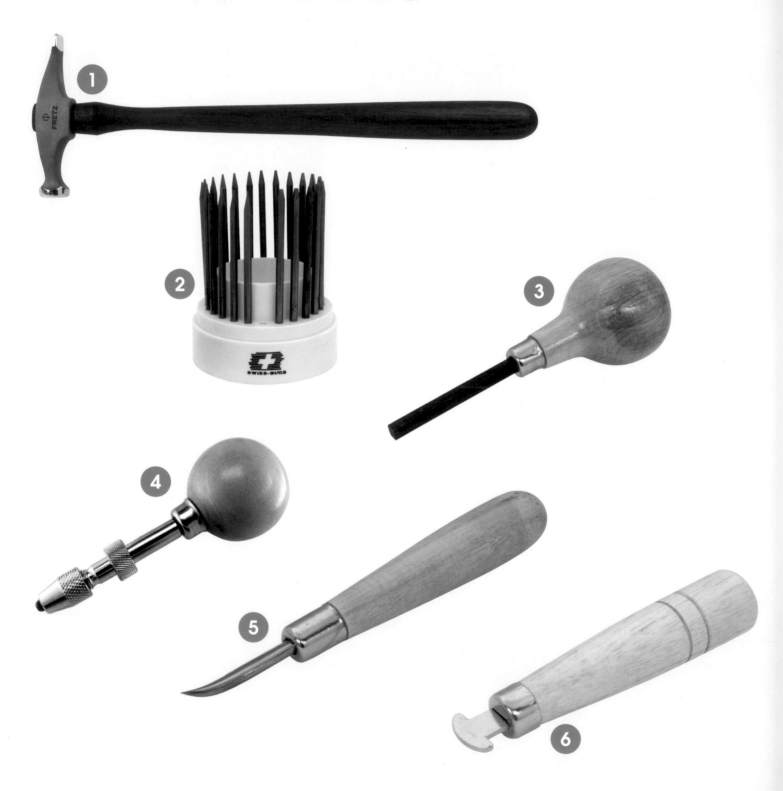

1. **Jeweler's hammer:** This is a well-balanced hammer used for light work and it is especially useful when setting cabochon stones in conjunction with a little punch.

2. **Set of beading tools:** These have different-sized concave ends, which are used to make a little round bead after a grain has been raised to set a faceted stone. They are held in a little handheld pin vise.

3. **Claw pusher:** This handheld pusher is used to push over the claws on a faceted stone.

4. **Handheld pin vise:** Used to hold any small drills, beading tools, diamond drills, or cutters.

5. **Burnisher:** A burnisher is a polished stainless steel tool with either a straight or curved end. It is rubbed firmly against the sides of metal to produce a shine.

6. **Rocket pusher:** This is used to push down the edges of a cabochon setting, using a side-to-side rocking motion.

7. **Collet former:** A cone that has been made for a faceted stone is placed into the right-sized depression in this block and formed to a uniform shape with the punch.

8. **Ring clamp:** The wedge is taken out of the bottom of this tool and the top is opened to receive the shank of a ring. The wedge is then reinserted into the clamp to tighten the ring for setting a stone.

9. **Hammer head:** This can be fixed into the pendant motor. When it is operated it has a little hammering action, useful for going around the edges of a setting to close it down.

CHEMICALS

1

MYLANDS

By Appointment to Her Majesty Queen Elizabeth II
Manufacturers of French Polishes, Stains and Wax Polishes
John Myland Limited, London

CRAFTSMANS RANGE
Wood Finishes

BLACK POLISH

2

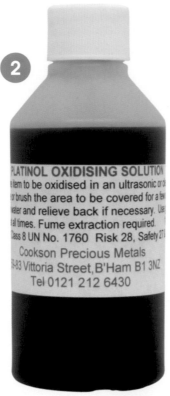

PLATINOL OXIDISING SOLUTION
item to be oxidised in an ultrasonic or
or brush the area to be covered for a
water and relieve back if necessary. Use
al times. Fume extraction required.
lass 8 UN No. 1760 Risk 28, Safety 27

Cookson Precious Metals
9-83 Vittoria Street, B'Ham B1 3NZ
Tel 0121 212 6430

3

"VITEX" SAFETY PICKLE SALTS
For removing oxides from Gold and Silver 1000
grams
Use 50 grams per litre at 30-80C

Un No   Cookson Precious Metal
2811   59-83 Vittoria St, Hockley
7681381   B'Ham BI 3NZ TEL 0121 233 8101
PG II 8.1

"VITEX" SAFETY PICKLE
REFER TO INSTRUCTIONS ON DATA SHEET
Causes Burns. Irritating to respiratory system. In case of
contact with eyes rinse immediately with water & seek
medical attention. Wear suitable protective clothing, gloves
& eye/face protection.
In case of contact or feeling unwell seek medical advise.
SEE HEALTH & SAFETY DATA BEFORE USE

4

PUMICE POWDER
1 Kg

5

BN H917
EXP 09 12
500ml

Protect from light.

6

Contact with acid liberates toxic gas. Causes burns. In case of
contact with eyes rinse immediately with plenty of water & seek
medical advice. Corrosive caustic preparation. Treat as sodium
hydroxide or sodium hydroxide solution. EMERGENCY ACTION:
Spillage. Absorb in earth/sand. Disposal: Through approved effluent
system. First Aid Skin & eyes OR ingestion, consult a Doctor
Ref: T2262680   UN NO. 3262   1/2 KG
YOUR LINK TO A WORLD OF TOOLS MATERIALS CLOCKS & EQUIPMENT

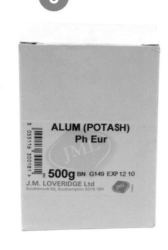

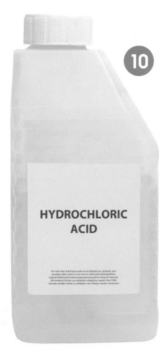

1. **Stop-out varnish:** This is painted on grease-free surfaces prior to etching. It can be thinned if necessary with mineral alcohol. It can be removed easily by heating with a gentle flame.

2. **Solution for oxidizing:** Various branded products are available alongside traditional chemicals such as liver of sulfur to artificially darken the surface of metals.

3. **Safety pickle:** This is used for pickling after soldering. It will remove oxidation and also any flux residue. It works faster if it is warm.

4. **Pumice powder:** This is used with a toothbrush and mixed to a paste with water to clean metal after soldering and pickling.

5. **Sulfuric acid:** This is sometimes used to pickle gold. It can be used to pickle silver, but less toxic substances should ideally be used. (See p. 285 for more information on using acids.)

6. **Potassium sulfide lumps:** One lump added to a cupful of very hot water is enough to oxidize any immersed pieces to a dark gray/black. As the solution cools, it becomes less effective.

7. **Acetone:** This is used to remove unwanted glue and to clean away residue polish.

8. **Alum:** These white crystals are added to hot water to act as a safe pickle. This solution should be used warm to be effective.

9. **Household ammonia:** A small amount of this is added to the water with liquid soap in an ultrasonic machine (see p. 51). It is basically a grease remover.

10. **Nitric acid/hydrochloric acid:** Nitric acid is used for etching and, sometimes, pickling gold; hydrochloric acid is used to etch copper.

CASTING TOOLS

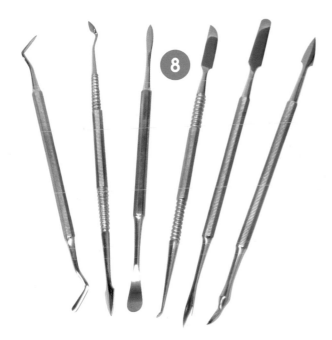

1. **Flasks:** These are used in conjunction with a rubber base to hold wax models. They are then filled with investment powder and left to dry before placing in the kiln for the wax burnout.

2. **Fine charcoal:** This fine powder is added to metal when doing a melt up, and is also used in the fabrication of balls for granulation.

3. **Small crucible:** This is used to melt metal and then pour it out into an ingot maker. Scrap pieces or casting grain are placed in the crucible with flux powder and a little charcoal powder before the melt up begins.

4. **Arm for holding crucible:** This adjustable arm allows for both small- and medium-sized crucibles to be held for the melt up.

5. **Cuttlefish:** These provide an ideal mold for casting. They can be purchased from most pet stores. Try to find thick ones, which can be cut down easily through the middle.

6. **Aluminum mold:** These come in two different sizes and fit together precisely for casting. There is a little line on the outer edge of the top and bottom pieces, which should always be lined up before casting.

7. **Casting sand:** This dense sand is used to pack out aluminum molds. It should be stored in an airtight condition, and any burned areas after casting should be thrown away.

8. **Wax-carving tools:** These usually come in a set and are used to shape and form soft wax.

9. **Block wax:** Wax comes in all different shapes and sizes. You can cut what you need from a large wax block, or you can purchase it already smoothly sliced.

ELECTRICAL TOOLS

1. **Polishing motor:** Arms are fixed to this machine's spindle and will receive all types of polishing mops, texturing steel mops, abrasive mops, etc. This should be used in an area with an extractor fan or, at least housed in a box to reduce the amount of polishing dust. Always wear a face mask.

2. **Ultrasonic machine:** This is used to clean work after polishing. Household ammonia and liquid soap is added to water in the machine and the work is held in a little basket that comes with it. The dial for the ultrasonic is then turned to as many minutes as are required. Avoid putting your hands in the liquid when the machine is on. The ultrasonic sound can apparently damage bones.

3. **Barrel polisher:** The stainless steel media shown on p. 41 are placed in this barrel together with cleaning medium and water. The lid is then secured and the machine switched on. The barrel then turns on the revolving rods.

4. **Electric drill:** A small electric drill will usually be sufficient for the workshop. This is a safe and easy tool to use. Always hold work firmly when drilling—a movable vise table can be used together with this drill to do this. Or, if you are not drilling something with straight sides that can be held in a vise, place the work on a block of wood instead for drilling.

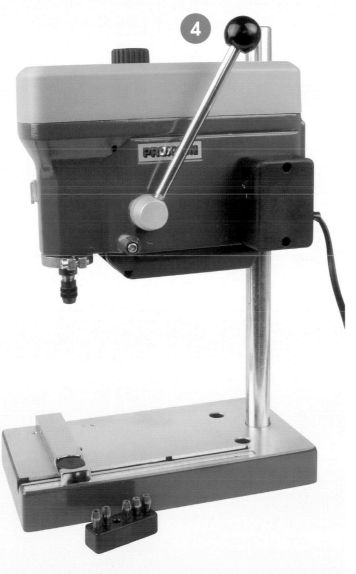

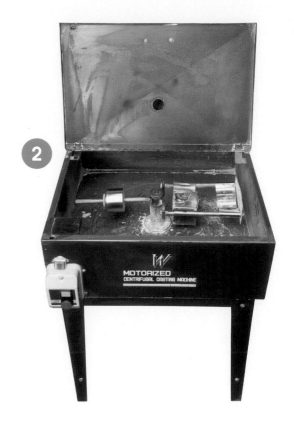

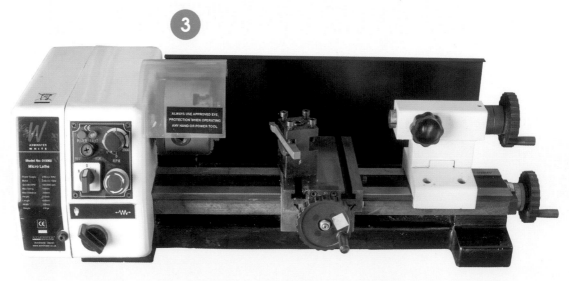

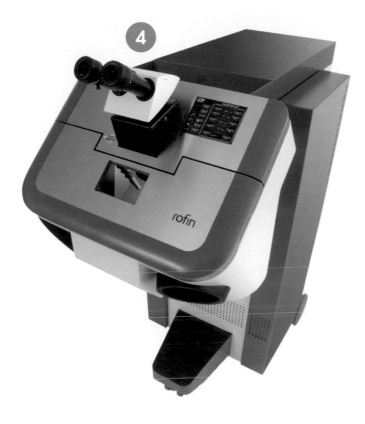

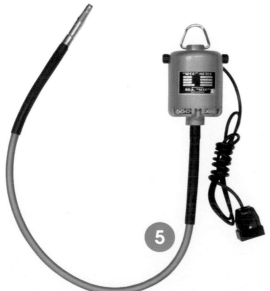

1. **Kiln:** Kilns are expensive, and unless you are going to be doing enameling or lost-wax casting, you will not need one. A gas kiln gives slightly better results for enamelers, but gas bottles should be stored outside the workshop.

2. **Lost-wax casting machine:** This is a machine used in the workshop for casting objects made using the lost-wax method. It is enclosed within a steel box for safety.

3. **Small lathe:** This can be used to cut anything from wax to silver, brass, and aluminum.

4. **Laser welder:** This machine is now becoming very common in small workshops. It uses a laser beam to weld together two parts made of the same material. The two sides being welded are held so that they are touching but with no pressure between them.

5. **Pendant motor:** This motor is operated with a foot pedal. The motor itself should be hung above the bench within easy reach. Many different-sized tools can be fitted into the end head for a variety of purposes.

2. METALS AND THEIR USES

Metals can be divided into two main groups. The first group is composed of "precious" or "noble" metals, while the second group of metals is referred to as "base metals."

The noble metals include platinum, palladium, gold, and silver, which are those most generally used by jewelers, and then others such as rhodium, iridium, osmium, and ruthenium, which are more likely to be used as alloys or plating materials. The noble metals are very resistant to chemical reaction and corrosion. All these metals are "nonferrous," which means that they do not contain iron, so are not prone to rusting.

The base metals are less resistant to corrosion and occur more commonly. These include aluminum, copper, lead, mercury, nickel, tin, and zinc. These metals are also nonferrous. Iron and steel also belong in the base metal group but are "ferrous," i.e., they contain iron and therefore will rust.

Metals are identified by their appearance, color, and weight, as well as other specific characteristics. Ductility refers to the capacity to be drawn out into wire, or stretched through a rolling mill. Malleability describes how easily a material is worked, i.e., extended by beating or hammering. Conductivity is the capacity for transmitting heat.

KEY TERMS

ATOMIC WEIGHT: The weight of 1 atom of a metal compared with 1 atom of water.

SPECIFIC GRAVITY: The ratio of the weight/mass of a given volume of metal to that of an equal volume of water.

Specific gravity is a useful figure to know when working out the weight of a piece of metal. For example: A piece of silver 1 mm thick, 120 mm long, and 80 mm wide will weigh in grams: 1 x 120 x 80 x **10.5** (specific gravity of silver) = 100.8 g. The same size piece of aluminum will weigh: 1 x 120 x 80 x **2.7** (specific gravity of aluminum) = 25.9 g.

(When working in inches, specific gravity may be converted to ounces per cubic inch by multiplying by 0.52686.)

The metals covered in this chapter are organized in order of frequency of use in jewelry-making.

Opposite: Knitted nylon-coated steel wire necklace with crocheted tendrils and gold fill, by Meghan Riley.

Symbol
Ag

Atomic number/weight
47/107.9

Specific gravity
10.5

Melting point
1760°F (960°C)

SILVER

In its pure form, silver is a soft white metal classed as 999.9 silver. For jewelry purposes, this metal is too soft to be practical, so 75 parts of copper are added to the pure silver to make 925, known as "sterling silver."

From time to time, different alloys of silver come on the market to fill a particular need, but in this book, sterling silver is the metal used throughout.

Lower grades of silver between 800 and 900 are commonly used for jewelry in places such as India, Thailand, Pakistan, and Afghanistan. This can be due to the difference in cost and the methods of reclaiming scrap, but an alloy of 800 parts silver to 200 parts copper when reticulated (see p. 204) can produce fantastic folds and contours as the fine silver surface is moved by the interior when it reaches a certain temperature.

FOR TUTORIALS SEE:
Annealing   p. 118
Hallmarking   p. 218
Soldering   p. 120

IMAGE CREDITS
Left: Sterling silver cast and filed rings, by Regine Schwarzer.

Bottom left: Sterling silver lost wax-cast earrings, by Mary Walke.

Center: Sterling silver wax-carved necklace, by Michelle Chang.

Opposite
Top: Silver metal clay pendant, by Esmeralda Woestenenk.

Bottom left: Hand-cut sterling silver and topaz pendant, by Elan Lee-Vance.

Bottom center: Laser-cut sterling silver necklace, by Sakurako Shimizu.

Bottom right: Pierced and blackened sterling silver brooch, by Sabine Amtsberg.

WORKING WITH SILVER

SOLDERING

There are five different solders for silver: enameling solder, which has the highest melting point, followed by hard, medium, easy, and extra easy, each one in turn needing a little less heat in order to flow.

Hard solder flows between 1370 and 1450°F (745 and 790°C); for easy solder it is between 1300 and 1340°F (705 and 725°C). The areas being soldered need to have a good fit and should be clean and dry. Silver will become a bright orange-red as it is being soldered.

Medium solder can be used between hard and easy, but it should be cut into very small paillons, with more of these used around a solder join than those of hard or easy in order to get the best flow.

ANNEALING

Annealing takes place at a temperature of around 1110°F (600°C). This will show as a dull red appearance on the metal.

After it is annealed, silver is quite soft and will work fairly easily. As it is being worked, because of the copper content, it will gradually become harder. It should then be annealed again. After annealing, enough time should be left to turn off the flame and replace the torch before quenching and pickling.

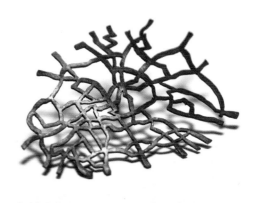

FIRESCALE

After all soldering has been completed on a silver item and it is polished, an area of darker color within the polished silver may appear, which will spoil the overall effect. This is known as "firescale."

When working with sterling silver, firescale is an inevitable part of the process, unless the metal has a protective layer of anti-oxidizing agent applied before every heating. Fine silver (999.9) does not oxidize (turn black) when it is heated, but 925 silver, which is alloyed with copper, will as heat is applied. The reason for this is the copper content. As mentioned on p. 74, when copper is heated, it turns black and can produce a flaky surface.

Further hard polishing may eliminate firescale, but it will also diminish some of the precise dimensions of the work. Luckily, there are other ways of dealing with it.

By annealing and pickling an item several times, a layer of fine silver will build up. This will not have any copper content in it, and therefore it will not have a firescale. However, the surface must not then be filed or polished, as either action will break through the fine layer, exposing the firescaled layer underneath.

A fine stone called a "Water of Ayr" stone can be dipped into water and worked into a paste over the stained area. This is a particularly good way to get rid of the scale—the stone is so fine that it leaves the surface pretty much scratch-free, and it only needs buffing up afterward. It may take quite vigorous working to eliminate the stain completely.

Before each heating, the silver can be painted all over with flux, or an anti-oxidation agent. This can be a bit tedious and awkward when soldering because there has to be an area between the flux used for the soldering and the flux preventing the firescale, which is therefore left unprotected. This method is usually more practical on large silverware than on small pieces of jewelry.

The whole finished item can be either silver-plated (this is a fine silver surface electroplated onto the finished item), or, for a very bright finish, a rhodium plate can be applied.

Lastly, the item can be "bright dipped." Great care must be taken with this method, as it involves the use of nitric acid. The item is dipped in a solution of 4 parts water and 1 part nitric acid; it will quickly turn black. The piece is then removed and rinsed under running cold water, then brushed with a soft brass brush and liquid soap until the silver surface reappears. This is repeated until the silver no longer turns black but stays "bright." The copper content will have been etched from the surface.

Opposite: Solid silver round wire ring, by Cynthia Nge.

Left: Hand-fabricated sterling silver rings, by Kirsten Muenster.

Symbol
Au

Atomic number/weight
79/197.2

Specific gravity
19.3
22 karat = 17.7
18 karat = 16.5
14 karat = 14.5
 9 karat = 11.5

Melting point
1945°F (1063°C)

GOLD

In its pure form, gold is—for me anyway—the most beautiful, soft, lustrous, tactile metal of all. Its durability means that thousands of stunning examples fabricated over the last 6,000 years or more can still be seen in museums today.

Gold remains the most desired metal today. Currencies have been, and to a certain extent still are, based on gold. In times of economic uncertainty, gold always increases in price as investors move away from other commodities and into this most durable of metals. Gold is highly malleable and ductile. It is less conductive than silver or copper, which means that when soldering gold the heat can be applied just around the area to be joined, without, as with silver, having to heat the whole piece. Pure 999.9-quality gold is rarely used for jewelry. The higher-karat golds are alloyed with other metals such as silver, copper, cadmium, platinum, and palladium, while golds lower than 15 karat typically have zinc and nickel as part of their makeup. For jewelry purposes, gold is available in several karats:

24-KARAT: pure gold. Being very soft this is rarely used on its own for an entire piece. It is typically used to add decoration to a stronger metal, and can also be purchased in very thin sheets known as gold foil. (Gold leaf used for gilding wood and plaster is too thin for jewelry.)

22-KARAT: an alloy of 22 parts pure gold and 2 parts other metals—usually copper or silver. The color is a buttery yellow or, if the alloyed metal is mainly copper, it will have a slightly redder look. This is used extensively in Eastern and Middle Eastern jewelry. It is a beautiful metal to work with but, owing to its high gold content, is too soft for delicate pieces.

18-KARAT: an alloy of 18 parts pure gold and 6 parts other metals, such as silver, copper, and palladium. Varying the amount of these alloying metals produces different colors.

WHITE GOLD

This color results from adding silver, palladium, and/or platinum to pure gold. It is suited to delicate work, being malleable yet strong. After finishing and polishing, it is usually rhodium-plated (see p. 100) to maintain a bright finish. Soldered lines can remain visible in white gold; the rhodium plate helps disguise these.

RED GOLD

This color is achieved by alloying more copper than silver to pure gold. It can become hard when working, so it should be regularly annealed.

GREEN GOLD

A small amount of cadmium mixed with copper and silver is the alloy for making green gold. It is not used very often, but it is malleable and has a very pretty appearance.

YELLOW GOLD

This is usually an alloy of just copper and silver. Yellow gold is the most commonly used in 18 karat; it is easy to work with and malleable.

LOWER-KARAT GOLDS

Lower-karat golds—14 karat, 10 karat, and 9 karat—are all used in jewelry. The lower the karat, the less fine gold makes up the content. These golds are also available in different colors, and the same guidelines apply when annealing, quenching, and soldering.

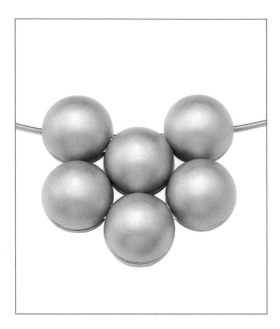

FOR TUTORIALS SEE:
Annealing   p. 118
Finishing   p. 164
Hallmarking   p. 218
Soldering   p. 120

IMAGE CREDITS
Left: Gold pendant, by Niessing.

Center: Champlevé enameled hand-engraved gold rings, by Rachel Emmerson.

Opposite
Top: Gradiated gold disk necklace, by Niessing.

Bottom left: Hand-forged, gold-plated silver ring, by Sabine Amtsberg.

Bottom center: Gold ring, by Niessing.

Bottom right: Bezel-set tsavorite in white gold ring, by Lilia Nash.

WORKING WITH GOLD

SOLDERING

White, red, and yellow gold all have solders to match their colors. The solders are available in hard, medium, and easy and are applied in the usual way (see p. 120).

To achieve a neat solder join in gold, the pieces to be soldered should have a really close fit (gold solder will not run and fill gaps the way silver solder may do), and the paillons of solder should be quite tiny. Using more tiny pieces rather than fewer bigger pieces will give a much better result.

- Low-karat easy solders will melt between 1200 and 1330°F (650 and 720°C).
- High-karat easy solders will melt between 1290 and 1320°F (700 and 715°C).
- Low-karat hard solders will melt between 1390 and 1460°F (755 and 795°C).
- High-karat hard solders will melt between 1450 and 1525°F (790 and 830°C).

ANNEALING

Annealing takes place between 1200 and 1380°F (650 and 750°C). A dull red color can be seen in all the different colored golds when annealing.

QUENCHING

Different alloys of gold need quenching at different times after annealing. The options are as follows:
- Quench straight after turning off the flame.
- Quench once the metal has cooled to black heat (i.e., at about 840–930°F/450–500°C).
- Do not quench but allow to air cool.

If your alloy feels hard to work after annealing and quenching in the usual (first) way, try either the second or third method until the metal feels soft. This applies to all colors and all karat golds.

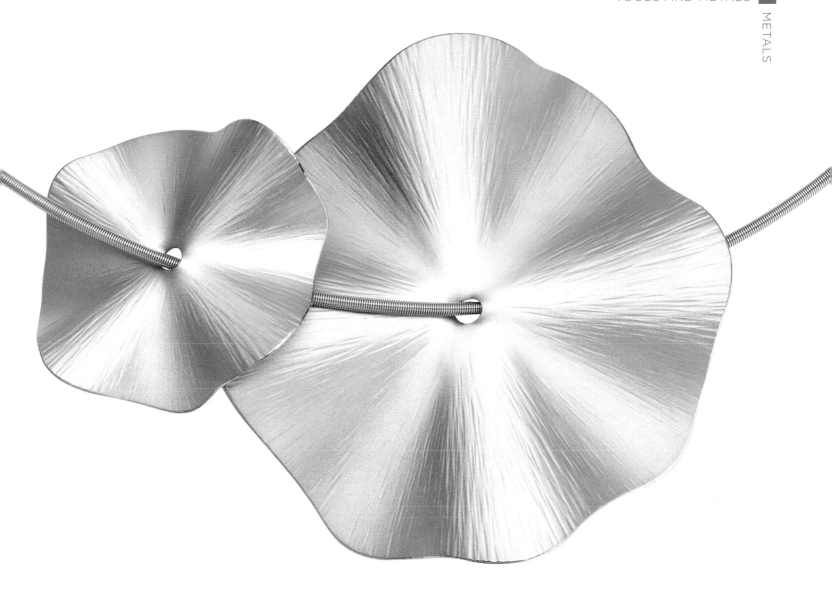

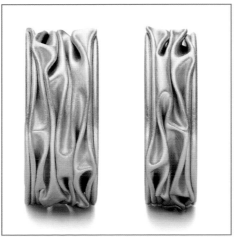

Symbol
Pt

Atomic number/weight
78/195.1

Specific gravity
21.5
950 platinum = 21.1

Melting point
3217°F (1769°C)

Color
Whitish gray

PLATINUM

Platinum has only been used extensively in the jewelry world for the last hundred years or so. Its strength and resistance to oxidation, plus its attractive color, make it a very practical and desirable metal.

Platinum is a strong, comparatively heavy, and malleable metal. It polishes to a very high, bright finish. It is not very conductive. It is highly resistant to oxidation and retains its polished finish even after soldering temperatures are applied, which makes it a perfect metal for intricate work, where finishing each piece to a high polish, before soldering to another, is not compromised. Due to both its strength and malleability, platinum has traditionally been used for setting diamonds; its color also offsets the brilliance of the stone beautifully. Its strength allows for finer dimensions than would be possible with high-karat golds or silver. Pure platinum, 999, is rarely used for jewelry because, like other pure precious metals, it is too soft. Platinum for most jewelry manufacture is an alloy of 950 parts platinum and 50 parts copper. For a casting alloy, the 50 parts would be made up of a mixture of copper and cobalt.

Other alloys of recognized quality are:
• 850 parts platinum and 150 parts iridium
• 950 parts platinum and 50 parts rhodium

When purchasing platinum, it is a good idea to find out what the alloy is, since different alloys have slightly different working properties. Your supplier should be able to provide you with the relevant information.

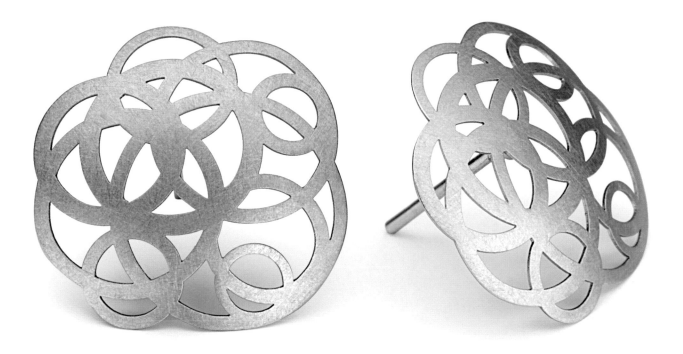

FOR TUTORIALS SEE:
Annealing   p. 118
Finishing   p. 164
Hallmarking   p. 218
Soldering   p. 120

IMAGE CREDITS
Left: Platinum earrings set with tzavorites and diamonds, by Gordon Aatlo Designs.

Center: Gold and platinum rings, by Niessing.

Opposite
Top left: Matte-finished pure platinum pendant with green tourmaline and diamonds, by Gordon Aatlo Designs.

Top right: Hand-fabricated platinum and gold pendants set with tanzanite, by Gordon Aatlo Designs.

Bottom: Wax-carved platinum and antique diamond ring, by Anna Bario.

WORKING WITH PLATINUM

CONTAMINATION

Working with platinum is, in most ways, similar to working with other precious metals—it does most of what they will do. The difference is in the way platinum is handled, as contamination with other metals or materials, such as charcoal blocks, is very detrimental. (Charcoal blocks contain charcoal and, as is the case with palladium too [p. 70], they will, when heated, contaminate platinum.)

Platinum should therefore be kept very clean as it is being worked. After contact with metal tools in the workshop—i.e., rolling, hammering, drawing down wire, etc.—it should be pickled in a warm nitric acid solution (10 parts water, 1 part nitric acid) to make sure there is no contamination. Better still, clean your tools before using them with platinum, or have tools specifically for platinum. Any particles of other metals that are accidentally deposited onto platinum will, when heated, burn and leave small holes in the surface of the platinum, which will then be difficult to remove.

ANNEALING

Annealing in the correct way (see p. 118) is important. If the annealing temperature is not reached or is not maintained sufficiently, the metal can become brittle and take on an orange peel-like appearance.

SOLDERING

Platinum has a high soldering temperature, which requires special soldering torches. These can either be a mixture of oxygen and propane, or oxygen and hydrogen. Special dark goggles are worn when soldering platinum, as the intense yellow light of the metal at high temperatures is harmful to the eyes.

POLISHING

It is a good idea to keep a separate set of files for platinum work, and, if this is not possible, other files should be brushed with a file cleaner before use. Fine abrasives of 800, 1,500, 4,000, and up to 8,000 are used to polish the surface. These are available either as finishing papers or polishing wheels and they should all be used exclusively for platinum. Polishes should be for white metals—tripoli and hyfin for a general polish, and for a high finish, a green or white rouge containing chromium or aluminum oxides.

Symbol
Pd

Atomic number/weight
46/106.4

Specific gravity
12.0

Melting point
2826°F (1552°C)

Color
Silvery white

PALLADIUM

This bright white metal, similar in appearance to platinum, is a relative newcomer to the world of jewelry making and has only recently been given its own mark of quality.

Palladium that is 95 percent pure is usually alloyed with ruthenium and iridium, which are palladium group metals. Palladium is often used to form the alloy "white gold," the other component being silver.

Palladium belongs to the "noble" group of metals (see p.55). It has a lower density and specific gravity than either platinum or white gold. For a precious metal, it is fairly light, so designs that would otherwise feel a little heavy in gold or platinum can be very well suited to palladium. It can be forged, and the advantage over white gold is that it does not need plating after finishing as it holds a beautiful white shine, which does not deteriorate as plating inevitably does.

Recently, in order to promote palladium, there have been some sponsored competitions to discover just what can be achieved and how inventive jewelers can be with this underrated metal. The difference in cost alone—compared with high-karat gold and platinum—should have the buyers queuing up to purchase items made of palladium, but as of yet this has been frustratingly slow. However, with more exposure and with beautiful, innovative designs becoming more and more available, hopefully this situation will change and palladium will be seen as a true addition to the precious metal market.

FOR TUTORIALS SEE:
Casting   p. 168
Finishing   p. 164
Hallmarking   p. 218
Soldering   p. 120

WORKING WITH PALLADIUM

Although palladium does not really oxidize, it will, when exposed to sulfurous conditions, take on a bluish hue, and temperatures greater than 1470°F (800°C) can produce a palladium oxide on the surface.

CASTING

Palladium does not "fill" (have the same density in the mold) as well as other precious metals do, as it has a tendency to be slightly porous. If possible, arrange the casting to be done in smaller, separate units, which can then be joined together afterward.

SOLDERING

Solder joins, too, can be slightly porous when hard palladium solder is used, so try to have fewer solder joins than when working with other metals.

At 2826°F (1552°C), the melting point of palladium is quite high. As with platinum (see p. 68), special goggles should be worn when soldering, as the heat is very intense and harmful to the naked eye.

Charcoal blocks should not be used when soldering palladium because the carbon they contain will contaminate both palladium and platinum, making them brittle. Therefore, special soldering blocks should be kept exclusively for both metals. Palladium does not need flux to solder and can be soldered with the lower platinum solders, some white gold solders, as well as special palladium ones. Due to some gold content in these solders, the solder line will remain just visible, but after cleaning and polishing, a smoothing over with a burnisher will help to reduce it.

Palladium can be hammered and rolled easily, and can also be drawn down in fine wire.

Symbol
Cu

Atomic number/weight
29/63.5

Specific gravity
8.9

Melting point
1981°F (1083°C)

Color
Brownish red

COPPER

Copper is an extremely versatile, easy-to-work metal, and it is therefore commonly used in a wide range of different applications.

The green roof of Chichester Cathedral in Sussex, England, like that of many old buildings, was made from copper panels that, when they were first in place, were the true golden-reddish color of clean copper. Over the years they have absorbed the sulfur in the atmosphere around them to become the magnificent green we see today.

For artists, most print work begins life with an etched copper plate, while many people suffering from arthritis wear a copper bangle, believing that it will relieve their symptoms.

Copper also has a high conductivity rate—the inner core of electrical wire, for example, takes advantage of this property, being made up of many strands of fine copper wire. Many plumbing fixtures, too, are made from copper tubing, as it is easy to bend and yet sturdy enough to withstand the rough treatment that it may go through when being installed.

Copper oxidizes readily when it comes into contact with air, and when it is being annealed or soldered it will produce a black, sometimes quite flaky oxide. Due to its high melting point, it is almost impossible to melt with the ordinary gas flame generally used by jewelers.

As it is a nonprecious metal, the use of copper in the jewelry workshop is fairly limited. It is more commonly used to make a model or mock-up of a piece that will then later be made in silver or gold. However, when used

for its color, it provides a beautiful contrast with the precious metals. In countries where there are hallmarking regulations (see p. 218), copper cannot be soldered together with a precious metal. It can, however, be used as a seperate metal, and in this capacity it is often seen as a background metal for enamels, which are then set like a stone would be into a silver or gold setting. It is also used to make hollow ware such as candlesticks, bowls, jugs, etc., which, when completed, are usually silver-plated.

When worn next to the skin, copper tends to leave a rather blackish-green mark, which probably accounts for it not being used to a great extent for jewelry. Copper is also one of the most important elements alloyed in varying small quantities to precious metals, either to increase their hardness, give a richer color, or lower the karat of gold.

FOR TUTORIALS SEE:
Etching   p. 260
Finishing   p. 164

IMAGE CREDITS
Left: Copper and sterling silver pendant, by Elan Lee-Vance.

Center: Patinated copper necklace, by Elan Lee-Vance.

Opposite

Top: Patinated copper clay pendant, by Anna Siivonen.

Bottom left: Hammered and oxidized copper and sterling silver ring, by Elan Lee-Vance.

Bottom center: Stamped copper, nickel silver, and aluminum pet ID tag, by Melissa McGraw Petrusch.

Bottom right: Hammered copper and sterling silver ring, by Elan Lee-Vance.

WORKING WITH COPPER

HAMMERING

Copper should be annealed before hammering, as it will then be beautifully soft and respond well to the blows of the hammer. However, it hardens quite quickly, so as soon as it becomes difficult to move the metal it should be annealed again. It will spread well and is very useful as a practice metal for a precious metal item. The surface of copper will take on the marks of the hammer, so use a wooden mallet to shape it over stakes and mandrels if the desired result is a smooth finish.

ETCHING

Copper is etched very successfully with a solution of 4 parts water to 1 part nitric acid. This solution etches quite quickly, so it can suffer from slight undercutting. For a slower etch, a solution of ferric chloride can be used: 10 fl oz (300 ml) of hot water is poured onto 9 oz (250 g) of ferric chloride granules and mixed until dissolved, then enough warm water is added to make it up to 20 fl oz (500 ml). The solution is kept warm to allow the etching process to develop.

POLISHING

After soldering, copper can just be quenched in water, and the surface, which will be oxidized, can be cleaned with a coarse 240 wet/dry paper. However, it can also be pickled, which will eventually clear the surface of oxides. Any file marks can be removed with wet/dry paper (ranging in grade from 240 through 400, 600, and 1,200) and then polished. Keep any mops seperate for nonprecious metals. Copper can take on a really good shine by using a tripoli polish followed by a rouge polish.

When copper is left in air, it will oxidize quite quickly, so after polishing the surface, it can be treated with a thin layer of palm oil, a wax polish, or a clear lacquer. The oxides can also be cleaned off with a special polishing cloth or impregnated wool.

Symbol
An alloy of copper
and zinc

Gilding metal
Cu95–Zn5 (alloy of 95 parts
copper and 5 parts zinc)

Red brass
Cu85–Zn15 (alloy of 85
parts copper and 15
parts zinc)

Yellow brass
Cu65–Zn35 (alloy of 65
parts copper and 35
parts zinc)

BRASS

Brass is an alloy. The main component is copper, and zinc is then
added in varying proportions to create different colors of brass.

These different alloys (see box, above) have slightly
different characteristics. The most commonly used brass
in the jewelry workshop is yellow brass, which can be
used very effectively for chased and repousséd pieces
(see p. 188). It is very malleable and, when worked, will
stay softer for longer than copper. When polished, it can
look quite similar to gold, but with a slightly "harder"
quality to its appearance.

Models made for castings are often made from brass,
and it is a very useful metal for making "mock-up"
pieces as it behaves in quite similar ways to silver
when being heated and shaped. It is soldered with
silver solder.

For costume jewelry, which is often plated with silver
or gold, items can be made from brass with a lower
zinc content.

Gilding metal, essentially brass, is 95 percent copper and
5 percent zinc and is commonly used to make models
and mock-ups in the workshop. It is a soft workable
metal available in sizes down to 29 gauge (0.3 mm).

Brass is often used as a contrasting metal when making
mokume gane (see p. 240), giving the appearance of a
gold layer but without the cost of gold.

WORKING WITH BRASS

When I first started my jewelry training, the metal I worked with was "nickel silver," and I thought I was making my pieces with a slightly lower grade silver. I learned much later that nickel silver is actually yellow brass with nickel added, so there is no silver content at all! Nevertheless, it behaved in a very similar way and was a good, cheap way to make my first pieces. Nickel is rarely added to any metal that is going to be worn, as it produces some nasty allergies.

PIERCING

Piercing brass is very similar to piercing copper. It feels quite coarse but cuts easily, and, as with every other nonprecious metal, the dust and filings should be kept separate from any precious metals.

FILING

Brass files easily, and all grades of silver solder can be used to join it with other metals. It is difficult to enamel, but when alloyed with a very low percentage of zinc, it is possible. It oxidizes in air, so until it is polished it looks a rather dull, patchy yellow. When worn close to the skin it can leave dark "oxidizing" marks on the skin.

PATINATION

Brass can be chemically oxidized with potassium sulfide to turn it black, and there are other chemical products that will produce a green or bluish color. These are usually a mixture of nitric acid and copper sulfate and should be handled with great care.

Note: Silver solder throughout this book refers to the solder especially made for silver, not the solder that is supplied on a coil or on a round rod used in the plumbing industry.

Symbol
An alloy of copper and tin

FOR TUTORIALS SEE:
Casting   p. 168
Lost-wax casting   p. 174

IMAGE CREDITS
Left: Forged and patinated bronze ring, by Stephanie Maslow-Blackman.

Center: Bronze clay earrings, by Anna Siivonen.

Bottom: Oxidized bronze chain bracelet, by Kirsten Muenster.

Opposite
Left: Oxidized bronze clay pendant, by Anna Siivonen.

Right: Sterling silver and bronze brooch, by Elan Lee-Vance.

BRONZE

Bronze gave a whole age of human history its name, and little bronze artifacts, such as brooch pins and hair ornaments, continue to reveal themselves in the ground, having been dropped or hidden many centuries ago.

It gives me a terrific sense of time when I hold one of these brooches and imagine it securing a Bronze Age woman's or man's cloak around them. They look so beautiful with their green patina, built up over such an extraordinary length of time.

Bronze can be used to great effect as a contrasting metal, set against silver or gold—its rich brownish hue can look wonderful. Patination using an oxidizing agent will darken the bronze, while commercially produced mixtures of nitric acid/copper sulfate will give the aged green appearance that we associate with bronze carvings and sculptures.

WORKING WITH BRONZE

Bronze, like brass, is an alloy of copper. Between 10 and 20 percent tin is added to copper to make bronze, and it is primarily used as a casting material for larger objects, such as sculptures, although small castings for jewelry are becoming more widespread. Casting bronze is known as LG3 ("leaded gun metal") and contains some lead and zinc as well as tin. This helps to make it flow better when casting and makes it more malleable as it is being worked.

CASTING

For larger pieces, a model is made in either clay, wood, wax, or plastic. A rubber part mold is then taken of this model, and the inside of each part is painted with a layer of wax and rosin up to $1/4$ in (6 mm) thick. The outer mold is then removed and the wax/rosin model is prepared for lost-wax casting or an impression is made in sand for sand casting. After casting, the runners and risers (which are the equivalent to the sprues and air lines referred to in Casting, p. 168) are removed with a hacksaw and filed flush with the bronze. The shiny metal left by filing is then blended with the whole piece with different chemicals.

Thank you to Marcus Cornish for sharing his bronze knowledge and expertise.

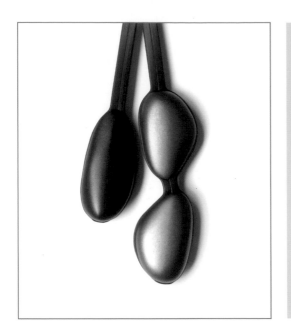

ALUMINUM

Aluminum is the most widely used nonferrous metal and is usually alloyed with other metals to provide a lightweight but durable metal.

For most purposes, aluminum is alloyed with a small amount of copper, zinc, magnesium, manganese, or silicon. Aluminum is a very good conductor of heat and electricity and also has very good malleability, which is what allows it to be thinned right down to foil thickness. (Its softness and low melting point do also present difficulties, however.)

The patination of metal surfaces can produce a variety of different colors—copper, for example, can be heated to become a deep red, and brass can be treated with chemicals to produce a blue or green surface—but this patina can wear off over time. Anodized aluminum, however, can permanently keep an applied color.

Anodizing is the process of using an electrical current to make the surface of the metal porous and accept colored dyes. Small pre-anodized quantities of aluminum can be bought and then treated in the workshop. Alternatively, it can be purchased already anodized, although once taken out of its packaging and exposed to air, the porous metal surface will begin to seal up again, so the surface must be colored quickly before this happens. An infinite number of shades can be painted on, and when resealed the color becomes an integral part of the surface and does not wear off.

As aluminum is such a light metal, items such as earrings and brooches can be proportionately larger, and with the variety of color palettes that are possible, very distinctive designs can be achieved.

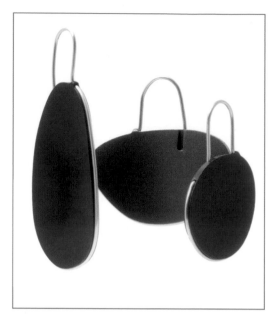

FOR TUTORIALS SEE:
Cutting and piercing   p. 114
Finishing   p. 164
Joins   p. 136

IMAGE CREDITS
Left: Anodized aluminum and sterling silver wire earrings, by Iris Saar Isaacs.

Center: Anodized aluminum and rubber lariat necklace, by Iris Saar Isaacs.

Opposite: Stamped and engraved anodized aluminum rings, by Meghan O'Rourke.

WORKING WITH ALUMINUM

Aluminum is worked in quite a different way from any of the precious metals. Owing to its lower melting point, any aluminum filings or small pieces that find their way onto precious metals as they are being heated will quickly melt into the host metal, leaving a series of disastrous little holes. Due to its low melting point, it is impossible to solder aluminum either to any other metal or to itself. The heat applied while soldering tends to melt the solder before the area round the join has had time to get hot enough. Any heat applied will also destroy the color (and the fumes given off are quite toxic). This throws up lots of practical issues, which have to be addressed in the design, such as riveting one piece to another, setting it like a stone with either a bezel or claw setting, or screwing it together.

CUTTING AND FILING

Any cutting and filing should be done on a clean pin with a fresh saw blade. The dust must be collected separately—take great care to ensure that it does not contaminate any other metal. Aluminum can be cut with a coarse blade in a piercing saw (a little beeswax on the blade before the first cut may help), although it will feel quite rough as the blade cuts through.

FINISHING

Aluminum is an ideal metal for turning on the lathe. It cuts easily and precisely, and the tools from both the lathe and the milling cutter will give a fine satin finish. Before anodizing it is given a bright finish either by polishing or chemically, with a bright dip solution of phosphoric acid, hydrogen peroxide, and water. Polishing by hand is done with wet/dry emery papers first, beginning with 240 and finishing with 800 or 1,200, and then using a stitched mop kept especially for aluminum, with either a tripoli polish or an all-purpose green polish. It can then be given a high finish with a soft mop and a rouge or finishing polish.

Thank you to Penny Warren for sharing her aluminum knowledge and expertise.

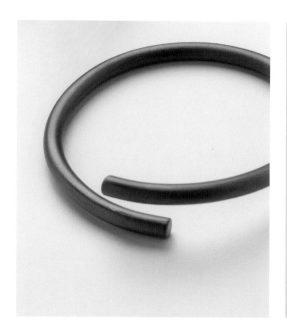

TITANIUM

Symbol
Ti

Atomic number/weight
22/47.9

Specific gravity
4.5

Melting point
3272°F (1800°C)

Color
Gray

TITANIUM

This corrosion-resistant metal is suitable for a number of different applications, but it is particularly appealing to jewelry makers because of the colors produced as a result of oxidation.

Titanium is a very light metal, but it is very strong for its size. It is very resistant to any corrosion, either in air or water, which makes it an ideal metal for industrial components, such as aircraft engines and ship propellors.

One interesting fact that I have only just discovered is that the "star" in a star sapphire or ruby is produced from impurities in titanium dioxide, which occurs naturally in the earth.

Titanium belongs to a group of metals known as "reactive" metals. These metals develop an oxide film when charged with electricity. A beautiful array of colors can be applied to titanium by exposing it to different voltages. This alters the thickness of the layer of titanium dioxide covering the surface of the metal as soon as it is exposed to the oxygen in the air. Niobium is the other member of this group that is used by jewelers.

FOR TUTORIALS SEE:
Joins   p. 136

WORKING WITH TITANIUM

Care must be taken when working with titanium; particles of titanium, if allowed to contaminate saw blades and files used for precious metals, can ignite and burn.

MELTING TITANIUM

The surface layer of titanium oxide affects how the metal can be heated. If it is heated in air as ordinary metals are, the oxide layer will cause it to burn and melt before it reaches its melting point. Therefore, any work with titanium should be carried out separately. Melting the metal is only possible in a vacuum, which is very difficult to do in a jewelry workshop!

SOLDERING

Titanium can not be soldered unless it has first been plated with a solderable metal, such as silver, but then the layer of oxides will not be able to be exposed to electricity to obtain remarkable colors.

Fittings for jewelry purposes can be riveted or screwed on, or, in the case of some aluminum jewelry, glued on.

Symbol
An alloy of tin and lead, brass, or copper

FOR TUTORIALS SEE:

Casting	p. 168
Etching	p. 260
Finishing	p. 164
Soldering	p. 120

PEWTER

Although not a strong metal, pewter is soft and easy to work. As it is much cheaper than precious metals, jewelers are coming up with ever more interesting ways to use it.

Pewter is an alloy, consisting mostly of tin, with lead, brass, or copper. It can be cast to produce large or small objects. There are two different types of pewter—one contains lead and the other does not. The most commonly used is lead-free; it oxidizes less than leaded and polishes to good shine. (If using pewter to make cups, there should be no lead present, due to its toxic nature.)

Pewter is very versatile and can be cast, hand-formed, etched, repousséd, pressed, and more. When designing a piece, remember that pewter is softer than most metals. For example, if hanging a pewter design off a silver ring, the hole the ring goes through must be made thicker so that the silver ring does not quickly wear the pewter away.

Thank you to Fleur Grenier for sharing her pewter knowledge and expertise.

WORKING WITH PEWTER

PEWTER AND SILVER

If just a small filing of pewter is transferred to silver and the silver is heated, the pewter will eat through it to create a pitted hole; the more it is heated, the bigger the hole will become. Avoid this by keeping a separate set of tools and polishing mops for use with pewter.

CASTING

Pewter starts to melt at around 430°F (220°C); to attain a good casting it should be cast from 540°F (280°C). It can be cast directly into a rubber mold, which means your pattern can be made of any material, as there is no heat involved. Incorporating rings into the casting will make it stronger.

ETCHING

Ferric chloride creates a shallow etch in 20 minutes, or a deep one in hours. Electrolytic etching, using salt water and a car battery charger, creates a shallow etch in three minutes.

HAND-FORMING

The techniques for this are the same as for other metals. However, there is no need to anneal pewter, as it is soft to start with and does not work-harden. A sheet of less than 20 gauge (0.8 mm) can be quite soft.

SOLDERING

Due to its low melting point you will need to use a low-melting-point solder and flux. You do not heat the whole piece—only the area that you are soldering, otherwise the low melting point will cause the entire piece to melt quite quickly. For a completely seamless join a strip of pewter can be cut and then melted into the join. This can take a bit more practice and really only works on thicker-gauge sheet or castings.

Symbol
An alloy of nickel, copper, and zinc

Color
Silvery white

FOR TUTORIALS SEE:

Casting	p. 168
Finishing	p. 164

NICKEL SILVER

The earth's core is formed of molten nickel iron, so nickel is found in locations where molten material from the deepest rocks have punched their way through into the crust.

The name "nickel silver" is in fact a misnomer, as it contains no silver at all—it is actually a copper alloy with nickel and zinc added, usually 60 percent copper, 20 percent nickel, and 20 percent zinc. It has a silvery-white color and is a strong, malleable, and ductile metal.

Nickel silver was once used more extensively in the jewelry trade, but its usage declined when it became apparent that it produced skin allergies in many people, in the form of rashes and irritation.

Nickel itself was once alloyed in white golds in different karats, but it is rarely used for this purpose nowadays.

The pure metal is produced from nickel-iron-sulfide minerals that when smelted, have the sulfides (or clay nickel oxides) reduced. In industry, it is a key additive to iron to make stainless steel. The more nickel, the better the quality of steel.

Thank you to Nick Castleden for sharing his nickel knowledge and expertise.

WORKING WITH NICKEL SILVER

Nickel is most commonly used today as a base metal for costume jewelry, which is then plated with silver or gold. Nevertheless, this practice is less popular than it was, owing to nickel's allergic nature, so silver-plated earwires, for example, should not really have any alloy of nickel in them.

Despite this issue, nickel silver is an easy metal to work, polishes well, and is resistant to oxidation. Its joins can be soldered with sterling silver solder, which makes it a useful addition to the workshop when making models for castings or patterns and mock-ups for jewelry designs.

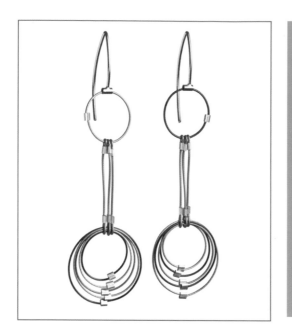

IMAGE CREDITS
Left: Nylon-coated steel earrings with gold fill, by Meghan Riley.
Bottom: Iron ring, by Janos Varga.

Opposite
Top: Iron ring with gold inlay, by Janos Varga.
Bottom: Knitted nylon-coated steel bracelet, by Meghan Riley.

CARBON STEEL

Symbol
No symbol as it is an alloy. Iron and carbon; will oxidize and rust

Specific gravity
7.85

Melting point
2687°F (1475°C)

Color
Gray

STEEL

Steel is an alloy of iron and carbon in varying proportions. Various other metals can then be added to steel to create alloys with specific characteristics.

Stainless steel is a harder metal than any of the precious metals used in jewelry making and can be used in several different ways—as a stand-alone metal, alongside other metals for a variation in color, or as a pattern maker. It does not oxidize, which means that it will not rust.

One of the most common elements on earth, iron has been used by humans since ancient times. As a ferrous metal, it is prone to rust.

Carbon steel is a hard metal and, as a result, is generally used for toolmaking (see p. 262). Tool steel, which is usually bought as rod in varying diameters, should be the correct alloy of iron and carbon, strong enough to withstand the use it will be put to after annealing and tempering. Carbon steel is quite brittle and, as a result of oxidation, can build up a lovely rough surface. This can then look very effective when it is combined with a smooth precious metal.

STAINLESS STEEL
Symbol
No symbol as it is an alloy. Chromium or a mixture of chromium and nickel is added to iron to make stainless steel; it does not oxidize.

Specific gravity
7.9

Melting point
2750°F (1510°C)

Color
Silvery gray

IRON
Symbol
Fe

Atomic number/weight
26/55.85

Specific gravity
7.87

Melting point
2797°F (1536°C)

Color
Steely gray

FOR TUTORIALS SEE:
Cutting and piercing   p. 114
Forging   p. 194
Toolmaking   p. 262

IMAGE CREDITS
Left: Heat-blackened steel brooch, by Meghan O'Rourke.

Center: Laser-cut, powder-coated stainless steel brooch, by Iris Saar Isaacs.

Opposite
Top: Anodized titanium, zincalume steel, and oxidized silver earrings, by Meghan O'Rourke.

Bottom: Necklace made from a steel jet brake plate, silver, stainless steel, and plastic set with citrine, blue topaz, and lapis lazuli, by Dauvit Alexander.

WORKING WITH STEEL

CUTTING CARBON STEEL

Carbon steel and tool steel are either cut with a handheld hacksaw or a large floor-standing motorized hacksaw. As these metals are supplied in rather large dimensions, larger saws and blades are needed to cut through them. Tool steel rod can be shaped on a sturdy metalworking lathe.

CUTTING STAINLESS STEEL

For workshop purposes, the maximum thickness of stainless steel to be cut by hand with a piercing saw should be no more than 11 gauge (3 mm), as it is so hard. Ideally, if using the steel for cutting a pattern, 20 gauge (1 mm) should be sufficient. A coarse blade—either a 0, 1, or 2—should be used and the full length of the blade allowed to do the work. When cutting stainless steel with a guillotine saw, the thickness of the metal able to be cut will depend on the size of the guillotine. For a small one used in the workshop, I suggest that between 20 and 14 gauge (1 and 2 mm) would be the maximum. The same applies to cutting with a small scroll saw (fretsaw).

USING STEEL/IRON

Steel is usually attached to precious metals using means other than soldering. Bear in mind that assaying and hallmarking (see p. 218) becomes a problem when mixed metals are soldered together. Nevertheless, this gives the opportunity for creative thought! Hooks, rivets, screws, nuts, and bolts are all useful ways of joining two pieces of metal. Or, steel can be hammered and curved around a precious metal piece. If the steel is dark, it provides a wonderful color contrast when used together with gold or silver.

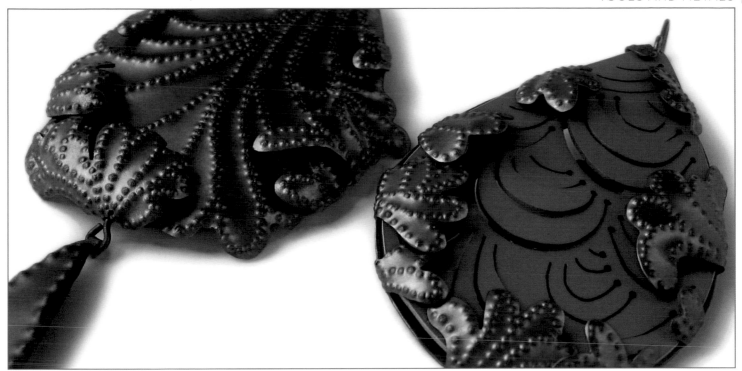

HEATING STEEL/IRON

Carbon steel is shaped while it is red hot. To get a
good idea of how to work with the metal, go watch a
blacksmith at work, and if you are offered the chance
to have a go with their tools, take it. It takes practice to
place the hammer in precisely the right spot and at the
right moment, but it is great fun to try. As it is being
worked, the metal loses its red color and malleability,
so to keep it soft enough to work it has to be reheated
repeatedly. This is done in a coke-fired or electric forge,
which is kept hot during the whole fabrication process.
The hot metal is held in a long pair of tongs or pliers and
shaped on an anvil. It is finally cooled by being placed
directly down into a bucket of water.

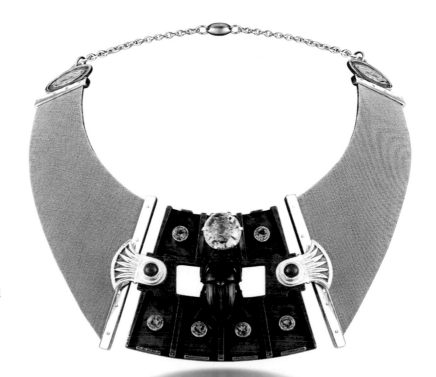

Symbol
Sn

Atomic number/weight
50/118.7

Specific gravity
7.3

Melting point
449°F (232°C)

Color
White

IMAGE CREDITS
Left: Patinated earrings made from sterling silver and a recycled tin can, by Carrie Crocker.

Opposite
Left: Earrings made from a vintage tea tin, by Betsy Menson Sio.
Center: Bracelet made from woven tin, by Betsy Menson Sio.
Right: Earrings made from a vintage tin can, by Carrie Crocker.

TIN

Tin was one of the earliest metals to be known and used—it is a component of bronze and has been used for this from as early as 3500 B.C.

Tin is a beautiful soft white metal with a very low melting point. It is nontoxic, not readily tarnished, and can either take on a bright polish or a textured finish. Tin can be worked in a similar way to pewter (the majority of pewter consists of tin; see p. 90).

In Cornwall, England, tin is traditionally associated with a tenth wedding anniversary, and Cornish tin has shaped the landscape and heritage of southern Britain for thousands of years.

Thank you to Erica Sharpe for sharing her tin knowledge and expertise.

FOR TUTORIALS SEE:
Cutting and piercing   p. 114
Finishing   p. 164
Soldering   p. 120

WORKING WITH TIN

When heated, tin bonds very readily with other metals, especially gold and silver (even at very low temperatures), and this is irreversible, so keep tools used for tin separate, use a different work bench, and vacuum up any dust and filings.

SOLDERING
Tin can be joined using a plumbers' type solder and low heat. Larger pieces are created using fold joins (see p. 138).

POLISHING
Polishing can be achieved using a series of increasingly fine abrasive papers followed by a jeweler's mop or a handheld pendant motor mop. Tin can also be tumble-polished with fine steel shot in a barrel polisher (see p. 51).

MALLEABILITY
The softness of tin means that it is easily dented, scratched, or bruised, so avoid anything too thin or intricate (e.g. pendant loops, hinges, catches). Rings and bangles must be heavy and not detailed.

Use a leather mallet to avoid denting the tin when hammering; steel hammers will mark it more readily. Bending and rolling can be done without softening, using pliers, your hands, hammers, and rolling mills. Listen for the "cry of tin"—the sound of the crystal structure shearing as the tin is worked!

Symbol
Rh

Atomic number/weight
45/102.9

Specific gravity
12.4

Melting point
3567°F (1964°C)

Color
White

IMAGE CREDITS
Left: Rhodium-plated brass chain, by Delia O'Farrell.

Opposite: Black rhodium-plated white gold ring with diamonds, by Anna Bario.

FOR TUTORIALS SEE:
Finishing   p. 164

RHODIUM

Rhodium is a hard white metal, similar in color to platinum. It can be worked and forged while it is still red after heating, but for practical jewelry purposes its main use is as a hard-wearing and shiny plate over other white metals.

Rhodium is most commonly recognized as the high-shining electroplated addition to items made in either white golds or silver. White golds on their own can look slightly gray, so the addition of a rhodium plate will enhance their appearance. When it is used over silver, rhodium will prevent the natural oxidation that would otherwise occur. It will, of course, also cover any remaining firescale (see p. 61).

Unfortunately, with wear, a thin rhodium plating will wear through, leaving the rather duller-colored metal underneath. So for items such as rings, and possibly earrings, rhodium plating may need to be redone after a year or so. After plating, the item should not come into contact with alkaline cyanide solutions, which will etch the thin layer away.

WORKING WITH RHODIUM

Work to be plated is usually sent out to a specialist. The preparation of items to be plated, however, should be meticulous. All scratch marks should have been removed, and the surface of the metal to be plated should be as shiny as you want the finished surface to be. If a polished finish is required, then the item must be polished, cleaned, then wiped over with acetone or a similar solution to remove any fingerprints or polish residue. Any areas that do not require polishing can be "stopped out" with any stop-out fluid that does not require heating to remove it.

A plated surface can be anything from 3–10 microns thick, depending on the cost of the metal used for plating. As this surface is very fine, no more finishing is required; if any abrasives were used at this stage, they would significantly reduce the fine surface.

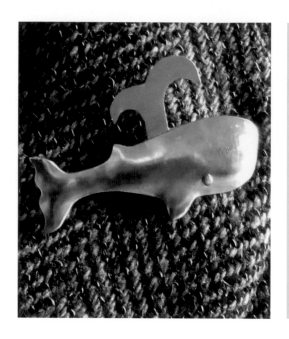

Symbol
Zn

Atomic number/weight
30/65.4

Specific gravity
7.131

Melting point
786°F (419°C)

Color
See text

IMAGE CREDITS
Left: Zinc and brass whale brooch, by Emmanuelle Le Fur.

Opposite
Top left: Zinc earrings by Malou Paul.

Top right: Polished and varnished zinc cubes on a cotton necklace, by Emmanuelle Le Fur.

Bottom: Etched zinc earrings, by Malou Paul.

ZINC

Zinc's main use in jewelry is as part of an alloy; it is added to precious metals to lower their melting points and to improve their flow as they are being cast.

Pure zinc is a whitish-blue color, but when it is left in the air it develops a thin oxidized coating, which leaves the metal with a dull gray appearance. Zinc is the metal added to copper to make brass (see p. 78). The more zinc added, the lighter the color of the brass. It is also the main additive in silver solder—the higher the proportion of zinc, the lower the melting point of the solder will be. Galvanized steel is steel with a top layer of zinc. This has many different uses where weather-resistant materials are required. It can, however, be affected by sulfuric and hydrochloric acids, which will remove the oxide layer to leave a whiter surface.

WORKING WITH ZINC

Zinc is fairly malleable between 210 and 300°F (100 and 150°C), but once it exceeds that temperature it becomes very brittle and can be pounded into powder form. Zinc is easy to melt, but do not breathe any vapor that might sublime from the pot as you are melting it in (turn on the ventilation fan over your stove, or do it outside, and you should be fine). Buy zinc ingots instead of powder, as the powdered stuff is more likely to be accidentally inhaled, and is also flammable. Zinc is quick to oxidize (either by burning or by dissolving if you put it in seawater) so keep away from flames. Jewelry containing zinc should not be worn if the wearer is going to come into contact with salt water.

INTERVIEW: JINKS MCGRATH

Jinks McGrath has worked as a designer/jeweler for over 40 years. She creates one-off pieces, using precious metals and distinctive gemstones, in her workshop in East Sussex, England, where she also holds regular classes and exhibitions.

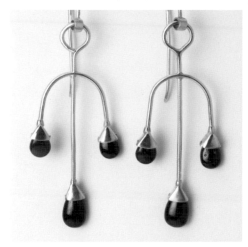

Describe your working environment

I have always managed to have my workshop close to where I live. This has been wonderful—at the start of my career I was always "at home" when my children came back from school, and it has continued, with visits from them and the rest of my family. For a few years I shared my workshop. Although this provided me with some interesting stimulation, it became a distraction, with too many breaks. Now I work on my own, which I love.

Can you describe a typical day in the workshop?

In the morning, I turn on the pickle and gas, and either pick up where I left off, or look at all my stones to see which one is speaking loudest to me. Most designs are in my head, and I only occasionally commit them to paper. Once I make a start I am quite open to changing a design if I feel it will be an improvement. Before I go away anywhere, I always tidy my bench. I love to come back and find it all ready for me to start afresh.

Do you enjoy teaching?

Teaching and writing books about making jewelry has been, and still is, a large part of my working life. Through the books, I have been invited to teach in some wonderful and extraordinary parts of the world. It is humbling to be able to pass on skills to young people, whose future without them would be limited, both creatively and financially.

What have you learned from your travels?

One of the things I love most about visiting and learning from fellow jewelers in different parts of the world is that wonderful feeling of familiarity as I step into their workshops. It may be that an oxypropane torch is not an option, and electricity is only available for a couple of hours a day, but, whether they anneal and solder on an outside hearth or sit at a bench that is a small box on the floor, there is still a common identity to be shared and a love of the materials to delight and inspire us all.

Jinks was interviewed by Angela Koo

Opposite
Top left: Rough-cut lapis lazuli necklace with silver and gold.

Top right: Handmade gold chain with emerald drop.

Bottom left: Handmade yellow and white gold chain with small sapphires.

Bottom center: Double ring with pink tourmaline and flat-cut emerald.

Bottom right: Silver bangles with rough-cut lapis lazuli.

Above: Gold earrings with ruby drops.

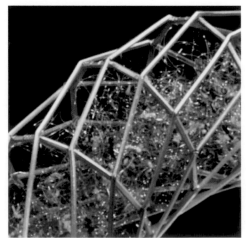

INTERVIEW: GIOVANNI CORVAJA

Having trained in both Italy and London, goldsmith Giovanni Corvaja now operates from a restored fifteenth-century building in the historic town of Todi, Italy, where he both teaches and creates his own art jewelry.

What, if anything, characterizes your design approach?

A piece of art should speak to the heart, not just the brain. To do so it has to talk in the language of the heart, which is very simple. Achieving simplicity, however, can be very difficult—we are born simple but become more and more complicated as we grow! Simplicity requires skill and the stripping away of all unnecessary complications.

What do you consider the purpose of your work to be?

Art consists of transforming an ordinary experience into an aesthetic one—one that acts through all the human senses. Usually one experiences things only through space, time, and causality, but in an aesthetic experience one transcends these aspects and perceives the universal essence of an object.

How does this relate to jewelry in particular?

Jewelry for me is all about beauty. Often we perceive beauty without decoding it: we just feel attracted toward something—because of the regularity of some minute details, the harmony in the proportions, the degree of finishing even at microscopic levels. Seeking beauty is a very positive and enriching process—a balance between correcting imperfections while also looking for inherent beauty and enhancing that. Nevertheless, to achieve a beautiful result, a high degree of precision is often required. Of course pure beauty is an abstract and absolute concept that can never be reached, but I think that an artist should always aim higher than what is realistic. I believe beauty is a fundamental necessity for a human being, like eating or breathing.

What part do materials play in your creative process?

I aim to make objects that will last forever. Gold or platinum are perfect in this sense—not only do they possess great beauty in themselves but the incorruptibility of these materials, if carefully preserved from mechanical damage, makes them eternal.

Why did you choose to become a goldsmith in particular?

Gold is my obsession; it is a symbol of evolution and perfection, and it expresses the best aspects of nature and creation. I work to acquire the maximum possible knowledge of it.

Making jewelry is probably the best solution I have found for enabling me to be constantly in contact with gold—this magic element, this miracle of nature.

Opposite
Top: Gold and platinum brooch.
Bottom left: Gold brooch.
Bottom center: Gold, platinum, and glass enamel bracelet.
Bottom right: Gold brooch.
Above: Gold and enamel ring.

SECTION 2
TECHNIQUES

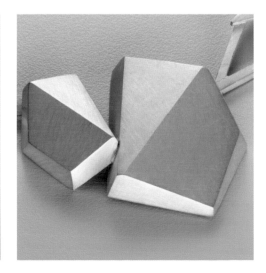

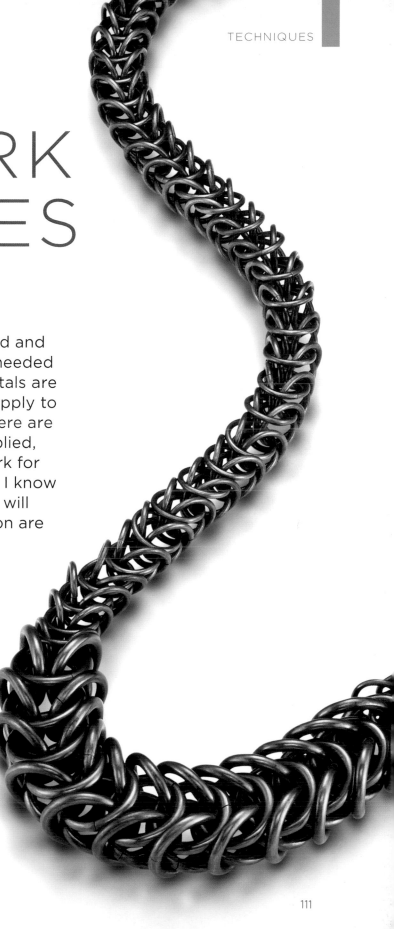

3. BASIC METALWORK TECHNIQUES

To pursue life as a metalworker/jeweler, there are several basic techniques that need to be understood and conquered. In this section all the basic techniques needed to start working with precious and nonprecious metals are provided. There are a few hard and fast rules that apply to metalworking techniques, but on the other hand there are plenty of different ways that techniques can be applied, and what works for one person may not always work for another. Here, of course, I am suggesting ways that I know work for me, but of course there will be others that will work equally well. All the tools needed in this section are referred to in Chapter 1.

Previous page, from left to right:
Engraved cast gold ring, by Neta Wolpe.

Hammered silver chain bracelet, by Cynthia Nge.

Stretched silver necklace, by Beth Pohlman.

Pierced silver ring with diamonds, by Michelle Chang.

Cast gold ring, by Doron Merav.

Cast silver necklace, by Regine Schwarzer.

Opposite: Hand-cut, drilled silver pendants on silk cord, by Meghan O'Rourke.

Right: Oxidized bronze chain, by Kirsten Muenster.

MEASURING

I have a picture in my workshop made for me by a friend many years ago, which reads: "Twice measured is once cut." It is a true and constant reminder to me and all those who study in the workshop that checking a measurement for a second time, just before cutting, is always a good idea.

To get an accurate size for a ring, the finger is first measured with a metal ring sizer. These come with both narrow and thicker bands, and in full and half sizes, from A to Z. Avoid measuring a finger with a piece of string—this can be very misleading. Different climates can also affect a person's finger circumference, so this may need be taken into account. A ring that fits well is one that is hardly noticeable when it is on and, contrary to what most people think, a finger is not round—some rings, when worn over a period of time, will take on the actual shape of the finger. Once the ring size is known, the length of metal needed to make it can then be calculated.

Formulae for measurements, i.e., the circumference of circles and ovals, can be found on p. 288.

MEASUREMENTS FOR A RING
LENGTH
1. Place the ring sizer on a tapered ring stick and push it down as far as it will go. Take the reading here. **(A)**
2. Cut a length of binding wire, wrap it around the ring stick, and twist to tighten it. Remove the wire, cut through opposite the twist, then straighten the wire. This is the measurement for the inside of the ring. **(B)**
3. You must also account for the ring's outer measurement. Measure the thickness of the metal being used for the ring with a spring gauge. Add twice that measurement to the length of the wire. This is the length of metal required for the ring. Lay the wire along the metal and mark the extra length required with the dividers. **(C)**

WIDTH
4. Measure the ring's width by opening out the dividers to the width required. Place one point against the straight edge of the metal and firmly draw a line of the required length with the other point. **(D)**
5. Cut the strip with a piercing saw.

THICKNESS
6. The thickness of a piece of metal is measured with a spring gauge, vernier, or micrometer. Open up the gauge and place the metal between the two measuring points on the gauge, or read from the digital screen. **(E)**

MEASURING STONE HEIGHTS
This is necessary when making a collet or bezel to fit around a stone (see p. 244). For a cabochon, look at the profile of the stone to see where it starts to curve over.
1. Place the stone on a flat surface and hold a ruler up against it to measure the height required for the collet. **(F)**
2. Mark this on the metal in the same way as for the width of a ring.

MEASURING EQUAL LENGTHS
1. To cut wire or sheet into equal lengths, open out the dividers on the steel rule to the length required.
2. Starting from a straight edge, place one end of the dividers against the end of the wire and mark off the distance on the wire. **(G)**

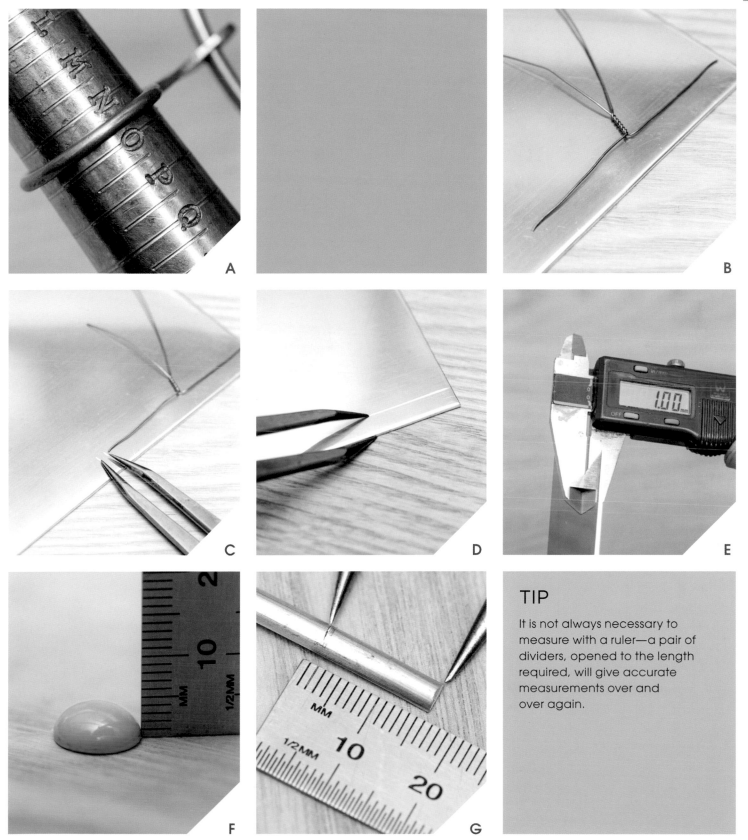

A

B

C

D

E

F

G

TIP

It is not always necessary to measure with a ruler—a pair of dividers, opened to the length required, will give accurate measurements over and over again.

CUTTING AND PIERCING

Cutting (with a guillotine, snips, shears, and cutters) and piercing (using a piercing saw) are essential basic skills for the jeweler. Learning to use these tools with ease will make these pleasurable tasks.

The frame size of a piercing saw can vary, but the most commonly used have a cutting depth of about $3^1/_2$ in (90 mm), and the distance between fittings is approximately $4^1/_2$ in (110 mm). Larger frames are useful for cutting farther into the metal sheet, but these are usually fitted with standard-size blades. The most important part of sawing is choosing the correct blade gauge for the metal you are using. As a general rule, there should be three teeth to the thickness of the metal (see p. 17 for more on saw blades). Always make sure that your fingers are not in the way of the blade or shears.

USING A PIERCING SAW

Cutting out, or piercing, is done sitting at the bench. Hold the metal on the wooden pin in the center of the workbench.

FITTING THE BLADE

1. Take the saw blade, with the teeth facing toward you and running downward, and fasten it into the top screw fitting of the piercing saw. Push the saw against the bench to bend it slightly. Fasten the bottom of the blade into the lower fitting and tighten it so that, when plucked, it makes a ringing twang. A loose blade breaks easily and does not cut well. **(A)**

STARTING A CUT

2. Place the blade at a slight angle to the metal and steady it in that position with the thumb or forefinger of the hand holding the metal. Draw the saw gently downward to get started and, as it starts to grip, change the angle of the saw to the metal so that it becomes 90 degrees. **(B)**
3. Once the cut has been established, the saw should just drop through the metal without any forcing. Keep the hand holding the saw relaxed. The best cut will be achieved when the whole length of the blade is used.

CUTTING

4. Keeping the blade upright and at right angles to the metal, let the saw do the work on the down stroke. **(C)**
5. To cut a curve, keep the blade moving and gently turn either the metal, the saw, or both, but keep the movement flowing. Jerky movements will break the blade.

CUTTING RIGHT ANGLES

6. Saw up to the right angle you wish to cut. Using the back of the blade, and keeping the up and down strokes flowing, push back gently into the corner while carefully turning the saw through 90 degrees. When done, move forward again with the saw. **(D)**

PIERCING

Begin by drilling a hole large enough for the saw blade to go through near the edge of shape to be cut out.

1. Draw the shape on tracing paper and place it on the metal. Thread the blade through the hole, keeping the top side of the metal facing the top of the saw frame. **(E)**
2. Support the metal so that it does not weigh on the blade as you fasten the bottom of the blade tightly. Then gently hold the metal in the saw as it is placed into position on the pin, ready for cutting out.
3. When cutting a very small angle, cut up to the point from one direction then go back, then cut up to the line of the angle and back into the corner from there. **(F)**
4. A piercing saw can also be used like a file. When the use of a needle file is restricted due to a very small opening, gentle strokes with a piercing saw along uneven edges will remove high spots and smooth out unevenness. **(G)**

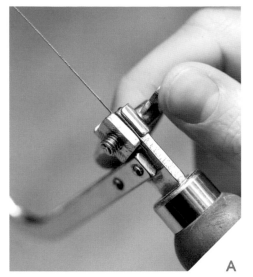

A

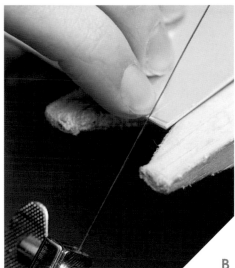

B

C

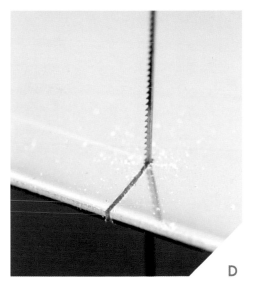

D

TIP

Lasers provide another way of cutting metals. If sending work away to a specialist to be laser-cut, you will need to supply a CAD drawing of your design.

Softer metals, such as brass, copper, and silver, can also be cut using a water jet. Check that the intricacy of your pattern will survive the process.

E

F

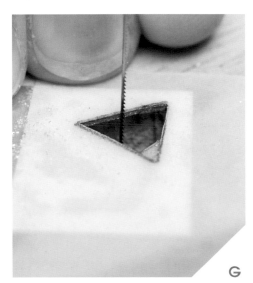

G

COPING SAW

This saw has a larger frame, thicker blades, and larger teeth, so is useful for cutting plastics, wood, and waxes.

THE GUILLOTINE

A guillotine should be fastened securely to the bench before use, and there should be a pin lock fitted so that the blade does not move until required. Draw or scribe a line on the metal, then line it up with the start of the raised blade. Hold the metal firmly in one hand with the line clearly visible, then slowly draw the blade down along the line, pushing the metal along in the same direction until the cut is complete. The blade of the guillotine should always be stored in the flat position.

SHEARS AND SNIPS

Large shears can be used to cut a straight line through metal. To make life easier, fasten one handle of the shears into a vise and work the other handle with your hand to make the cut. Tin snips are used by hand to cut thinner metal, no more than about 19 gauge (1 mm) thick. However, these will leave a slightly raised edge that will need to be filed down. Snips are used for cutting up strips of solder, then top cutters are used to cut across the strips to create tiny squares, or "paillons."

SCROLL SAW

A scroll saw (also often referred to as a fretsaw) uses an electric motor to drive a vertical blade up and down. A piece of metal is held by hand on the flat steel table of the saw and carefully guided along the line that is being cut. These machines are small enough to have in the workshop but need very special care when being used, especially with metals of 13 gauge and under (over 2 mm) thick.

PHOTOETCHING

Photoetching is used for both cutting and etching (see p. 281). The process can be carried out in the workshop but is usually done by a specialist. A CAD drawing of the exact pattern, cut, and/or area to be etched, as well as the depth desired for the etch, must be supplied (the cutting and etching can be done at the same time). The maximum depth that can be cut is approximately $1/8$ in (2 mm).

CUTTING SPECIFIC METALS
GOLD

Be as economical as possible when cutting gold, and make sure that all the dust created by the saw is not mixed with any other metal. Lower-karat golds are slightly "coarser" to cut than the high karats; 22 and 24 karat are very soft and bend easily, so they should be well supported when piercing. On a thickness of 23 gauge (0.6 mm) or less, use a fine 04 or 06 blade.

COPPER

Copper is a good metal on which to learn to use a piercing saw. Before making the first cut, rub a little beeswax onto the blade to help ease it into the metal. A 01 or 1 blade is suitable for most thicknesses of copper. The copper can be cut either annealed or in its hard state, although if less than 18 gauge (1 mm) and well annealed, it may bend quite easily as it is cut.

ALUMINUM

Aluminum is a coarse metal to cut, so use a blade of 1 or 2. It is also a very light metal so cutting it will be quite easy. Saw marks on the edges can be removed with a file kept especially for aluminum. It is absolutely essential that any filings of aluminum do not come in contact with any of the precious metals.

Opposite: A selection of tools.

ANNEALING

Annealing is the process of heating a metal with a soft flame to reduce the stresses that have built up as the metal has been hammered, curved, bent, twisted, or stretched.

As they are worked on, most metals harden to a point where they are likely to crack or break. Annealing usually takes place after piercing but before any other work begins, as metal bought from suppliers is often supplied hard. To avoid oxidation, cover the metal with flux. After quenching and pickling, the flux is removed, so apply a further coat before the next annealing. Also consider when to anneal:

AFTER CASTING: At this point a piece is usually quite hard and, if worked before annealing, could easily crack. So always anneal after any type of casting. With some large castings it may be prudent to anneal more than once.

AFTER SOLDERING: When making a bracelet, for example, bending will take place after annealing. However, as the metal is heated for soldering, it may start opening again at the join, making soldering impossible. If annealed just prior to soldering, the join will stay together.

SHEET SILVER

1. Place the silver on the soldering block and heat it with a large, soft flame. Start with the end of the silver facing toward you and place the flame around this area; the metal will start to oxidize and go black, but keep moving the flame around until you start to see a dull red color. Then move the flame over the rest of the piece, making sure the dull red color is applied to the whole sheet. **(A)**
2. Quench and pickle the piece to remove the oxidation. **(B)**
3. On subsequent annealings the oxidation will not appear so strongly, and on further annealings the surface will become quite "white." **(C)**

WIRE

If wire bends easily there is no need to anneal it until the bending starts to make kinks in it. Wire should be rolled into a coil for annealing, then carefully heated with a soft flame using a circular movement.

1. Use insulated pliers to turn over the coil so that the underside is also evenly annealed.
2. For fine wire—24 gauge (0.5 mm diameter) or less—coil it up into a little dish and heat from underneath until a dull red appears on the wire **(D)**

GOLD

Between 1200 and 1380°F (650 and 750°C), a dull red color can be seen in all the different-colored golds when annealing. Different gold alloys are quenched at different times after annealing—right after turning off the flame, or once the metal has cooled to black heat. A piece can also be left simply to air cool.

PLATINUM AND PALLADIUM

Due to their high melting points, these must be annealed with an oxy-propane or oxygen–hydrogen torch with a hot oxidizing flame. Let the metal reach a reddish-orange glow and hold there for 2–3 minutes. Special glasses must be worn, as the heat is harmful and the color is so intense that the metal will be visible only through these lenses. **(E)**

COPPER AND BRASS

These anneal in a similar way to silver. The oxidation can appear quite flaky. Quench it in water but pickling is unnecessary, as most of the oxidation will clean off with emery paper or a pumice powder paste. **(F)**

A

B

C

D

E

F

TIP

Platinum and palladium should be placed on a high-temperature soldering block kept exclusively for these metals. The block should not be made from charcoal, though, as particles from the block may contaminate the metal, causing it to fracture.

SOLDERING

Soldering is joining one piece of metal to another. Solder, combined with an anti-oxidizing agent, commonly known as "flux," is what is used to achieve this.

Solder has a slightly lower fusing temperature than the melting temperature of the metal it is used on. When heat is applied, the metal on either side of the join needs to become hot enough to allow the solder to run. The solder then becomes part of the metal, thus securing a join. Precious metals have different temperatures at which solder will run, so solders are made specifically for different metals—most will have a corresponding "hard," "medium," and "easy" solder.

Hard solder, which has the highest melting point, is used first and for as long as possible for subsequent joins. This is followed by medium solder (a slightly lower melting point), and lastly by easy solder (even lower). Less commonly used are enameling solder, which has the highest of all melting points, getting very close to the melting point of silver, and extra easy solder, which is often used in repairs but which will show more easily as a slightly different color line due to its alloys.

Do not place solder between the join, as this will make a gap and the solder will tend to go to one side; similarly, do not sit a piece that is being soldered to another (e.g., a collet) on top of your paillons (chips of solder) as this, too, creates a gap.

A SILVER RING JOIN

1. Make sure the join is as close as possible and everything lines up so that very little filing will be needed after soldering. **(A)**
2. Mix up a little flux/borax and paint it in between the join. Place a paillon of solder on the soldering block and position the ring so that the join is sitting right on top of the solder. **(B)**

3. Gently heat the whole ring; the flux will start to bubble. With further heat this will dry off and the join will become clear again. At this point, watch the heat increase until the paillon of solder moves upward to fill the join. You will see a bright silvery line as it does so. **(C)**
4. Make sure the solder has fully run before withdrawing the heat, and then quench in water before pickling.

SOLDERING A DOME TO A FLAT BASE

If you try to solder a dome to a base by laying paillons of solder touching both, inevitably the solder will just run straight onto the dome. This is really annoying! So, a little pre-soldering is required here.

1. Turn the dome upside down and paint flux around the base. Take tiny paillons and lay them at approximately $3/16$-in (5-mm) intervals on top of the flux. **(D)**
2. Keeping the dome upside down, heat it until the solder just runs and forms little mounds.
3. Quench, pickle, and dry the dome, then rub the underside on a flat file until the solder pieces are just visible. **(E)**
4. During the soldering the air will need an escape hole (see Tip), so it is a good idea to have a hole drilled in either the dome or the base before proceeding. Reflux the base of the dome and position it on the silver sheet.
5. Cut a little sliver of solder and place it close along the join, so that as the piece is heated up you will see it run and know that the rest of the solder will now run. **(F)**

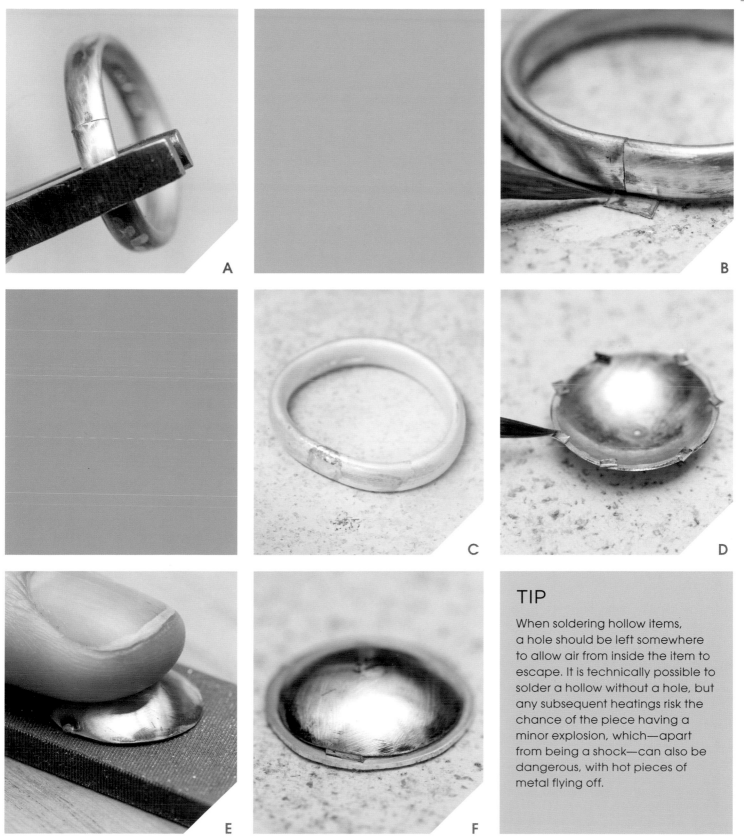

A

B

C

D

E

F

TIP

When soldering hollow items, a hole should be left somewhere to allow air from inside the item to escape. It is technically possible to solder a hollow without a hole, but any subsequent heatings risk the chance of the piece having a minor explosion, which—apart from being a shock—can also be dangerous, with hot pieces of metal flying off.

SOLDERING A SMALLER PIECE TO A LARGER ONE

Here, we are soldering a collet for a stone (see p. 244) onto a sheet metal backing.

1. Flux the underside of the collet and place it in position on the silver. **(A)**
2. Cut up little paillons of hard solder and place them at intervals around the base of the collet. They should all touch both the collet and the silver base so that they run onto both of them. **(B)**
3. Flux the join already made in the collet and make sure there is a paillon of solder directly next to it. As hard solder will be used again (for the join of the collet), this prevents the solder of that join from leaking out to help solder the base.
4. Introduce the flame slowly, from a slight distance, to dry the water in the flux, then gradually bring in the heat. Concentrate on the outside and the base sheet (the heavier of the two parts). If heat is concentrated on the collet, all the solder will run onto it and not form a join. Both pieces must be at the same temperature for the solder to run into the join. **(C)**
5. If it is hard to concentrate the flame on the larger piece without too much heat touching the smaller piece, it can be heated from underneath by holding it up with a pair of insulated tweezers or balancing it between two soldering blocks, and heating it from beneath. **(D)**

SOLDERING SPECIFIC METALS
PLATINUM

Platinum should be placed on a special soldering block kept aside for this metal only, and tweezers should be made of tungsten. As platinum does not oxidize, work may be finished to a high level before soldering. Joins should be closely butted and will not require flux. Hard, medium, and easy solders are available, but large joins are welded together by placing a bit of platinum through the join and filing to shape after welding.

GOLD

White, red, and yellow gold all have solders to match their colors. These are available in hard, medium, and easy and are applied in the usual way. To achieve a neat join, the pieces to be soldered should have a close fit (gold solder will not run and fill gaps the way silver solder may), and many small paillons of solder will give a better result than fewer bigger pieces. (See p. 64 for the melting points of gold solders.) In jewelry, 14-karat, 10-karat, and 9-karat golds are all used and are also available in different colors, and the same applies when annealing, quenching, and soldering.

COPPER

In the jewelry workshop copper is soldered with silver solder. The first solder join is fluxed as normal, using hard solder. Subsequent joins can then be soldered with medium and easy silver solders. As the solder join will be a different color from the copper, it is better to use a number of small paillons than a few larger ones. Excess solder can be filed away, but too much solder around a join will always show. The silver solder will run at the same temperature as when it is being used on silver, i.e., around 1380–1430°F (750–780°C) for hard solder and 1300–1340°F (700–725°C) for easy. Since copper has a high melting point, there is very little danger of melting it when soldering.

A

B

C

D

TIP

Joins to be soldered should always be clean, which means no oxidation from previous heatings and no grease. Also make sure that there is no residue from the pickle which is likely to spill out onto the join.

SWEAT SOLDERING

When soldering one solid piece to another you will need to sweat solder.

1. Clean the underside of the top piece and cover it with flux. Place several paillons of solder around the edges and then in the middle, and heat them until the solder spreads. **(A)**
2. Quench and pickle, and after drying use a flat file to reduce the "bump" of the solder until it is only just visible. **(B)**
3. Reflux the piece—but do not overdo the flux as this may cause the top piece to move out of position—and lay it on the bottom piece. Lay a couple of tiny pieces of solder close into the seam so that you can see when the solder is running. **(C)**
4. Introduce the flame very gently to dry the flux. Then increase the heat until the solder has run. When done carefully this method of soldering one piece to another is very neat, which should mean that the bottom piece will not need any filing or cleaning to get rid of solder marks.

STICK SOLDERING

When there is a very large join that will require a lot of solder, a method called stick soldering is used.

1. Flux the join in the usual way and place one or two large paillons on it. Then cut and flux a long, thin strip of the solder to use and hold it in a pair of insulated tweezers. Before starting to heat up the piece, it is a good idea to check the position of the hand holding the stick solder and try to make sure that either the wrist or elbow is supported somehow; this will help guide the solder to where it needs to go.

2. Heat up the piece until you see the paillons just starting to run, then bring in the stick and run it as steadily as possible along the join. If the temperature is correct, the solder will flow immediately. If not, it will be a bit sticky and run up itself, so just keep the heat on the piece until it flows again. **(D)**

SOLDERING FITTINGS

When soldering something quite small to something large, such as a wire to the back of an earring, a little flux with a paillon of solder is placed on the main piece.

1. Flux the little wire on the bottom and then hold it with insulated tweezers at the right angle so that when it is lowered it will sit straight on the base. **(E)**
2. Heat up the main piece and, as the solder flows, keep the heat at that temperature (do not increase it). Lower the wire down carefully into the puddle of solder and hold it there until you see the solder come up around the base of the wire.
3. Withdraw the heat, still holding the wire in place, and when you are quite sure the wire is firm, lift it all up and quench it.

A

B

TIP

Pick soldering can be used for intricate joins and repairs. This method uses a metal pick to add a tiny amount of solder exactly where it is needed.

C

D

E

FUSING

Fusing is joining one piece of metal to another without the use of solder.
The metal is heated so that the surface just starts to melt and move.

Fusing is not an entirely predictable process, so trying it out first on pieces of scrap is highly recommended. Different metals can be fused to others to give a contrast in color. However, do not try fusing silver to copper, as silver has a lower melting point than copper and so will just become a puddle of molten silver. Likewise, 9-karat gold will behave in a similar fashion if it is fused to silver unless great care is taken when heating it. Because of the unpredictable nature of fusion, the appearance of a fused piece is very organic; too much heat and you will finish with a total melt, and not enough heat will give a rather disappointing surface. Fused pieces will be heavily oxidized so they need a long time in the pickle to clear it. To finish with a shine, a piece can be brushed with a soft brass brush using liquid soap and water.

MAKING A BALL
Make a small indent in a charcoal block with a drill or round-ended former, and place a small piece of the chosen metal in it. Use a hot reducing flame on the piece until it starts to roll up into a ball; keep the flame on it as it starts to spin. At first there will be a little dirt spinning with it. With the continued heat this will disappear and the ball will become clear. Withdraw the heat and allow it to settle. When the color has gone, remove it with tweezers and pickle. **(A)**

FUSING SCRAPS TO A BASE
1. Clean a base piece and paint it with a layer of flux. Place some scrap pieces, pieces of wire, or sheet cut especially to create a desired pattern onto the base piece.
2. Bring a soft flame slowly in to allow the water in the flux to evaporate and then increase the heat overall. The whole piece needs to be hot before concentrating the heat as the fusing commences.
3. The surface will start to look shiny in one place, so concentrate the flame there and only move it along as you see the surfaces fuse together with the obvious appearance of a silver line. Keep the heat along the whole piece until it has all fused. **(B)**
4. Pickle until all the oxidation has cleared and then clean with a brass brush, liquid soap, and water. **(C)**

ROUNDING OFF WIRE ENDS
To make little balls or rounded ends on wire, cut the required length of wire and hold it vertically using insulated tweezers. Dip the end in a little flux and then hold it, again vertically, in the flame at its hottest point, i.e., where the blue tip meets the orange flame. As the tip starts to melt it will start to run up the wire and form a little ball. The size of the ball depends on the size of the wire—if it gets too big for the wire, it will drop off. **(D)**

FUSING A JOIN
If a ring is being joined by fusing, the join must be really tight or, even better, a little overlapping. Flux it, then apply heat until the surface becomes shiny and the fusion is visible. If the join is overlapping, there is a greater surface area to fuse together, which makes a more certain join. This can be smoothed out afterward by hammering. **(E)**

FUSING WIRE
A design of wirework can be laid out on the soldering block and fluxed where the fusing will take place. You should heat the whole area until one area just starts to show signs of surface movement, then you can concentrate the flame there until it is fused, before moving on to the next area. The temperature should be kept at near fusing on the whole piece throughout.

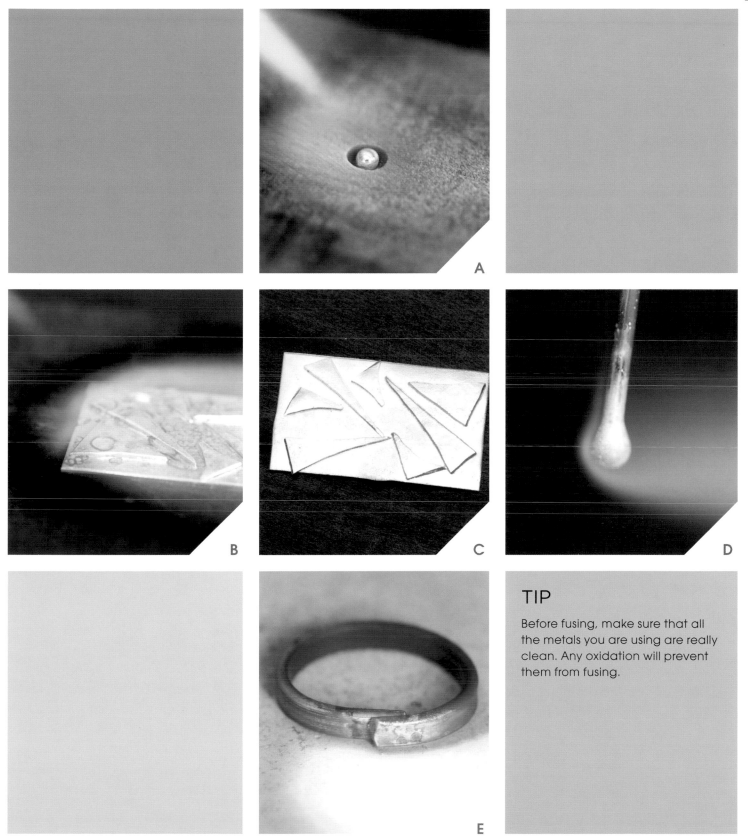

A

B

C

D

E

TIP

Before fusing, make sure that all the metals you are using are really clean. Any oxidation will prevent them from fusing.

FILING

Filing is the first stage of cleaning that must be done after working and soldering. Learning to use which file when, where, and how is an essential skill if a clean finish is required.

Files vary from the large rasp type to the small, very fine needle file, and choosing suitable ones can be quite a headache. I strongly recommend seeing and feeling any files before purchasing. Unless you know what you want, choosing from catalogs or online can lead to costly mistakes. The cut of a file is identified by numbers: 0 indicates a coarse cut, a 3 is medium, and a 6 is a fine cut. Large and medium files are made to be fitted into a wooden or plastic handle; needle files have no handle but are held at the smoother end. To fit a handle onto a file, the handle should have a small hole (smaller than the diameter of the file end, known as the "tang") drilled into it. Place the handle upright on the bench. Hold the file with the tang positioned over the drill hole, then push it down into the hole by banging it up and down on the bench until it is firmly in place. A file does not cut so much as scrape the surface of a metal. It is effective on the push stroke rather than the coming-back stroke; the small fillings are discarded at the top of the push.

FILING A STRAIGHT EDGE

To file a straight edge after a previous uneven cut on a sheet of metal, use a large, flat file. I find it helpful to hold the metal as close as possible to the edge of the pin or bench.

1. Hold the file sideways and work it in a very straight line, parallel to the pin, taking care not to work in an arc of any sort.
2. When the edge looks straight, hold it and the file together up to the light to see if there are any gaps. If there are, keep filing until the file and metal edge sit tightly together. **(A)**

FILING FOR A RIGHT ANGLE

There are many times when a right angle is needed in either wire or sheet metal. To achieve this, a triangular or square-sided file is used.

1. Mark a line with either a pen or scribe and place the edge of the file along it. Then file a groove down to a depth of just over halfway through the thickness of the metal. **(B)**
2. Secure one end and, holding the other with flat-nose pliers, bend the metal into the right angle. **(C)**
3. This bend should then have a little solder run up it before any further bending.

FILING AN INSIDE CURVE

After soldering a circle you will usually need to file away any excess solder on the inside with an oval or half-round file.

1. Hold the file with the right-hand edge gently against the inside area to be filed. Using a curving motion, gently push the file through until the left-hand side is closest to the metal. It is a sort of rocking, curving motion. **(D)**
2. Work from both sides of the circle with this file to make sure the filing is even.

FILING A STRAIGHT EDGE USING A VISE

1. Metal can be held in a vise to file a straight edge. As the filing is done on top of the metal, it is difficult to check whether or not the file is level. Hold the file in one hand at the handle and then at the tip with the other hand to keep it level. Keep checking that the file is not being allowed to "drop" at either end. **(E)**

A

B

C

D

E

TIP

Do not put any extra pressure on the tips of tapered files, as they will break very easily. Keep files for filing, not for taking lids off things! Avoid using them to stir any liquids, too, as they rust easily. Clean your files regularly with a proper file cleaner—a fine little metal brush with a wooden handle.

FILING A CONVEX CURVE

For any convex curve or edge, a flat file is used.

1. On an edge, push the file evenly along the curve, not across it.
2. If filing over a dome or spherical shape, you will need to work carefully to avoid creating flat areas. **(A)**

RIFFLER FILES

Riffler files are used when necessary for filing in a concave area. **(B)**

However, it is always better to make sure that the area is clear of excess solder or scratches before having to use these files. The trouble is that they themselves make scratches that then have to be cleaned—in rather inaccessible areas, this can be very time consuming and difficult. A small, abrasive tool fixed into the pendant motor is often preferable to a riffler file.

FILING TO STRAIGHTEN A JOIN

Sometimes, when bending up a strip of metal to be joined, the two ends may not be parallel, and therefore will not make a good join. Here, a small flat file can be used.

1. Pull the join area apart, just enough to place the edge of the flat file through, and allow the piece to spring back into position.
2. As the file is held between the join, move the file up and down until the two sides are parallel. Remove the file, and the join should now fit nicely together. **(C)**

USING A ROUND FILE

Round files are either parallel or tapered.

1. A parallel round file is extremely useful for filing grooves in preparation for making hinges. This can be done using a tapered file, but file the groove from both ends to try to keep it even.
2. If a drilled hole needs to be a little larger, a round file can be used to open it out, but take care to keep it moving around the hole, otherwise it will concentrate in one area, leaving a hole that is not round! **(D)**

USING A LARGE FLAT FILE

1. To achieve an even edge on a soldered ring shape, start by filing away any obvious unevenness. Hold the ring on the pin and see what needs removing and then file it away.
2. Now place it on a large flat file and file both edges until they are even. Then place a sheet of wet/dry paper on a flat surface and smooth both edges on the paper.

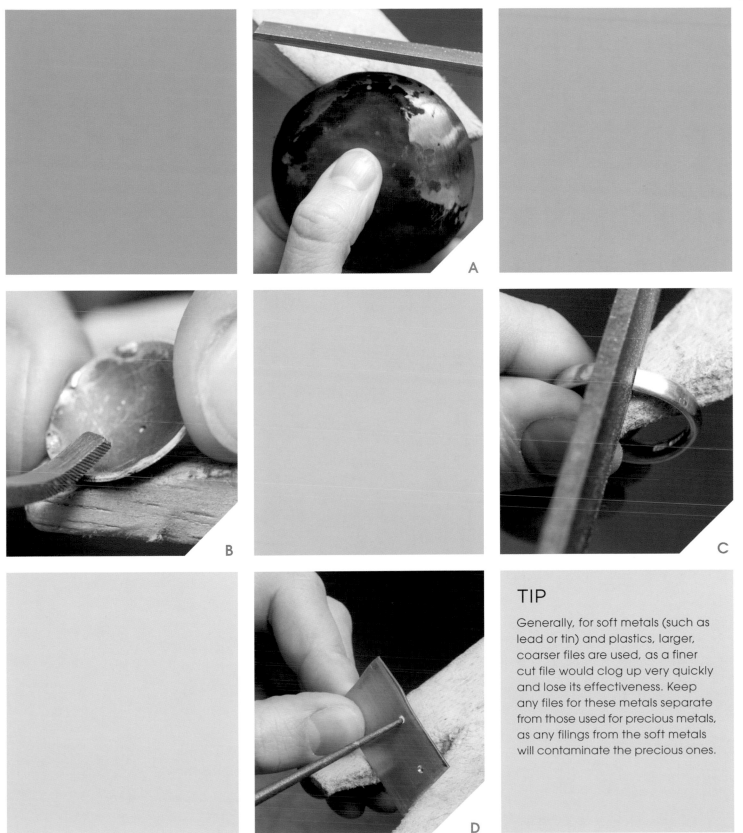

A

B

C

TIP

Generally, for soft metals (such as lead or tin) and plastics, larger, coarser files are used, as a finer cut file would clog up very quickly and lose its effectiveness. Keep any files for these metals separate from those used for precious metals, as any filings from the soft metals will contaminate the precious ones.

D

DRILLING

The jeweler has at his or her disposal many different types of drills for making holes in metal and other media.

The most traditional of drills is the "bow drill." Many jewelers still use this as their preferred hand drill, but it is restricted as to the size of drill bit that it can hold. With any hand drill, one hand works the drill while the other holds the metal steady, so a traditional woodworker's drill, for example, is difficult to use unless the metal is fixed to an unmovable base.

Most larger drilling is done with the use of pillar drills and flexible shaft motors. The pillar drill can only move in a straight line up and down, and the arm on the side of the motor is operated by hand. The metal is usually held in a small vise, which is part of the drill. If not, it should be held firmly and carefully with the other hand.

With the flexible shaft motor, or pendant drill, the drill is held in one hand and the metal with the other. Care should be taken to keep the drill at 90 degrees to the work—small drills break easily if they are subject to pressure at the wrong angle.

MARKING THE POSITION

1. Before starting to drill a hole, mark the position carefully using a sharp pencil.
2. Now place the point of a small punch with a sharp end right on this point. Use a ball-peen hammer to strike the top of the punch to make a noticeable impression. **(A)**
3. This impression will now give the drill a sure start, preventing it from wandering around and making unwanted scratches until it finds somewhere it can grip into—usually where you do not want it! It is also more likely to break if it does not have a good location point.

4. A center punch is also very useful for marking the spot. Hold the point of the center punch on the marked spot and press down hard. The tool is spring loaded, so as it is pushed, the point will hammer down, making a strong mark on the metal. **(B)**

FINISHING

After drilling, a small raised area can often be seen around the hole. This can happen when the drill is not very sharp.

1. Remove the raised area by taking a drill piece that is larger than the drill used and just twisting it around the hole on both sides of the metal. **(C)**
2. If the hole is being made for a rivet, it then needs to be "countersunk." Make this in the same way, but cut away more of the metal around the hole to leave space for the head of the rivet to be hammered into (see p. 136). **(D)**

A

B

C

TIP

It is a good idea to apply a little oil to a drill before using it. This will help prolong its life.

D

MAKING A HOLE

I have worked in several places—mostly in the East—where electricity is not always available and new small drills are wishful thinking. So other ways of making holes are normal. One of the best I have found is by using a sharp tool, such as a punch or scribe, which is not too broad at the tip end (so that the hole does not open up too much).

1. Simply hold the tool on the marked spot and give it a good blow with the hammer. This usually has to be worked from both sides and sometimes for quite a few blows, but it always works in the end! If a larger hole is required, it can then be cut using a piercing saw.
2. Make sure the work is held on something hard, such as a wooden bench, which, when it is marked by the tool (as it surely will be), it will not matter. **(A)**

MAKING A DRILL

Another way is to make a drill out of a needle or some other small piece of hard steel. You will also need a sharpening stone and some oil.

1. Break the end of the needle off with a pair of pliers. **(B)**
2. Now hold the needle at an angle of approximately 45 degrees, with the tip on the oiled stone. Rub it backward and forward until a "flat" is formed on one side. Then turn it over so that the opposite side is now worked at the same angle on the stone and another flat is formed.
3. The two opposite edges of the flat surfaces can now just be ground off on the stone, and the "drill" should be ready for use! **(C)**

FITTING A DRILL

A drill has to be held really firmly in the chuck for it to work. The chuck is the head into which the drill is fitted. On many hand drills the size of the chuck needs to be changed to fit the size of drill being used. As many as four chucks can fit one hand drill. Some drills come with just a single chuck that will close down very small, to hold a small drill bit, and then open up to hold a much larger one.

1. When fitting the drill, make sure that it is held in the center of the chuck. The easiest way to do this is to close the chuck just tight enough for the drill bit not to fit and then, holding the top end of the drill close, open up the chuck until the bit just fits in. Tighten it by hand and then—I usually use a pair of serrated-edge pliers for this—hold the main piece of the drill where it tightens with the pliers and turn it as hard as possible.
2. Most flexible shafts will be self-tightening; if not they will have a little hole that can be lined up and a small rod inserted to hold while tightening. Pillar drills will come with their own chuck key, which can be used to tighten the chuck.

USING A REAMER

When a hole is just a little too small it can be opened out with the use of a "reamer." This is a small steel tool that comes in different sizes and is about the length of a needle file. It is tapered and four-sided, and, when inserted into a round hole and twisted around, its sharp edges will remove some of the metal from the hole. **(D)**

DIAMOND DRILLS

These special drills come in all sizes and are used to make or open out holes in stones. As they are being used they should be kept lubricated and used very carefully, being raised out frequently to get rid of the dust made by the stone.

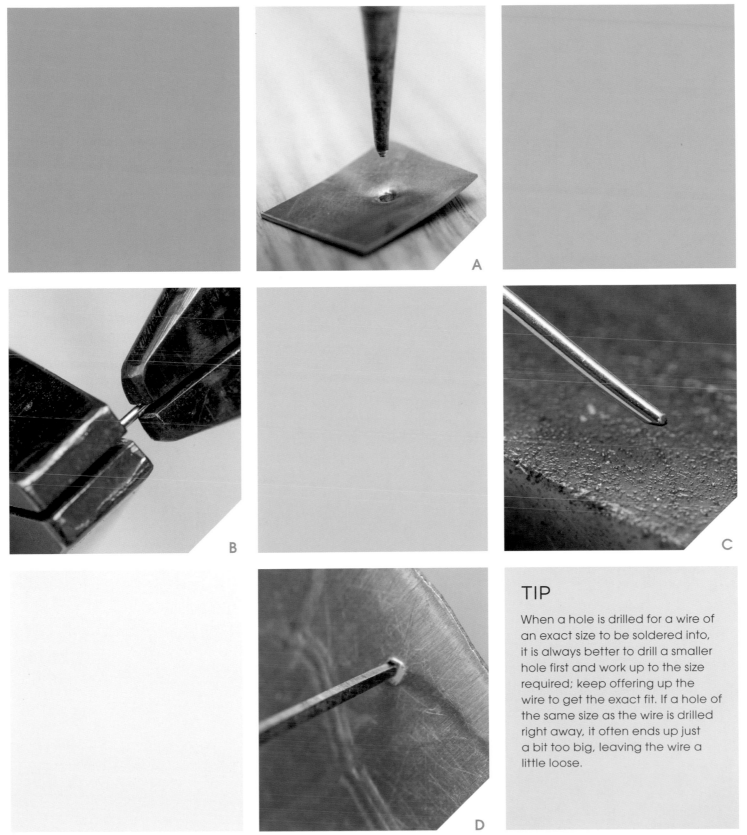

A

B

C

D

TIP

When a hole is drilled for a wire of an exact size to be soldered into, it is always better to drill a smaller hole first and work up to the size required; keep offering up the wire to get the exact fit. If a hole of the same size as the wire is drilled right away, it often ends up just a bit too big, leaving the wire a little loose.

JOINS

When one thinks of joins in metalworking, soldering naturally springs to mind. But, of course, there are lots of different ways of joining pieces of metal.

It is sometimes necessary to join pieces together when the use of heat would be impossible, for example, when a stone has already been set and an attachment needs to be made. There are several different ways to do this. The main thing is to make sure that, whichever method is used, the join is secure and cannot loosen. You can also make a choice about whether your join is going to be visible or invisible. Sometimes a join that is obvious is a really interesting part of the work; at other times, it looks better to have an "invisible" join. Before joining any work together it is always a good idea to make sure that each part is finished as well as possible, so that any cleaning up after joining is kept to an absolute minimum. Using just the right amount of solder is one way to keep everything around a soldered join really clean so that it needs virtually no filing.

RIVETS

A rivet is a wire that is fitted through holes that have been drilled in pieces of metal to be joined.

1. The holes should line up exactly and the top and bottom holes should be countersunk (see p. 132) on the outer sides. (A)
2. Cut the wire so that you have a length that will protrude about $1/16$ in (1 mm) either side of the hole. (B)
3. File both ends so that they are flat, then place the whole piece on a small anvil or flat plate, balanced on the rivet on the underside. (C)
4. Use a small punch with a rounded point at one end to initially spread the top of the rivet outward. (D)
5. Now use a punch with a broader end to spread the top farther. (E)

6. Turn the whole piece over and use the pointed punch on the other side of the rivet to spread it. Once both ends of the wire have spread enough and are sitting down into the countersunk area, the join has been made. Bear in mind that to hold something steady, or to stop it from turning around, a second rivet may be needed. The rivets can be filed level with the work and should not be visible.

VISIBLE RIVETS

The wire used for these rivets has one end that has been "balled" up.

1. Where the ball forms there will be a slight shoulder. File this away so that the ball will sit neatly on the surface of the metal. (F)
2. Cut the wire so that just the right amount is protruding through to the top piece, and file it straight. (G)
3. Use the broader punch to start spreading the top of the wire, then use the ball end of a small hammer or a round punch to form the curved head of the rivet. (H)
4. Finally, file the two heads until smooth.

PINNING

Pinning is similar to riveting, except that the pin is not spread at either end. It is usually used in a hinge, where the removal of the pin may be required at some point. The pin has a snug fit, and to pull it all the way through the hinge join, one end can be filed into a long point so that it slips through easily. The rest can then be pulled through with a pair of serrated-edge pliers.

A

B

C

D

E

F

G

H

FOLD JOINS

One piece of metal can be joined to another by means of a fold. This will inevitably be thicker where the join is than the rest of the metal, but this could be part of the design.

1. The metals to be joined should not be too thick—preferably no more than 22 gauge (0.75 mm). Make sure that the ends to be joined are straight, then draw a line approximately $^3/_8$ in (10 mm) from the ends to be joined, and parallel to them. These lines can be made a bit deeper with a triangular file or a lozenge engraving tool. **(A)**
2. Place one strip of metal in the safe jaws of the vise—far enough down that the scribed line is sitting parallel to the top of the vise. Tighten up the vise and then use a mallet to hammer down the top of the metal.
3. Remove the piece from the vise and place it on the flat plate. Hold it right up into the bend of the first piece, then hammer the bend down over it. Tighten this fold in the vise. **(B)**
4. Bend the second piece of metal (along the groove) back over the first piece. Tighten it firmly in the vise. **(C)**

HOT JOINS

A hot join is made either by soldering or fusing, and some joins are stronger than others.

1. When joining two pieces of sheet metal of the same height together, a "scarf join," which gives the greatest contacting surface area, should be used. **(D)**
2. When fusing a ring shank together, a "lap join" can be used. The two ends cross over each other and should be touching all the way along before fusing begins. The double height of the fused area can be hammered down afterward. **(E)**
3. When soldering an ear post to the back of an earstud, a greater surface area can be achieved by broadening out the pin (i.e., balling up one end and then filing half the ball away). **(F)**
4. Alternatively, a small length of tubing, with the same inside diameter as the pin, can be soldered onto the back first and then the pin soldered into that. **(G)**

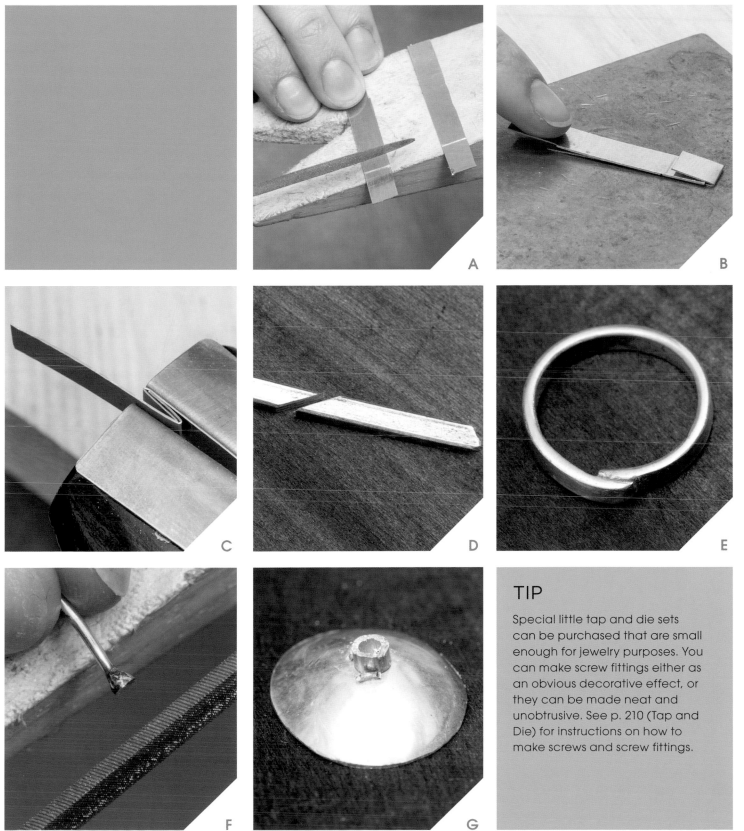

A

B

C

D

E

F

G

TIP

Special little tap and die sets can be purchased that are small enough for jewelry purposes. You can make screw fittings either as an obvious decorative effect, or they can be made neat and unobtrusive. See p. 210 (Tap and Die) for instructions on how to make screws and screw fittings.

HINGES AND FITTINGS

Handmade fittings can really enhance a piece of jewelry. There are really no hard and fast rules about how they should look, only how they work and, of course, whether they work well!

Of course it is quicker and possibly cheaper to buy fittings, but you may find that the sizes that are available may not always be appropriate for the work involved. There are several ways of making your own catches, hinges, clasps, links, and hooks, but the scope of this book does not allow me to show them all. Here are just a few to get you started.

Basically, fittings need to be attached to pendants, brooches, necklaces, bracelets, earrings, and cuff links, while hinges are mainly used on boxes, lockets, and straps, although they can also be used as a fitting on any of the above.

PENDANTS

When working with a pendant, the first thing to work out is where the fitting will go. If the pendant needs to hang straight, for example, the center of balance should be marked, as this is where the loop for the chain will go.

1. Find a steel ruler or similar slim piece of metal and hold it on edge on the bench. Place the pendant on the top edge of the ruler and balance it. Note where the center comes and then mark it with a pencil. Obviously, you would need three hands to do this simultaneously, so mark it once you have taken it off the ruler! **(A)**

2. The simplest fitting for a pendant is a jump ring soldered to the top. But there are a couple of things to consider first. If the jump ring is soldered on face on, there needs to be another jump ring fitted through that for the chain to go through, which can make rather a long drop.

3. An alternative for a jump ring soldered like this is to make a bail to hang from it. Draw a shape approximately like this on tracing paper, transfer it to the metal, and then cut it out carefully using a piercing saw. **(B)**

4. Anneal the shape. Draw a line across the middle and fold the piece down over a former of approximately $1/8$ in (3 mm) diameter. **(C)**

5. Bring the bottom edges together, file a little round groove across the edge, and solder a jump ring in place, leaving it open at about 2 o'clock. **(D)**

6. Slip the open jump ring through the one on the pendant, and solder the join with easy solder. The jump ring could be soldered on directly in line so that the chain can go straight through, but if it is being soldered onto a collet, will it impede the setting of the stone? **(E)**

7. A wire loop (three-quarters of a jump ring), or a wider loop made from a small strip of 25-gauge (0.5-mm) sheet, could be soldered onto the back of the pendant so that it is not visible from the front. **(F)**

8. A wide pendant could have fittings on each side so that it hangs better. **(G)**

A

B

C

D

E

F

G

TIP

How about using a piece of tubing instead of a jump ring? Just make sure that the chain fits through it!

MAKING AN S-CATCH

The simplest fastening for a necklace or bracelet is an S-catch. These always look nice, if a little predictable. Here is how to make one.

1. Using an annealed length of wire, longer than you need—between 8 and 18 gauge (1–3 mm diameter), depending on the size of your necklace—start to turn one end a little using half-round pliers. **(A)**
2. Now use round flat pliers and go back along the wire a little; wrap the wire around the widest part, bringing the wire right around to create a curve.
3. Now place the pliers at the same distance on the straight side of the wire. Bring the wire around to make another curve to match the first. **(B)**
4. Flick out the end and then pierce away the remaining wire. The ends can then be filed to shape.
5. After soldering onto the necklace, the curved ends of the catch can be hammered gently on the flat plate to give them more tension. **(C)**
6. If this catch is being used for a bracelet, solder a little ball onto the inside of the opening so that the fixing ring has to be pushed past this ball to open and close the bracelet.

MAKING A T-BAR CATCH

This catch can be used on a bracelet or necklace, or simply made as a decorative piece in itself to hang at the front of a chain. It is important when using this fitting on a bracelet to make sure that the T-bar cannot loosen. On a necklace, the weight of the chain will keep the pull of this fitting in a downward direction.

1. Always use a size of wire that is appropriate to the piece. Cut a length of wire a little bit too long for your needs. Solder three-quarters of a jump ring to the middle of the wire. **(D)**
2. Use a pair of half-round pliers to bend the soldered ring slightly downward. **(E)**
3. Make a ring with the wire (this could be flattened or have a border) with an inside diameter that is smaller than the length of the T-bar. **(F)**
4. Solder the link at one end of the necklace/bracelet to the ring, keeping it on the same plane. **(G)**
5. Solder a length of smaller chain to the three-quarter jump ring on the T-bar. This chain has to be small enough to fit through the ring. **(H)**
6. Adjust the length of the T-bar so that it can be pulled through the ring and then sit comfortably across it. The ends of the "T" can either be hammered out to finish the look, or have a couple of small jump rings soldered onto each end. **(I)**

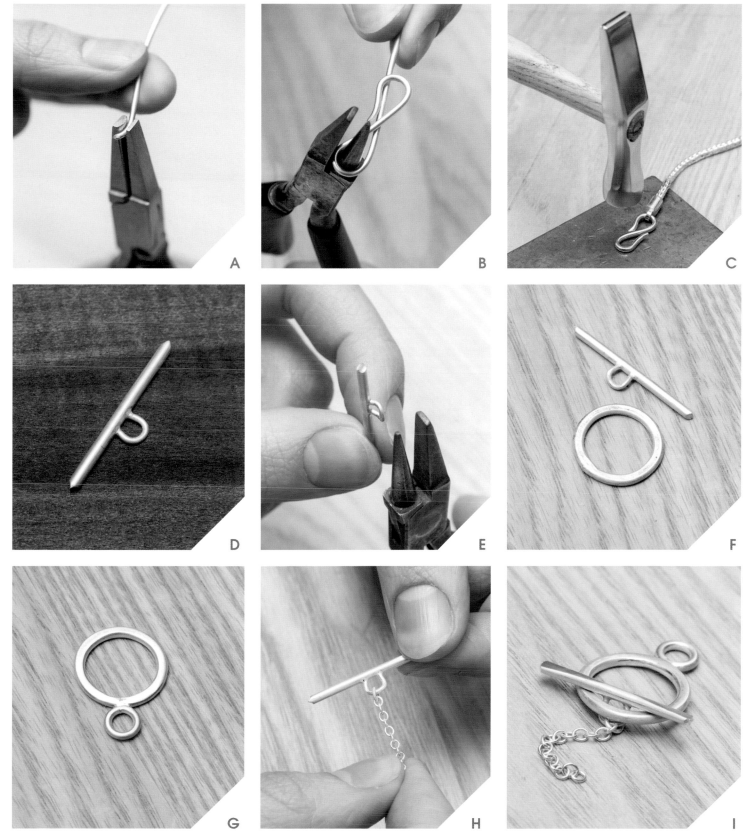

MAKING A TUBE BOX CATCH

If that is not a contradiction in terms! But sometimes a chain or torque, being round, will look neater if the box catch is also round.

1. Cut a piece of tubing, say $^9/_{16}$ in (15 mm) long, which is approximately the same diameter as the chain.
2. Take a piece of 19-gauge (1-mm) sheet metal and draw a circle lightly with a scribe that is the same diameter as the tube, mark the center, and then cut a circle just outside the scribed line—approximately $^1/_{16}$–$^1/_8$ in (1–2 mm) larger.
3. Now cut a T-shape slot into the scribed circle. The top of the "T" comes through the central horizontal line and finishes at each side approximately $^1/_{16}$ in (1 mm) before it. The leg of the T comes vertically down from the top to meet the horizontal line at 90 degrees. **(A)**
4. The cutout T will need to be able to accommodate the thickness of the catch, which can be made now.

THE CATCH

The metal for the catch bends back on itself to fit into the slot of the T. Choose a thickness of metal that will be appropriate to your fitting.

1. Cut a strip of the metal the same width as the top of the T and just over double the length of the tubing. At the halfway point, file a groove straight across. **(B)**
2. Anneal and pickle, then carefully bend the strip back on itself at the groove. **(C)**
3. Run a little hard solder through the groove.
4. Cut off approximately $^1/_8$ in (2 mm) of the open end on the top. **(D)**
5. Make a serrated tag the same thickness as the leg of the T and solder it halfway across the top of the catch. **(E)**
6. Now try fitting the catch into the circle with the cutout T, and make any adjustments to make sure it is a good fit.

THE TUBE

1. On one end of the tube, cut a slot for the tag. **(F)**
2. Now solder the circle with the T slot onto the tube, lining the slots up exactly. File around the edge. **(G)**
3. Solder a cap onto the other end of the tube and then solder on a fixing ring. **(H)**
4. The catch will now have a round plate soldered onto the bottom edge, which will correspond with the tube when it is closed. First, though, the serrated-edge tag needs to be trimmed enough to allow the round plate to be soldered onto the bottom edge. Finally, attach a fixing ring to the back of the round plate. **(I)**
5. After all the soldering is finished, hammer the tongue of the catch a little on a steel plate to make it springy. The catch should now fit nicely into the tube and make a good snapping noise as it fits into place!

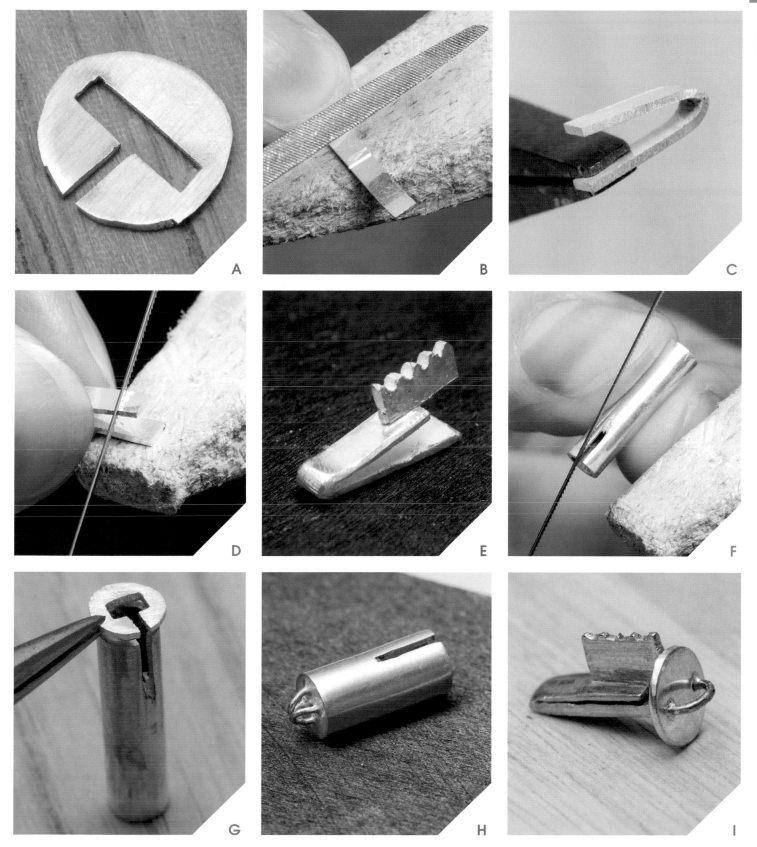

A

B

C

D

E

F

G

H

I

MAKING A HINGE

Hinges provide a flexible join between two pieces of sheet metal. The metal can either be straight sided or rounded, so a hinge will need to be made to accomodate this. The pin to keep the hinge in place can be either fixed or removable, becoming a catch.

HINGE BETWEEN TWO STRAIGHT SIDES

The two sides of metal need to have a groove filed along their edges where the hinge will fit. **(A)**

Chenier of a size that will sit neatly in the groove is then used to make the hinge. A short hinge usually only has three pieces of tube; longer ones have five or seven. If a stainless steel spring is used along the length of the hinge to help keep it closed, an even number is used, with one end piece soldered to one side and the other end to the opposite side.

CUTTING A FIVE-PIECE HINGE

1. Take a length of chenier just slightly longer than the sides being joined. Measure the length and divide it into five sections, marking them off with a pair of dividers or a marker. **(B)**
2. Remove half of the no. 2 and no. 4 sections with a piercing saw. **(C)**
3. Lay the tube along one side of the metal, with the removed areas facing down into the groove. **(D)**
4. Where the tube touches the groove, place some small solder paillons on each piece and solder them together.
5. Now thread the saw blade through the gap left by the no. 2 and no. 4 sections and remove the remaining area, so that there are now three pieces of tubing soldered in line along the groove. **(E)**

6. Hold this piece up to the opposite side and mark off the gaps where no. 2 and no. 4 match up. **(F)**
7. Cut two pieces of chenier to fit between the marks and check with the opposite side to make sure it all lines up before soldering them on.
8. Remove the sharp edges on the sides of each piece of chenier very lightly with a flat needle file to ease the movement of the hinge. Place them together and push a piece of wire through to join it all up. Cut off the wire, leaving about $1/16$ in (1 mm) at either end, then use a little punch or the ball end of a hammer to spread the top and bottom of the wire to fix it in place. **(G)**
9. The outside edges, at the point at which the hinge opens, may need to be filed a little at a 45-degree angle to achieve the full movement.

SPRING HINGE

This type of hinge is used when a lid or something similar needs to spring back into position easily. You will need to retrieve a little strip of very fine sprung steel, which can be found in old watch and clock mechanisms.

The hinge is slotted together and the steel, which should be just longer than the whole, is laid flat along the inside of the hinge and then the top end is plugged with a piece of tapered wire, which can be tapped down into it. It should have a snug fit. The same is done with the other end, and the wire plugs are filed flat.

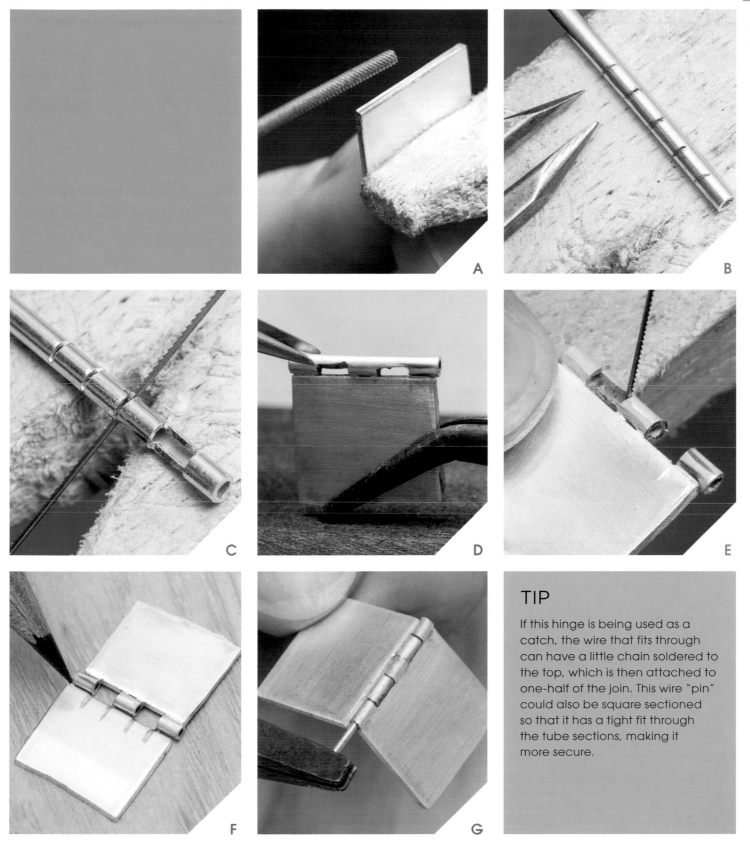

A

B

C

D

E

F

G

TIP

If this hinge is being used as a catch, the wire that fits through can have a little chain soldered to the top, which is then attached to one-half of the join. This wire "pin" could also be square sectioned so that it has a tight fit through the tube sections, making it more secure.

EARRING FITTINGS

Any piece of metal wire that goes through the ear should be biologically inert. Copper, brass, and nickel should definitely be avoided. Bear in mind, too, that some people also react to silver and, occasionally, lower-karat golds. Stainless steel and titanium can also be used, although they cannot be soldered to precious metals. Most earring fittings can be purchased but, if you want an individual look it is worth taking a little time to make your own.

EAR WIRES

1. Solder a length of 18- to 20-gauge wire (1 to 0.8 mm diameter) onto the back of an earring. After fixing, bend it with pliers into a sort of kidney bean shape and round the end so that it is comfortable when it goes through the ear. **(A)**
2. Fuse a length of wire into a ball at one end, then loop this through a ring attached to the eardrop. Shape this as for Step 1. **(B)**
3. A longer length of wire can be soldered to the top of an earring and then bent around so that it goes up the ear and down behind it. This needs to be hammered to make it springy, to hold it in place.
4. A twist can be made at the front of the loop to make a ring from which an earring can hang. The end is then taken behind and curved to make a little catch for the other end of the wire to catch into. **(C)**
5. An O-shaped earring has a hinged wire at the top that opens to fit through the ear. It is shaped like this so that there is some tension when it is being held in place on the other side. **(D)**

EAR CLIPS

Although these days most people do have their ears pierced, there is still the occasional call for clip-on earrings. Clips can be uncomfortable if they are too tight, and of course if they are a little bit loose there is more likelihood of them coming off without the wearer noticing, so they have to be just tight enough. The most comfortable ones I have come across are wire clips.

The curved wires are held in a cradle that is soldered at an angle to the back of the earring. The cradle is thick enough to have a small hole drilled through both sides, and the bottom of the wire, making the clip, is pushed together and held between the two sides.

The wires also have small holes that line up with the others, and then a smaller wire is pushed through to make the rivets. **(E)**

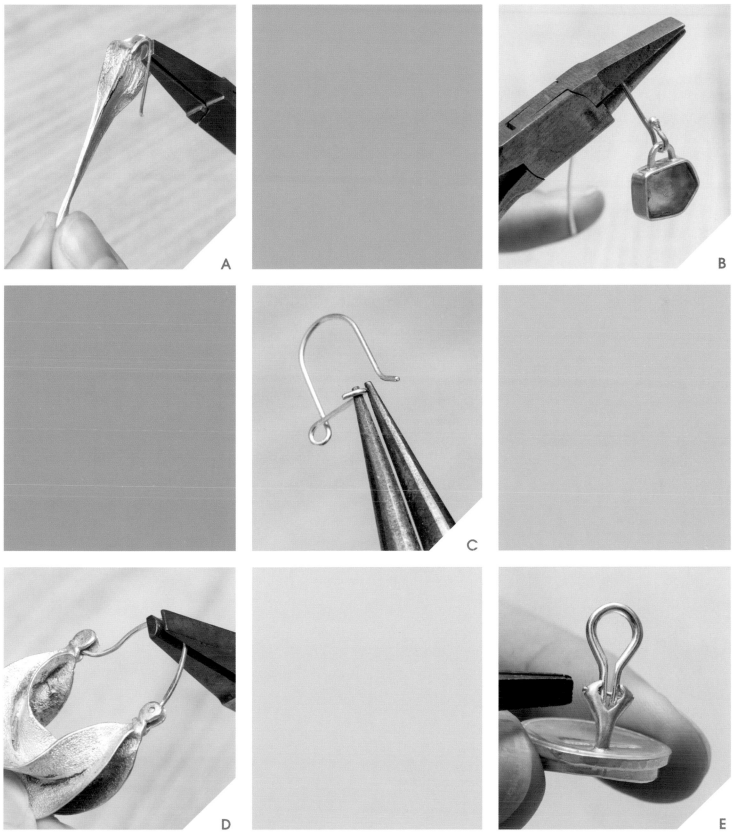

A

B

C

D

E

MAKING AND WORKING WITH WIRE

Wire can be bought or made in many different shapes and sizes—round, triangular, oval/rectangular, and square, to name just a few.

Round wire can be shaped by pulling it through a drawplate with differing patterns and drawing it down to less than 26 gauge (0.4 mm), when very fine wire is required. As wire is being drawn, it should be kept annealed, as it will stretch more easily when it is soft.

A drawplate, with round holes going down from about 12 to 28 gauge (2–0.3 mm), is an invaluable piece of equipment in the workshop. Being able to make a piece of wire of the right diameter, however long or short, saves us from having to keep all sorts of different gauges in stock. The drawplate should be held firmly in the safe jaws of a large vise. Keep the vise clear of the holes in the drawplate, though, because they can deform if squeezed.

USING THE DRAWPLATE

1. File one end of your wire to a long point, like a sharp pencil, then anneal it. Melt a little beeswax on it so that it will pass through the plate more smoothly. **(A)**
2. Find a hole in the drawplate just smaller than the wire's diameter. Push the pointed end through and grip it with a pair of serrated-edge pliers. Pull the wire through smoothly. Continue working down, one hole at a time, keeping the end filed, until the desired diameter is reached. Anneal the wire when it starts to feel springy.
3. To anneal very thin wire, make a coil and tuck the two ends in so it does not spring apart when heated. Place it in a round tin and heat with a gentle oxidizing flame from underneath. Turn it over during heating for an overall anneal. **(B)**

4. Any long piece of wire can be annealed by coiling then turning while heating. Make sure no single part gets too hot and melts.
5. Thicker wire can be laid along a soldering block, heated at one end until it turns a dull red, then the flame worked along the wire as the color appears. **(C)**

MAKING GOLD WIRE

1. Using 18-karat or higher gold scrap (high-karat wires are easier to make than lower), remove any solder traces. This can be identified by heating gold to just below annealing point, then letting it air cool. Solder will show as a darker line. **(D)**
2. Pickle, rinse, and dry. Place the gold in a crucible fastened in a heat-resistant holder. Add a pinch of flux powder suitable for using with higher melting temperatures (such as Tenacity no. 5). Add a pinch of finely powdered charcoal and a small piece of a higher-karat gold if desired. **(E)**
3. Have an iron ingot maker heated and ready, with a piece of casting sand pushed into it to determine the ingot's length. Melt the gold with a hot flame (ideally an oxygen/propane mix) until it forms a shimmering ball, then pour it into the former. **(F)**
4. Tip the ingot onto a soldering block and quench it when it has lost any pink color. It can now be placed in the square slots of a rolling mill and rolled down until it is small enough to pass through the drawplate. Anneal regularly—cracking can appear if the metal becomes too stressed.

A

B

C

D

E

F

TIP

When annealing wire, try not to anneal from side to side as it is much more difficult to see whether the flame has been worked evenly along the wire; failure to do so will result in a very uneven anneal.

STRAIGHTENING WIRE

Wires can become quite bent and twisted as they are stored. This can be annoying when a nice straight piece is required, but it can be easily rectified by:

- Annealing the wire
- Fastening one end into the vise
- Holding the other end in a pair of serrated-edge pliers and giving it a sharp pull **(A)**

You should now have a straight piece of wire, which will need annealing before any shaping or bending.

BENDING AND SHAPING

First of all, use the right pliers!

1. Half-round/flat pliers are used to make curves and bends, the curved side of the pliers being held on the inside of the curve being made and the flat side on the outside. This will prevent any marking. **(B)**
2. Round-nose pliers are used to make loops and small "S" shapes by pulling the wire around the nose. Bear in mind, though, that if the wire is held tightly between the tips, it will leave marks on the outside of a bend. **(C)**
3. Flat-nose pliers are used to make sharp angles, hold a bend steady, or to close jump rings. **(D)**

MAKING OVALS

1. Make a jump ring and then solder it together.
2. Hold a pair of round-nose pliers inside the jump ring and open them up so that the round becomes an oval.
3. An oval former can also be used to create oval rings, or if there is nothing on hand, use two rods of the same size taped together along the sides to give an oval shape.

MAKING JUMP RINGS

You will need some sort of rod or tube to use as a former to make jump rings. The outside diameter of the former will be the inside diameter of the ring.

1. Anneal the wire. Tighten the former with the end of the wire into the vise.
2. Hold the wire and wrap it firmly and closely together around the former. **(E)**
3. Cut away any remaining wire. Make a mark using either a piercing saw or a marker at an angle right across the wires. **(F)**
4. You can either remove the former now, hold the rings up against the pin, and cut through them one at a time, or you can keep the former in place and just bring down one ring at a time and saw it off. **(G)**
5. Use two pairs of flat-nose pliers to bring the two ends of each ring together. **(H)**

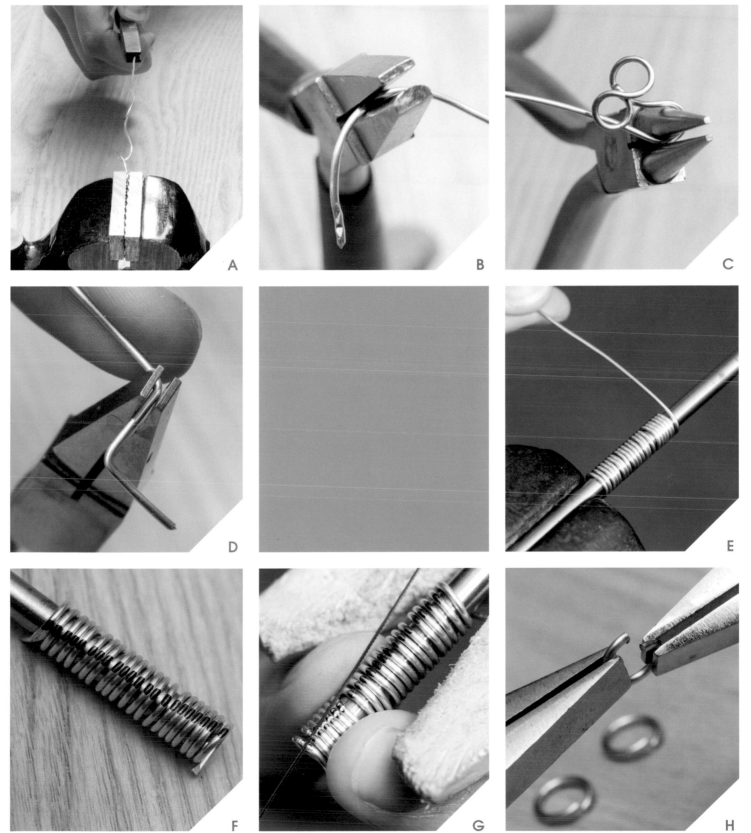

TWISTING WIRE

1. Take an annealed piece of wire of at least double the length needed for the twisted wire.
2. Fold it in half and fasten the two ends sideways in the vise.
3. Make a hook, maybe out of brass or steel, and fasten it into a woodworking drill.
4. Slip the end loop of the wire over the hook and, keeping the tension on the wire, start to wind it up using the handle on the drill until the desired amount of twist has been achieved. **(A)**
5. If a woodworking drill is not on hand, place a rod through the loop and carefully, keeping an even motion, turn the rod until the desired amount of twist has been achieved.
6. After removing from the hook and the vise, the twist will untwist a little. It should be soldered to prevent further unraveling as it is bent.
7. Lay the wire along a soldering block and flux it along the whole length.
8. Cut tiny paillons of hard solder, place them closely along the twist, and solder up. **(B)**

MAKING SPIRALS

1. To make a tight, flat spiral, find a piece of wood or plastic sheet approximately $3/8$ in (10 mm) thick and drill a hole—the same size as the wire being used for the spiral—straight through it.
2. Thread a piece of annealed wire through the hole so that there is an inch or so coming through the bottom. Lay the wood or plastic on top of the vise and tighten it up so that the wire is being held fast. **(C)**
3. Push the wire right over so that it lies flat on the wood and, using a pair of round-nose pliers, start the turn of the spiral. **(D)**
4. The rest of the spiral can be turned by hand, keeping the wires as close as possible. **(E)**
5. Remove it from the vise and cut away the central length.

HARDENING WIRE

After soldering, wire is soft and, if it is being used for a fitting of any sort, it will need hardening. There are several ways of doing this.

1. Harden an earstud wire by holding it with flat-nose pliers as close to the solder join as possible. Then use another pair of flat-nose pliers to hold the other end, leaving a little wire showing in the middle. **(F)**
2. Turn the flat-nose pliers (and the wire) through 180 degrees. Trim the end to size and file it to a comfortable rounded end. To help keep the butterfly fitting in place, a small groove can be filed right around the wire, about $1/8$ to $3/16$ in (3 or 4 mm) from the tip.
3. Harden a wire pin by holding it on the metal flat plate and rolling it along, while tapping it with a jeweler's hammer. **(G)**
4. Wire used for making hooks and catches can be hammered flat around the curve. This helps to keep them springy. **(H)**

A

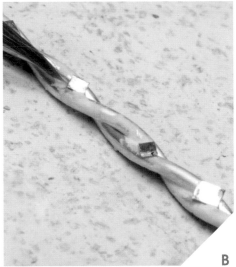

B

TIP

Fine silver wire can be joined to itself by fusing without the need for solder. The ends need to form a tight join and then be heated until the metal just appears to flow.

C

D

E

F

G

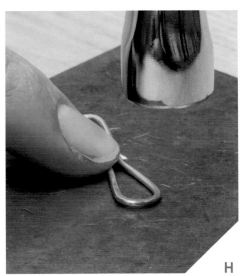

H

CHAINS

There are many varieties of machine-made chain available, but the time spent making one by hand is easily justified—it will bring both originality and value to a piece of jewelry.

Chains are always fascinating—the sheer size of some industrial chains makes me wonder how on earth they were made! Keep an eye out for chains that we take for granted in everyday life; they are often a good source of inspiration.

A chain can be a stand-alone piece, or made to enhance (not detract from) whatever will hang from it. Essentially a chain is a series of linked rings. For most jewelry purposes these links are soldered, although there are exceptions.

MAKING A CHAIN WITH ROUND JUMP RINGS

Making jump rings requires a "former"—keep a selection of steel rods of different diameters on hand. To hang correctly, the inside diameter of the links for a "cable chain" should be at least just more than double the thickness of the wire used. I usually make up a few links first in a cheaper metal to check sizes and appearance.

1. Choose a former. Anneal the wire and wrap one end of it around the former, then tighten the two together in the vise.
2. Keeping the wire under tension, wrap it as tightly as possible around the former until you have the right number of jump rings. **(A)**
3. Turn the blade in the piercing saw the other way up, so the teeth run up instead of down. Hold the rings with the former on the edge of your bench pin and slide a couple of rings down from the former as you start to saw through each one.

4. Make sure your filings drawer, or skin, is nice and clean so that the rings can be found easily as they come off! Cut through one at a time, cutting at a slight angle.
5. Use two pairs of flat-nose pliers to close the rings. Use a side-to-side movement rather than pushing them together.
6. Count the number of jump rings and select about half of them to solder. Lay these on the soldering or charcoal block so all the joins are placed at the same angle. This is to make sure you know where every join is. **(B)**
7. Flux each join, then cut lots of very small paillons of hard solder and place them on top of each join. Solder each one at a time, leaving the flame on the ring just long enough to ensure the solder flows evenly across the join. Clean the rings in the pickle.
8. When they are clean and dry, take one unsoldered ring and slip two soldered rings into it. Hold it with a pair of stainless steel tweezers so that the join to be soldered is isolated, flux it, and place a small paillon of hard solder across the join. Aim the flame slightly above the ring until the solder flows across the join. **(C)**
9. Do this until you have several units of three rings, and then join those together with another jump ring so that you have sets of seven. Continue in this way until you have the full length of chain.

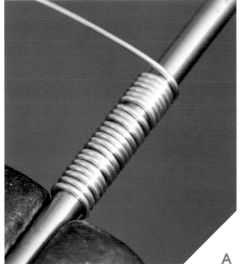

A

B

C

USING SPECIFIC METALS

GOLD
The higher the karat, the easier it is to work: 24-karat gold is very soft, needs little or no annealing and can be fused without solder; 22-karat gold may be fused or soldered but the ends must be close together or they will pull back when heated; 18-karat gold should be annealed as soon as it starts to feel hard; use hard solder when closing jump rings for chains.

PLATINUM
As platinum is strong, very fine wire can be used for jump rings and chains. The join must be very close fitting, with a small piece, $1/64$ in (0.4 mm) thick, of the same alloy of platinum held between it for soldering. Use separate tools and soldering blocks, kept aside for platinum only.

PALLADIUM
Jump ring joins must be very close fitting. Use hard palladium solder (no flux is needed). After soldering and pickling, palladium may lose its brightness; it can be restored with fine abrasive paper. Tools and soldering blocks should be kept seperate. Over-heating when annealing platinum or palladium has a detrimental effect on the metal surface. Once annealed, you should be able to reduce these metals by 70 percent before annealing again.

COPPER
Copper wire can be drawn down through a drawplate (see p. 150) until it is very fine, but it must be annealed constantly to keep it soft. Use silver solder—use the minimum amount to avoid a splotch of silver over the join.

TIP
When pickling very small items such as jump rings, granulation balls, ear wires, etc., pop them all into a small container that will fit inside your pickle, then lower it down carefully, using a pair of brass or stainless steel tweezers so that it fills up with pickle. Leave for five minutes or so, then carefully remove.

MAKING A CHAIN WITH HAMMERED LINKS

To make a chain with hammered or flattened links, solder the jump rings before hammering.

1. Place the rings on a metal flat plate and either place a smaller flat plate over the rings and hammer that evenly until the rings underneath are flat, or flatten them one at a time with the flat side of a ball-peen hammer.
2. Cut through the join where it was soldered and link it into the other flattened rings. Resolder the join.

MAKING A CHAIN WITH OVAL LINKS

1. Either use an oval former in the same way as for making round links (see p. 156), or make round links and slip a pair of round-nose pliers inside each ring and pull the pliers apart to form the desired oval shape. **(A)**
2. To make a twist in the middle of an oval link, do a test first to ensure the correct length of wire—it will shorten as it is twisted. Make the oval link. Use a pair of flat-nose pliers to hold one end of the link, and another pair to hold the other end, and then make the twist. **(B)**

FLAT CHAIN 1

There are several ways to make a chain that will sit flat against the body, the simplest being to make a flat oval link that will join two circles together.

1. Cut a strip of metal to a width appropriate to the design of the chain and a little longer than the intended finished link. Solder the two ends together and file away any remaining solder.
2. Stretch the two ends of the link with round-nose pliers.
3. Cut through the link at the join and slot two links of the chain into it, then resolder it up again. **(C)**

FLAT CHAIN 2

1. On each side or end of the main links for a chain, solder a very small piece of chenier (tubing). File the top and bottom of the chenier to form a U-shaped angle. **(D)**
2. Choose some wire that fits through the chenier to make some jump rings, and then fit them together and use easy solder to close the ring. **(E)**

FLATTENING A CABLE CHAIN

1. Make a chain as usual using either round or oval rings. Hammer a headed nail onto the end of a wooden board and slip one end of the chain over it. Allow the chain to hang from the nail, working down it with your hand to ensure it is all sitting in the same direction. **(F)**
2. Now fix the other end of the chain so it is pulled tight.
3. Pick up the chain carefully and lay it out flat on a metal plate. You can then pass it gently through the rolling mill, taking care to maintain tension as it goes through.

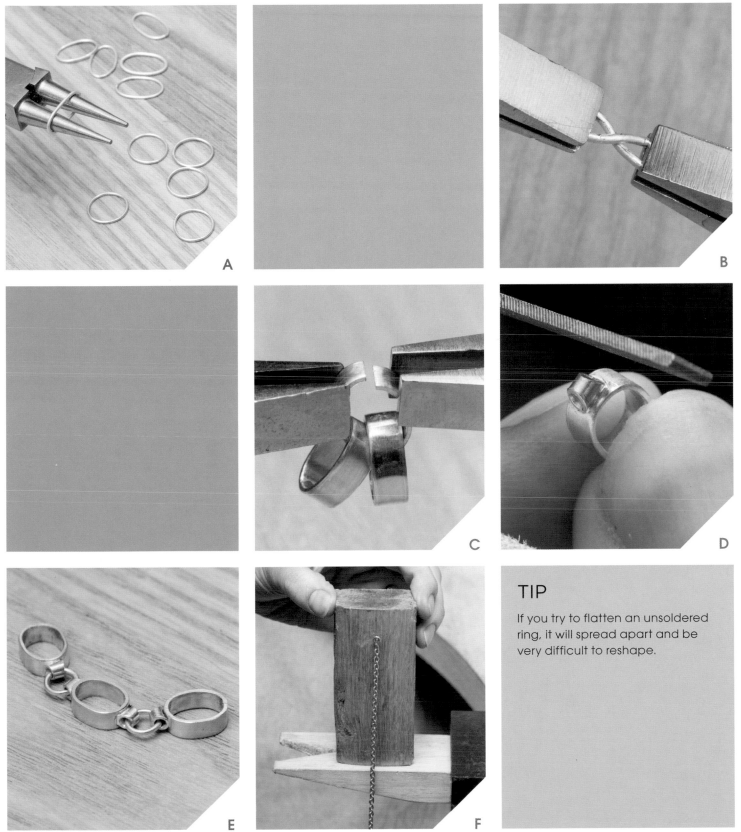

A

B

C

D

E

F

TIP

If you try to flatten an unsoldered ring, it will spread apart and be very difficult to reshape.

LOOP-IN-LOOP CHAINS

Although they can be time-consuming to make, loop-in-loop chains are a great way of making a solid but totally flexible chain. They range from very simple to quite complicated, so we will just look at the basics here. Ideally, the metal used should not be an alloy, but as this is not always practical, keeping the wire annealed will make for a smoother chain.

1. The average diameter of wire used for a loop-in-loop chain is 22 gauge (0.6 mm) but this can vary, along with the size of the loops. Either make jump rings that will stretch to the length of the loops needed, or cut equal lenths of wire and solder the ends together.
2. Fine silver does not need soldering, which can save time when joining lots of hoops. The ends should sit very close together and the flame should be directioned over the join until the metal looks shiny across both sides. **(A)**
3. High-karat golds can be fused in the same way, but bear in mind that if the join is not really close together, one end will pull backward, making it impossible to rejoin.

A SIMPLE LOOP-IN-LOOP CHAIN

1. Take an 8-ft (2.5-m) length of 22-gauge (0.6-mm) round wire. Anneal it and make jump rings around a former with a diameter of approximately $5/16$ in (8 mm). Solder or fuse all the loops. Use a pair of round-nose pliers to spread them into slim ovals. **(B)**
2. Now use a pair of round-nose pliers to squeeze the two sides together in the middle. The loop will look like a figure eight. Squeeze all the loops in the same way. **(C)**
3. Use either a former held in a vise or a pair of round-nose pliers to bend the loop at the squeezed middle so that the top and bottom of the "eight" touch. **(D)**
4. Place a scribe or round-nose pliers through the open sides of the loop to "true" them up, then pass the next loop through the first and shape as above. Continue until the full length of chain is achieved. **(E)**

DOUBLE-LOOP CHAIN

A fuller flexible chain is made by using more loops. This will obviously use more metal, but the result will be a very beautiful and long-lasting chain.

You will need 20 ft (6.5 m) of 22-gauge (0.6-mm) round wire and a former approximately $5/16$ in (8 mm) in diameter.

1. Make all the jump rings as for the loop-in-loop chain, and shape them all in the same way. **(F)**
2. Start the chain with the second loop placed inside the first. Now, push the second loop down toward the first so that the third loop can be pushed through the space just created. **(G)**
3. Each time a new loop is added, it is pushed through the space made by the last but one loop.

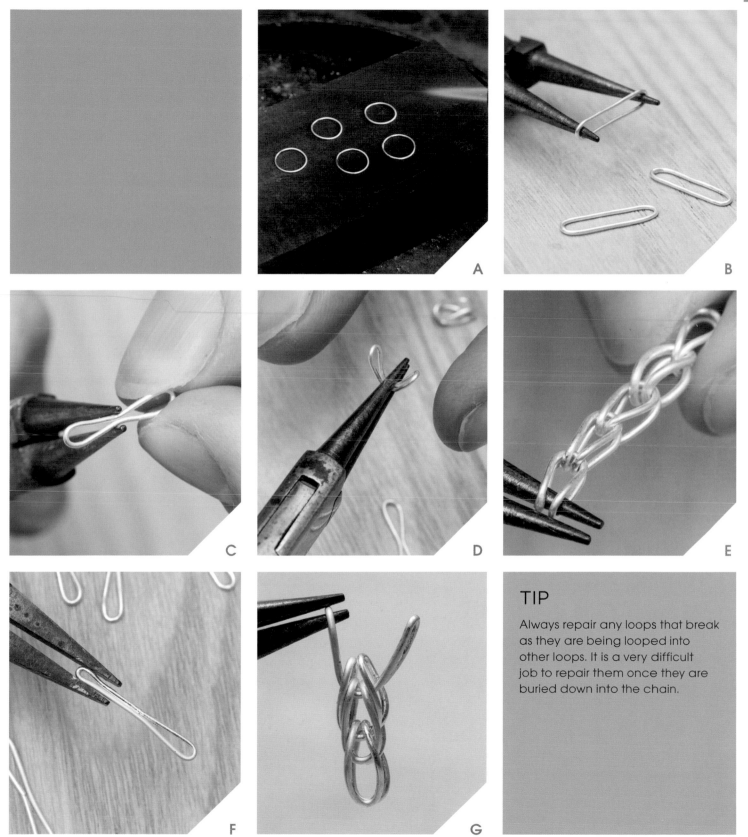

A

B

C

D

E

F

G

TIP

Always repair any loops that break as they are being looped into other loops. It is a very difficult job to repair them once they are buried down into the chain.

KNITTING NANCY

A Knitting Nancy is a wooden cylinder with rivets on one end and is used to weave wool to make a long, round knitted tube. You can make something similar to weave fine silver wire! I have used four loops here, but you can use more, depending on the size of your "reel."

1. Choose an empty cotton reel or similar-shaped article with a wide inside diameter. Fix four loops of wire in place. Bend the loops backward slightly to prevent the wire from slipping over them. Using fine silver wire—28 to 30 gauge (0.25–0.3 mm diameter)—wrap the end tightly around one of the loops to begin.
2. Now move to each loop in turn and wrap the wire from the inside to the outside of each. **(A)**
3. When you get to the second line, use a crochet hook or similar tool to lift the bottom line up and over the top.
4. Continue to create the required length for the chain. **(B)**
5. Loop-in-loop chains usually need smoothing out when finished, as it is difficult to maintain the same tension while making them. Drill holes of decreasing diameters through a thick piece of wood, secure it in a vise and thread a loop of copper—or similar—wire through the first loop of the chain. Pull the chain through the decreasing holes until it is smooth.

MAKING ENDS FOR CHAINS

As a handmade chain always has a beginning and an end, making two identical ends will give it a smooth look when finished. If the chain is fairly simple, with not too many loops, a jump ring can be looped through the loops and soldered. An S-catch can be attached to one of the rings. For a thicker chain, the ends need to fit the diameter, and these can be long, short, tapered, or parallel.

ROUND PARALLEL ENDS

Ideally, use a piece of chenier with an inside diameter matching the outside diameter of your chain, or make tubing yourself (see p. 206) with the correct inside diameter.

1. Cut two identical lengths and file one end of each so that they stand at 90 degrees on a little piece of sheet metal between 24 and 18 gauge (0.5–1 mm thick). Flux around the bottom where the join will be, and lay a few pieces of hard solder around the join. If you have made the tubing, reflux along the join line and add some extra pieces over the join at the base. **(C)**
2. Solder together and, after pickling, rinsing, and drying, cut away the excess metal from the chenier and file.
3. Make two jump rings with a diameter the same as the chenier and solder them with hard solder. Use a flat file on the solder joins. Balance the ring in the middle of the end of the chenier piece and use hard solder to fix it. Repeat with the other piece. **(D)**
4. Now file around the outside of the open end of the chenier to give it a graduated finish. **(E)**
5. Paint the inside of the chenier with flux and push the end of the chain into it tightly. Place some paillons of easy solder where the chain meets the end of the chenier and solder together. An S-catch can now be fitted. **(F)**

RECTANGULAR/SQUARE PARALLEL ENDS

If the chain is flat sided make the ends to fit.

1. Measure the sides of the chain with a pair of dividers.
2. Use this measurement to mark the bends on a metal sheet approximately 24 gauge (0.5 mm thick). Score the lines so they can be bent using flat-nose pliers. **(G)**
3. Now flux and solder this piece (using hard solder) to a base sheet that has one end bent up. **(H)**
4. Trim around the edges, then continue as for round ends, finishing with a clasp. **(I)**

FINISHING

Finishing involves removing marks and scratches, replacing them with finer ones until a surface has a uniform finish. An ultrafine polished finish is not always crucial, but a finish should always reflect the light in a smooth, pleasing way.

Solder residues, firescale (a staining left on the surface of metal after finishing, see p. 61), and random file marks or scratches should all be removed before a piece is "finished." This can all be done by hand, with small finishing papers and mops held in the end arm of a pendant motor, with larger brushes and mops on a polishing machine, or in a barrel or magnetic polishing machine (see Chapter 1). Working carefully, using the correct amount of solder, and making sure that joins are close and neat and that each stage of construction is cleaned and finished before moving onto the next will help to reduce the time spent cleaning up around difficult joins and removing file marks from awkward places.

PAPERS AND CLOTHS

Any remaining obvious scratches and previous file marks are removed from a piece using the appropriate grade and shape of needle file. A finer finish is then achieved using different grades of emery or wet/dry papers.

1. Emery papers are used dry. As the name suggests, wet/dry papers can be used dry or held under water or a running faucet as they are being worked across a metal surface. The coarsest papers are numbered between grades 110 and 240, and the finest is 1200, with grades in between of 400, 600, 800, and 1000. Finer "polishing" papers, or "crocus" papers, are used to give a high shine. These grades are also available on cloth instead of paper, and these are useful when more flexibility is required. **(A)**

2. When using emery papers in small and difficult areas, pieces can be cut from the large sheet and either wrapped around a needle file or a small piece of wood, such as a matchstick. **(B)**

3. There are also flexible files, known as "flexifiles," which look very similar to nail files but have four different grades (usually 240, 400, 800, and polishing) of paper on one file, and which will bend over and around curves, making them very practical. **(C)**

BRUSHES

1. On castings and items with textured finishes, use a soft brass brush with a liquid soap and water to achieve a nice bright shine. (If used on a smooth surface, the brass brush will leave quite obvious scratches, and if it is used without a liquid soap it will leave a yellowy tinge.)

2. An old toothbrush dipped in water and pumice powder and rubbed over metal will give a soft matte finish. This is a very good way of cleaning an item after soldering and pickling, as it will show any areas that need further work before finishing. **(D)**

3. A glass brush used with a liquid soap will give a very crisp, bright finish after pickling. These brushes are made with tiny fibers of glass, so always wear rubber gloves when working with them because the small fibers have a nasty habit of finding their way into your fingers if you do not!

4. A soft bristle brush used with water and liquid soap can be helpful as a cleaning tool, but this will not really give a special finish.

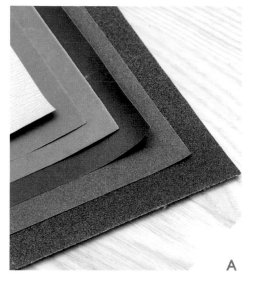

A

B

C

D

TIP

It is a good idea to wrap and stick emery papers to a flat wooden stick. In addition to helping to keep surfaces flat and even while hand polishing, this will also help to prolong the life of the paper.

USING SPECIFIC METALS

GOLD
When using gold, keep any filings separate. The color of high-karat gold can be enhanced by pickling in a hot sulfuric acid or hot nitric acid. Always have fresh water on hand so that a piece can be placed immediately into water after pickling. Do not take gold out of one acid and put it in another without a thorough rinse first.

PLATINUM/PALLADIUM
Special polishing heads, from mildly abrasive to very fine, are used in the pendant motor for these metals. For a highly polished finish, these must be used in the correct order. They are used after emery or wet/dry papers.

COPPER AND BRASS
These take a long time to clean in pickle, but will clean very quickly with a pumice paste or a brass brush and liquid soap.

ALUMINUM
This takes on a really good finish when turned on a lathe. As the metal is quite "grainy," work down through the wet/dry papers until you have a shiny, bright, smooth surface. Keep any files and filings separate from precious metals.

STEEL/IRON
Filing and sandpapering will produce a beautiful surface. These files are only really for use with nonprecious metals.

IMPREGNATED CLOTHS AND STRINGS

Special cloths impregnated with a fine "powder" will clean most metals. Either use the cloth like a duster or hold one corner in a vise and pull it tight, rubbing the piece along the cloth to give it a high polish. You can also thread the cloth through rings and other hard-to-reach areas. **(A)**

"Strings" are supplied in a ream and are fixed so that they can be pulled tight. Use a few strings at a time to get into tight holes and corners of your work. Drop some lighter fluid along the strings and rub on an all-purpose polishing wax, then pull tight while rubbing your piece up and down. **(B)**

LIQUIDS

Some liquids for cleaning metal can be abrasive, so test them first. The sole pupose of some liquids is to remove oxidation and brighten the look. Use these carefully; if an article is left in these liquids for more than a minute or so, it can actually worsen the look! When removed from the fluid it will be sticky, so wash it immediately with a liquid soap and water.

BARREL AND MAGNETIC POLISHERS

Esentially, both of these machines do the same job. A barrel polisher is a revolving drum that burnishes a piece of metal with small stainless steel media and a soapy compound. The stainless steel media and cleaning liquid in a magnetic polisher are activated by a magnetic field. This machine has no lid, so items can be added during use.

POLISHING MACHINES

A polishing machine has two horizontal shafts onto which different polishing mops, brass and stainless steel mops, and carborundum wheels are attached (see p. 41). There are several different mops used when a high polish is required, and each mop should only ever be used with one type of polish. When applying polish to a mop, it is better to apply little and often rather than applying loads and hoping it lasts until the polishing is finished. This tends to make streaks, which can leave annoying lines in the final result.

1. Start by using a bristle brush with a tripoli polish, which comes in a brown block and is fairly coarse and greasy. After polishing with tripoli, the piece must be cleaned and degreased before going onto the next polish. **(C)**
2. Now use a stitched or soft muslin mop together with a finer polish such as hyfin (a white block) or green polish, then clean and degrease the piece as before. **(D)**
3. The third and final polish should be a rouge, which will give the metal a high shine. Rouge is also quite a greasy polish so use a lambswool mop and dip the rouge into mineral spirits first before charging the mop, as this will make it slightly less greasy. **(E)**

PENDANT MOTORS

Flexishaft pendant motors have two heads into which different abrasive, cutting, drilling, and polishing tools can be fitted. The usual head is handheld; the tools are fitted into a constant chuck and tightened to fit. The alternative is a "hammer" head. This is used with small metal punch-type tools to work around a bezel and push it down when setting a stone. When used for finishing, there are literally hundreds of different wheels, mops, brushes, and burrs available for creating a polished or textured surface. These are able to polish in places that are inaccessible when using larger mops on the polishing machine. Take care, though—the surface area of a little mop is much smaller than a mop on the larger machine, so when used across a flat surface wider than itself, it tends to make a "groove" of its width, which is then very hard to remove. Very fine silicone heads are used to polish platinum and palladium. These do not need to have any polishing compound applied to them. Blue medium-abrasive heads are particularly useful for smoothing around the inside of a ring. The pink abrasive heads are much coarser and can be used to grind away excess solder and sprues left over from casting (see p. 168).

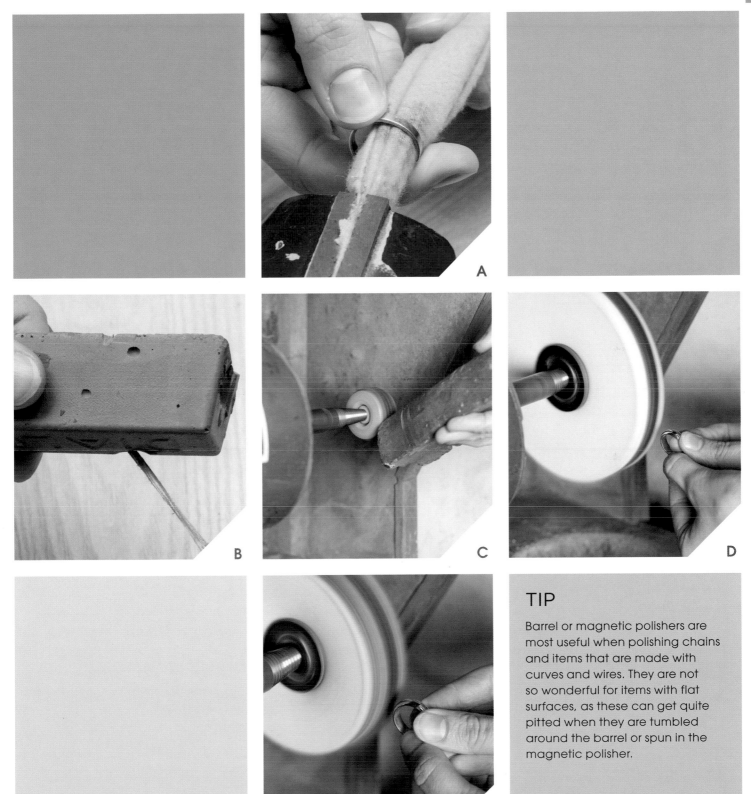

A

B

C

D

E

TIP

Barrel or magnetic polishers are most useful when polishing chains and items that are made with curves and wires. They are not so wonderful for items with flat surfaces, as these can get quite pitted when they are tumbled around the barrel or spun in the magnetic polisher.

CASTING

There are two reasons to choose casting when making something in metal: to produce a one-off piece, or to produce several—perhaps hundreds—of identical pieces.

A one-off piece can be cleaned and polished to use as is, or it can have a sprue added (a passageway for introducing molten metal to a mold), be cleaned and polished, and then get used as a model for further castings. In this section we look at creating a wax model as well as a few casting techniques suitable for the small workshop—cuttlefish, sand, and lost-wax. To find the weight of metal needed for a casting, you will need its specific gravity (SG). (If this is unknown, make a calculated guess by comparing it to a known one.) Then multiply the weight of the wax model by the SG of your metal—e.g., for a 2 oz wax model, you would need 20.8 oz of silver (2 x SG of 10.4) or 33 oz of 18-karat gold (2 x SG of 16.5). Always add $1/3$ oz (10 g) extra to allow for the sprue. This applies to all metals. Remember, too, that after a piece is cast it loses about 10 percent of its volume.

MELTING METAL

Place the metal in a crucible. If using scrap pieces, remove all signs of solder first, then cut them into small pieces. Fasten the crucible into a holder with a wooden handle and add a little flux powder. Aim a very hot flame directly at the metal so that it becomes shiny. Hold this until the metal's surface tension is reduced and it becomes a spinning mass. I now count to 20 to make sure that there are no unmelted pieces lurking in the mass, and to raise the metal's temperature a bit so that it stays molten as it is poured into the mold. If it cools too quickly, the casting will not be complete.

CARVING WAX MODELS BY HAND

A wax model can be used to produce a mold and from that, a finished piece. This can be done in the workshop (see Lost-wax casting, p. 174) or outsourced to a specialist company for casting. Wax is available in different thicknesses of sheet and wire, resembling the dimensions of commonly used metals. There are also blocks of wax for carving; various profile tubes for rings; solid waxes that, when heated in water, become soft and pliable in the hand; and very soft waxes that are used for repairs. There are also "sprue waxes," which are attached to all models —either thin rods to attach to a single piece or thicker ones, used where wax models are attached like branches all the way up a "tree."

Try holding a former in a vise and use this to make a ring by bending the wax over it. Heat the former (in water), dry, and lightly oil it to prevent the wax sticking. **(A)**

To avoid overheating, cut wax slowly with a piercing or coping saw. Once a rough shape has been achieved it can be refined with scalpels, files, and engraving tools. **(B)**

To make carving easier, warm tools by passing them through a small flame. Wax sheet can be softened by immersing it in hot water. This will then allow it to be manipulated without it cracking. For joining waxes together and "sprueing," pass the blade of a craft knife through a flame and place it between the two areas to be joined. This will melt the wax enough to hold it. Keep it in the same position until cool. **(C)**

It is easy, when first using wax, to make a model that is too heavy. Remember that most metal jewelry is fairly light. A wax ring with a thickness of $1/8$–$3/16$ in (3–4 mm) around the shank will look perfectly acceptable; translate that into metal, however, and it will become very heavy and require much tedious filing to get it down to lighter proportions.

A

B

TIP

Always have a reason for casting. If a piece can be made easily and accurately by fabrication, there is no reason to cast it. Casting is appropriate for designs that have some parts that are thicker than others, convex/concave curves, lifelike three-dimensional models, surface textures, and pieces that cannot really be made any other way.

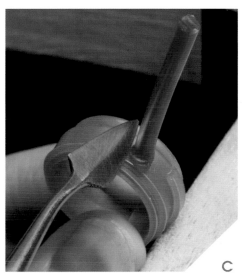

C

CUTTLEFISH CASTING

Cuttlefish bones can be bought at pet stores, from jewelry suppliers, or found on the beach. They have one hard side and one soft. Make sure they are dry before use, and choose bones that are nice and thick down the central area. To get the best use of very large bones, cut them in half and use each half for a separate casting. The dense white bone is cut in half lengthways. When compressed and then swept gently with a soft paintbrush, the lined pattern of the bone emerges, transferring beautifully onto the metal when it is poured in.

1. Cut away any hard bone on each edge. **(A)**
2. Cut across the top and bottom in a straight line. **(B)**
3. With a larger piercing saw, cut straight down through the middle, using a slightly pushing action and keeping the blade as smooth and straight as possible. **(C)**
4. With the two sides back together, draw a zigzag line in pencil across the top. If the cutting is very uneven, place each side on a sheet of wet/dry paper on a flat surface. Gently rub the bone down until the inside is smooth and flat, then fit the pieces back together again. **(D)**
5. Draw the area that outlines the pattern for the casting on one side of the inside bone, then scrape it out using a small metal tool. **(E)**
6. On the top edge of both sides, hollow out a sprue, or entry, for the molten metal.
7. Make sure there are no barriers between the sprue and the hollow area that will impede the flow of the metal.
8. Using a scribe, draw three or four air lines down from the pattern, which will allow the air to escape when casting. **(F)**
9. Place the two sides back together and fix binding wire around the top and bottom of the bone, then secure the cuttlefish firmly in a soldering tray. **(G)**
10. Place the metal in a crucible with a pinch of powdered flux and heat it until it forms a spinning ball. The metal must remain liquid and spinning as it is poured directly into the sprue area. **(H)**
11. Allow to cool for a moment before cutting off the binding wire, opening the two halves, and dropping the cast piece into some water. The piece is now ready to be finished. **(I)**

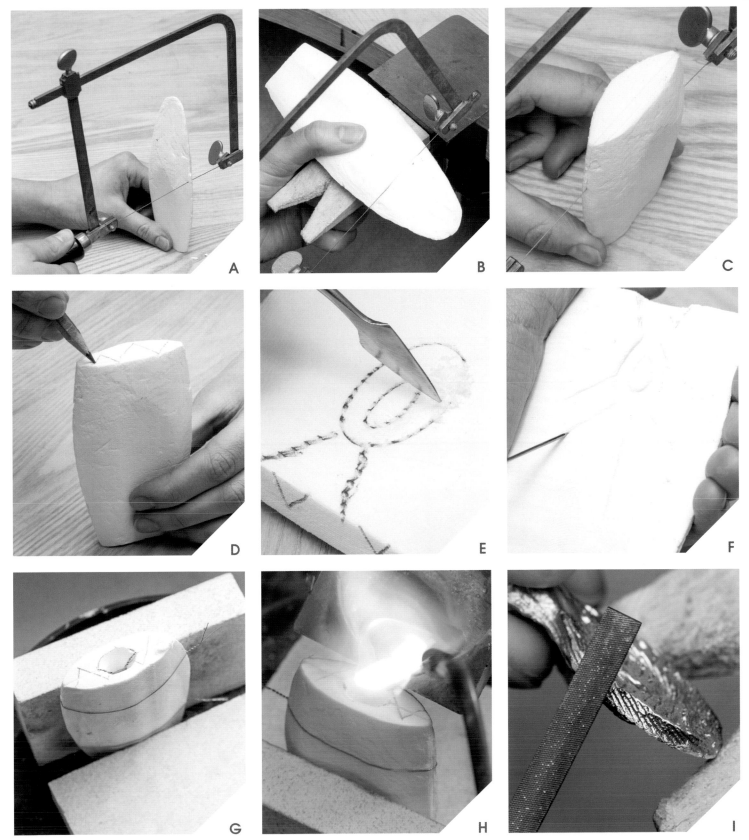

A

B

C

D

E

F

G

H

I

SAND CASTING

Sand casting has been used as a method of casting for many centuries. Silversmiths, when making large items or items with curves or angles not easily achieved by other methods, laid sand on the floor and made impressions into which they poured the molten metal.

Sand casting for jewelry is done in either wooden or metal molding boxes. These boxes come as two halves and are filled with a dense casting sand. The box is designed for either a horizontal or vertical pour of the metal, which passes through an area cut out through the sand at the top of the box (the sprue) into the hollow made in each half to produce the casting.

The casting shown here uses an aluminum flask with a horizontal spread.

1. Fill one half of the flask with the sand and compress it down as much as possible. Level off the top using a metal straightedge. **(A)**
2. Now press the model of the piece that is going to be cast into the sand until it reaches halfway down. **(B)**
3. Spread talcum powder thinly over the sand and the model. This helps separate the two halves cleanly.
4. Fit the other half of the flask on top, aligning using the marks made in both sides, then fill it with sand and compress it down as you did on the bottom half. **(C)**
5. Carefully pull the two halves apart and remove the model equally carefully, using a fine, sharp point so that the sand is not disturbed. **(D)**
6. Now cut an area for the sprue in the sand of the top half. Do this by first pushing through, from the side or top of the impression left, a drill of approximately $1/8$ in (2 mm) in diameter. **(E)**
7. Now remove a wider area from the top to allow for easy pouring. **(F)**

8. In the lower half, draw air lines out away from the impression and join them up with a circle, using the end of a scribe or similar tool. Then use a drill to make a hole from the circle down through the base of the box. This will allow the air in the impression to escape easily when the metal is poured in. **(G)**
9. Put the two halves back together again, with the marks lined up ready for casting.
10. Place the metal in a crucible with a pinch of powdered flux, and heat it until it forms a spinning ball. The metal must remain liquid and spinning as it is being poured into the mold.
11. Now separate the two halves to reveal the finished casting. **(H)**

A

B

C

D

TIP

Molten metal will not flow back on itself, so make sure that the pattern being cast flows downward, with no return. If the model has any curves that come back on themselves they will appear to be fine when they are pushed into the sand, but when removed, they will break up the sand, and therefore not result in a true copy.

E

F

G

H

173

LOST-WAX CASTING

This is a somewhat more involved process, but it too creates a space within a mold into which molten metal can be poured. Both robust and fine three-dimensional pieces are easier to achieve, and the quality of the casting is less porous than with cuttlefish or sand casting. The main advantage of this process is that once made, a model can be reproduced many times.

Centrifugal casting is the most commonly used method in small workshops. The metal is thrust at great speed out of a crucible at the center of the rotation and into a mold (away from the center) as it spins in a circular motion. This centrifugal force produces a denser, less porous result than is the case with poured molten metal, which relies on gravity alone. Casting machines come in different shapes and sizes, so I have just described the principle here.

The following exercise demonstrates making a wax model of a ring, attaching a sprue, fixing it in a flask, covering it with liquid investment, placing it in the casting machine, melting silver, then propelling it into the mold.

MAKING THE WAX MODEL

1. Cut out the basic shape of the ring from a bar of green or blue wax. Cut out enough to accommodate the widest part of the ring. **(A)**
2. Outline the pattern of the ring on the wax with a scribe. This will give you an idea of where the first cuts will be, or where to start filing. **(B)**
3. File the wax to shape. (Wax can be removed quite quickly with a special carving file.) Always bear in mind that silver weighs 11 times more than wax, so try to imagine what the ring will look like in metal. Wax can be filed until it is really quite thin. During casting, though, about 10 percent in volume is lost, so do make allowances for that. **(C)**

4. Attach a wax sprue. Hold the sprue over a gentle flame and, as it starts to drip, place it quickly onto the model. It should be attached to the heaviest area. **(D)**
5. Now weigh the entire piece and record this figure. Then use one of the following calculations to work out the metal required for the piece:
   SILVER: weight of wax x 11 + $^1/_3$ oz (10 g) to allow for the sprue
   10-KARAT GOLD: weight of wax x 13 + $^1/_3$ oz (10 g) for the sprue
   18-KARAT GOLD: weight of wax x 16 + $^1/_3$ oz (10 g) for the sprue
6. Fix the model and sprue into the rubber base of the flask. There should be a gap of at least $^3/_{16}$ in (5 mm) between the edges and top of the flask and the model. **(E)**

A

B

C

D

E

TIP

Models are usually carved or machined out of differing grades and colors of wax, but they can also be "found" objects that will burn out at temperatures of up to 1360°F (740°C).

THE INVESTMENT

1. Assess the amount of investment powder needed for the flask. The flask should be attached to its rubber base and the model securely sprued.

2. Fill the flask with water to within 3/16 in (5 mm) of the top. Pour this water into a large rubber bowl. **(A)**

3. Use a tablespoon to sprinkle investment powder on top of the water. At first it will just sink to the bottom, but once you have the correct amount, it will start to sit on the surface. Mixing and clearing away air bubbles should now take no longer than 10 minutes. If it does, you may need to start again, as the mixture will become too thick and sticky to pour properly. Give the mixture a really good stir, making sure you reach the bottom of the bowl and mix everything together well. **(B)**

4. Place the rubber bowl on a "vibrating table." Hold it down firmly and let as many air bubbles surface as you can. **(C)**

5. Squeeze the sides of the bowl to make pouring easier, and pour the investment carefully into the flask. **(D)**

6. Now put the flask on the vibrating table for a minute or so to allow any air trapped during the pouring to surface.

7. The flask should be left to dry overnight. In the morning, peel the rubber base away from the flask. As this is being done, you will see the base of the wax sprue. **(E)**

8. Place the flask in the kiln with the sprue end facing down. This will allow the melting wax to get out.

9. Switch on the kiln and hold it between 300 and 390°F (150 and 200°C) for about an hour. Then turn it up to about 750°F (400°C), and hold it at that temperature for about one-and-a-half hours. Finally, turn it up to 1300°F (720°C) and hold it for about one hour more. These different temperatures will allow sufficient time for a) the investment to dry out, b) the wax to melt thoroughly, and c) the investment to harden.

CENTRIFUGAL CASTING

1. Place the required amount of metal in the crucible. Cut out any existing solder and cut up scrap pieces so that they all fit comfortably. Sprinkle a pinch of powdered flux on top. Add an extra 1/3 oz (10 g) of metal to allow for the sprue. **(F)**

2. Wearing protective gloves, remove the flask from the kiln with a large pair of steel tongs. Hold it about midway around. Place it in the centrifugal machine and close up the crucible so that it is as close and as tight as possible to the sprue end of the flask.

3. It should now all be balanced and everything fastened tightly. The machine is primed ready for action, while the metal is being melted.

4. Once the metal is molten enough, with no small lumps remaining, activate the machine. Always make sure that there is nothing in the way of the centrifugal arm, which would cause it to stall.

5. When the machine has finished spinning and the bottom of the flask has hopefully turned from a lovely red to black, remove it with the tongs and plunge it into a metal bucket of cold water. A few swishes to and fro will disperse the investment, revealing the metal casting. **(G)**

6. Pickle it, scrub it clean of any remaining investment, and then remove all sprues with a saw. It will now need filing and polishing to finish it, either as a one-off original piece or to be sent away for a rubber mold to be made from it so that many copies can be produced if desired. **(H)**

A

B

C

D

E

F

G

H

TIP

The machine should be totally enclosed as it is spinning so that, in case of a breakthrough of the investment, any flying metal will be contained within the encasement.

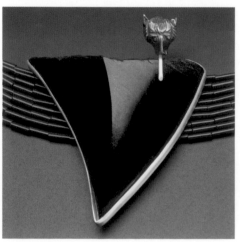

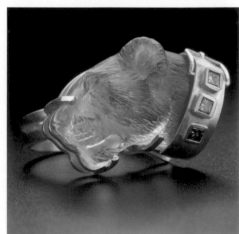

INTERVIEW: BARBARA CHRISTIE

British designer Barbara Christie created one-off works that featured unique and diverse combinations of tactile surfaces, construction methods, colors, and materials. She passed away in 2013.

What is a typical work day for you—is there a set routine?

My workshop has a disciplined of a 9 AM start. Taking Fergus (an extraordinary tabby cat) and a cup of tea with me, I head up the stairs and to my usual spot. My workshop is on the second floor, with nice large wooden windows overlooking a tree-lined avenue. Normally everything is packed away from the night before, as I like to start with a clean slate. So unpacking and getting my thoughts in motion is the next step. Then is my favorite part of the day—the making of the piece and all its technical complications.

I work solidly for the next couple of hours while listening to an audiobook—perhaps a thriller or something else that will provide easy "background noise." Lunchtime is then normally around half an hour—a play with the cat; a sit outside in the garden—and then back to the bench for another four hours or so. Afternoons can vary and may involve seeing clients for commissioned work or preparing for exhibitions.

How do you find working with clients?

Commissions are a large part of my practice, and the most enjoyable part of this work is interaction with the clients, many of whom have become friends over the years—and regular customers.

Can you describe your usual design process?

The piece I am involved with has always been carefully worked out in every detail, first by playing with the idea and concept, then planning it out on paper, and maybe making a model. The model is really meant to show me all the "technicalities." When it comes to designing the actual piece, the form is sometimes dictated by the combinations of stones available in my treasure trove, or it will sometimes follow a preconceived idea.

What materials do you use, and where do you source them from?

My materials are sourced overseas and from dealers coming into the workshop. Most of my materials are precious metals, but I do sneak in some rusty iron or steel too. Instead of using precious and semiprecious stones, I use Georgian glass, pieces of bone, meteorite, Damascus steel, and various types of granite. I cut some of my own material but often find inspiration in the natural forms and inclusions they offer.

Through all my years of working, I have never ceased to be amazed by the materials I have been able to find. I have thoroughly enjoyed working with whatever treasures have come my way, and long may it last.

Opposite
Top: Necklace with silver detail.
Bottom left: Silver and gold drop earrings with opals.
Bottom center: Coral necklace with carved head.
Bottom right: Gold ring with carved lion's head and diamonds.
Above: Gold ring with labradorite ammonite and diamond.

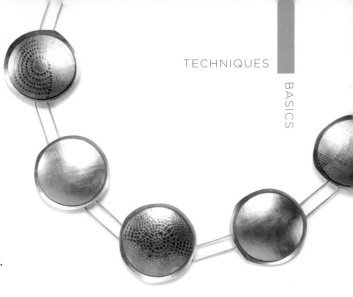

INTERVIEW: FELICITY PETERS

Australian designer Felicity Peters is internationally recognized for her development of the Korean art of keum boo, which involves fusing high-karat gold to silver.

What is it that appeals to you about metalsmithing?

I am passionate about my craft, and I love the fact that my craft comes from a long line of history and tradition. I am always in awe of what others before me have achieved in metalwork, and now I am in awe of all the wonderful creative forms and shapes that can be made using CAD design.

What is a typical work day for you?

My working days are seldom the same... I might start at about 8:30 AM, after I have checked e-mails. I do not "do" Facebook or Twitter, but I love seeing work and exhibitions posted online that others have seen whilst traveling. Perth, Western Australia, is the most isolated city in the world, so to have a handle on what is happening at jewelry fairs like Schmuck is marvelous.

My working day might then be finishing off a piece, repairing something, or working on a new commission.

How do you sell your work?

My work is generally sold through galleries, which is something I am grateful for. I feel that I need galleries to sell my work—working on my behalf, getting my pieces into collections or selling to private collectors. I prefer to spend my energies on making new work!

Describe your working environment.

When I am really busy I tend to work in quite a mess—tools on the ground where I can reach them, bits and pieces spread out around me. My benchtop is a very messy site. But I make sure I know where everything is! Whenever there is a hiatus, I will start from one end and begin cleaning up, hanging up the hammers, finding yet more boxes for storing samples or strange materials that I have sourced.

What is the best part of the day for you?

My favorite part of the day is going to my workshop. I am quite territorial about my space. In the wintertime I enjoy getting snug and warm and lost in a new technique. In the summer it is good to have the perfume of the roses and the sound of the kookaburras. And a ten-minute spell in the hanging chair will often help me solve a problem, or simply refresh my soul.

Has your work changed at all since you began?

My work has definitely changed over the years. In my student days I also made bold pieces, but mainly using copper and patinas as the key materials. Over the years I have acquired more and more skills: anticlastic forming with Michael Good, granulation with Giovanni Corvaja and Kent Raible, hydraulic forming with Susan Kingsley, enameling with Jamie Bennett and Hiltrud Blaich. My work now tends to be mainly semiprecious materials and usually reflects the results of the explorations that I have made through research and the skills that I have developed over the years.

Opposite
Top: Silver ring with gold argyle diamond.
Bottom left: Keum boo brooch.
Bottom center: Keum boo pendant.
Bottom right: Silver and gold keum boo brooch with enamel paint.
Above: Silver and gold keum boo neckpiece.

GALLERY

1. Plain and oxidized sterling silver necklace with wirework, by Beth Pohlman.

2. Gold-plated wire necklace, by Hannah Bedford.

3. Cut and pierced sterling silver pendant, by Mary Walke.

4. Filed gold ring, by Stephanie Maslow-Blackman.

5. Formed gold initial necklace, by Michelle Chang.

6. Cut and filed zinc and textile necklace, by Malou Paul.

1

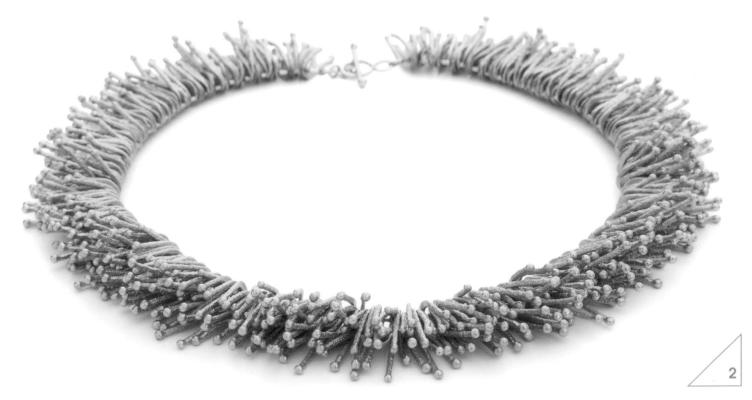

2

3

4

5

6

1

2

3

GALLERY

1. Pierced silver heart earrings,
   by Maria Apostolou.

2. Fused and drilled white gold ring,
   by Doron Merav.

3. Cast gold cuff, by Doron Merav.

4. Pierced gold ring set with a spessartite garnet,
   by Tamara McFarland.

5. Lost wax-cast, oxidized silver necklaces,
   by Kirsten Muenster.

4

4. SURFACE TREATMENTS

One of the many lovely aspects of working with metal is being able to start with a plain sheet where the surface is smooth, and then finishing the work with the surface in a totally altered state. In this chapter, we will cover just a few of the different ways to achieve this.

Opposite: Stamped sterling silver pendant on a silk cord, by Cynthia Nge.

Below: Patinated silver brooch, by Beth Pohlman.

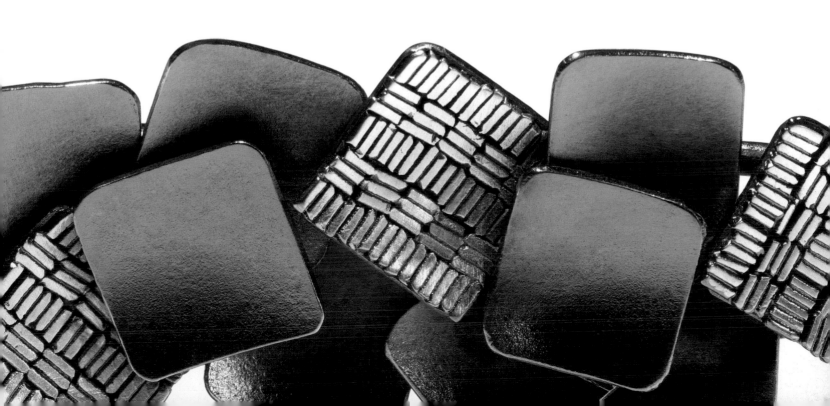

REPOUSSÉ AND CHASING

These two skills are usually worked in conjunction with each other. When combined, they enable you to create a three-dimensional piece by working with punches and chasing tools, beginning with a flat sheet of metal.

Repoussé is a French term meaning "pushed up." With this technique, a design is pushed up from the back of a metal sheet. Chasing then involves drawing detailed lines on the front of the sheet and defining the areas raised by the repoussé process. As the metal is formed into highs and lows it strengthens, so a thinner gauge of metal can be used—e.g., if you were using a 19-gauge (1-mm) thick sheet for a flat panel, when it is being repousséd, a sheet of 24 gauge (0.6 mm) would be sufficient.

Various steel punches are needed for this work. The most useful shapes are smooth round and oval-headed punches. A triangular or wedge-shaped head can be useful too. For chasing you will need small, blunt, chisel-shaped ends that can be hammered to form lines across the metal without cutting it. Patterned heads, featuring crosshatching, lines, circles, etc., can be used to define background areas.

Work is usually carried out on a bed of "pitch"—a mixture of bitumen, plaster, and a lubricant (tallow, beeswax, or linseed oil). Pitch gives as you work, yet it provides a supportive, firm background. If pitch becomes brittle and difficult to work, more lubricant is added; if it becomes too soft and gooey, more plaster is added. Pitch is kept in a thick metal container and heated to soften it so it is ready for use. As it heats it gives off heavy fumes, so work in a ventilated area.

WORKING A PIECE

1. Use a fine marker pen to mark the area on the front that will be pushed out from the back of the metal. **(A)**
2. Now fold down the corners of the piece and place it in the pitch. **(B)**

3. Strike a blunt chisel-type chasing tool repeatedly with a chasing hammer to follow the line. Hold the chisel at an angle—thumb on one side, fingers on the other, and touching the metal or pitch for support. **(C)**
4. Hit the top of the chisel with the flat side of the hammer. Use only enough pressure to create a smooth line, which will just show on the reverse side of the metal.
5. Turn the metal over and strike the repoussé tools and punches vertically to push into the areas marked out from the front. (Keep it all as smooth as possible. If the metal becomes hard to work, remove it from the pitch and anneal it.) **(D)**
6. Lift the piece and clean it. The pitch can be removed easily by standing the piece in a soldering table and playing a flame over it until the pitch has flaked off. (Avoid using soldering blocks, as pitch can contaminate them.) Now quench the piece. **(E)**
7. Redraw the pattern for the chasing on the front of the piece, then replace it in the pitch, front side up. Use chasing tools to push the metal back down along the lines, leaving the repousséd areas high. **(F)**
8. Backgrounds and details are achieved on the metal with marked punches held at right angles to the work. The back and front of the metal may need working over more than once. Make sure the piece is annealed before each side is placed face down in the pitch. During this process the sides of the metal will start to curl and distort.
9. Remove the piece from the pitch, then anneal, quench, and dry it. Place it top side up on a metal flat plate, and use a smooth oval punch to flatten out the sides. **(G)**
10. Cut the outside edge of the piece away with a piercing saw, and neaten it using files.

A

B

C

D

E

F

G

TIP

When chasing lines, take care not to hit the punch too hard—this can cause a split in the metal.

189

DOMING

Doming—also known as dapping—is a technique used for creating a concave or convex surface in a round or oval cutout piece of metal.

Doming is a commonly used technique in the workshop. It requires rounded or oval-ended punches, a round and oval doming block, and/or a floor-standing hardwood tree trunk section with round and oval depressions carved into it. Before doming, the metal being used should be annealed, and its diameter should be slightly smaller than the depression into which it is being sunk.

A "cake" of lead can also be used for shaping larger domes. Lead cakes are made by melting lead into a tin container. They provide a flexible support when hammering or doming annealed metals. Specific shapes, such as deep ovals or round stakes, can be oiled lightly and then sunk into the lead once it has been melted sufficiently. Lead should be handled with care, and beginners are advised to work with it under supervision until they are familiar with the technique.

MAKING A SPHERE

1. Set a pair of dividers to $^5/_{16}$ in (7.5 mm) and draw two circles on the silver. The dividers will make a mark at the center point, which can then be used later when drilling the hole. **(A)**
2. Pierce out the circles and file the edges smooth. Anneal and then pickle, rinse, and dry them.
3. Select a depression in the doming block with a slightly larger diameter than the circles. Place one circle over it. Position a wooden or metal round-ended punch over the center of the circle and use a hammer or mallet to strike the punch vertically until the metal touches the base of the depression. **(B)**
4. Now work the punch in a circular motion to shape the metal to the sides of the depression. The top edge of the metal can be worked around the base of the dome to achieve a really good shape. **(C)**

5. Now place the dome into depressions of decreasing sizes and work it in the same way to produce a tighter half sphere. When the desired shape is achieved, repeat all the steps with the second circle.
6. Use a large flat file to smooth the edges of the half spheres until they sit neatly together. **(D)**
7. Paint flux all around the edge of one side. Then cut about eight small paillons of hard solder and place them at intervals on the flux. Heat them until the solder runs. Pickle, rinse, and dry. **(E)**
8. Lightly file away most of the solder until it is almost flat with the edge. **(F)**
9. Drill a small hole (suggested diameter of $^1/_{16}$ in or 1 mm) in the center of both half spheres. **(G)**
10. Paint flux around the edge again and place the two sides together. **(H)**
11. Make a depression in a charcoal block to hold the sphere steady and place it down, ready for soldering. Check that the sphere is aligned all around, by turning the soldering table and checking each side.
12. Place two or three small pieces of hard solder right across the join. Heat the sphere gently to start with, and then increase the heat until they run. This will show when the solder in the edge is actually running.
13. After soldering, pickle the sphere, wash it thoroughly in running water, then shake well to dry. File away any excess solder and clean around the solder join with wet/dry papers or flexifiles.

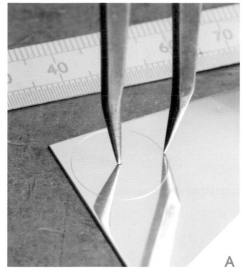

A

B

C

D

TIP

Any thickness of metal can be used to make a sphere, but the thicker it is, the harder it will be to form into a really good shape. This example uses 18-gauge (1-mm-thick) silver.

E

F

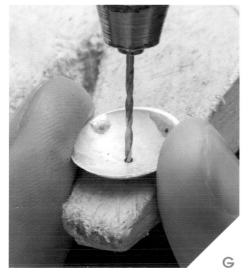

G

H

MAKING A SMALL DISH OR LARGE DOME

The larger dome example illustrated here is being formed in a carved-out depression in a floor-standing tree trunk. It uses a copper disk, with a diameter of around $2^1/_2$ in (60 mm) and a thickness of $^1/_{16}$ in (1 mm).

1. Cut the circle of copper and file the edges smooth. Anneal, rinse, and dry.
2. Hold the disk on one side of the rim and place the other side into the edge of the depression. Use either a curved wooden mallet or a round-ended hammer to strike around the edge, pushing it down into the depression and turning it to complete the circle around the rim. **(A)**
3. Now move the disk a little farther down into the depression and work a second round with the mallet or hammer, just below the first. **(B)**
4. Continue working in layers around the disk/dome, moving the hammer or mallet farther down each time until it follows the shape of the depression.
5. To get the sides to come up a little farther, anneal the piece again, rinse, and dry. Now place it on edge into the depression and use the hammer on the inside edge just under the rim, turning it until you have completed the circle. Continue working down into the disk/dome at this angle.
6. To smooth out any hammer marks, anneal the dome again and planish it. Now place a polished metal stake with a similar outline to the dome in the vise. Invert the dome so that it can now be hammered on the outside. Work a planishing hammer smoothly over the whole surface to flatten out the dents made by the first hammer, making sure you keep the hammer/metal/stake always in touch with each other. There should be a nice solid sound while doing this. **(C)**

MAKING A LARGER DOME USING A LEAD CAKE

For this larger dome you will need a metal stake the same size or larger than the dome you wish to make. Take great care when working with lead to ensure that it does not contaminate anything else in the workshop (see Tip).

1. Remove all the soldering blocks from the soldering tray and place the lead (held in the tin) into the tray.
2. Smear some oil over the shiny surface of the metal stake; this will prevent it from sticking and will protect it from being damaged by the lead. Have this on hand as you heat up the lead.
3. Heat the lead with a large flame until the area to be impressed has melted. The top will melt quickly, but it needs to melt to a reasonable depth and so may take a while. **(D)**
4. Remove the flame and place the stake directly down into the molten lead. Leave it there to cool. (This can be hastened by cooling it all with cold water.) **(E)**
5. When it is cool enough to handle, remove the stake. There will now be a good depression where it has been. The stake should be well cleaned before further use.
6. Cut a circle of matching diameter from the desired metal and file the edge so that it is smooth. Anneal, rinse, and dry. Place some soft cotton or absorbent paper towel into the lead depression to avoid any contamination to the metal. Now place the disk over the depression and use the stake and hammer to push it down. Continue working as you did for the sphere in the doming block. **(F)**
7. If you require a really smooth edge, file the piece carefully and finish it using wet/dry papers.

A

B

C

D

E

F

TIP

Any lead particles remaining on the surface of precious metals will, when heated, eat holes in the host metal. So precious metals that have made contact with lead must be cleaned before heating. For gold over 18 karat, boil in a 20 percent solution of nitric acid; for lower-karat golds and silver, warm in a solution of 1 part hydrogen peroxide and 5 parts acetic acid.

FORGING

A piece is forged when its shape is created by the action of rhythmical blows made with a hammer. The piece being forged can either be hot or cold, but for most jewelry and metalsmithing purposes the metal is annealed first and worked cold. The marks left by the hammer when forging create a lovely texture, but of course these can be filed to give a smooth finish if desired.

Hot forging is traditionally performed by blacksmiths working with steel and iron. Metal is placed into the glow of a red-hot fire until it is also red hot. It is then removed, placed on an anvil, and shaped with a metal hammer. As the metal cools it becomes harder to work, so it must be replaced in the forge to heat up again before continuing.

Precious metals can be forged when hot, but they lose their heat more quickly, so it is simpler to forge them after annealing and quenching, making sure that, as they harden by being struck, they are regularly annealed.

You will need a good sized—preferably floor-standing—anvil when forging, as well as a selection of hammers. When forging, the hammer should be kept as flat as possible to avoid leaving marks with the hammer's edge. When working more heavily on one side of the metal (to curve it perhaps, or straighten out an unwanted curve), keep the hammer slightly tilted to avoid unnecessary marks. Do not make the edges too thin when forging either—they will become uneven but can be filed to finish.

FORGING A RING

To make this ring, either begin with a section of round wire or rod that has a larger dimension than the finished item, or make an ingot using approximately 3/8 oz (12 g) of the metal for the finished ring. We will begin by making an ingot. Then we will make the ring.

MAKING THE INGOT

The purer the metal used in making an ingot, the better. For example, if 9- or 10-karat gold is melted and cast into an ingot the result will quite likely be brittle, porous, and hard to work. However, fine silver or gold of more than 18 karat will give a much better result. The metal should be clean with no trace of solder on it.

1. Place 3/8 oz (12 g) of either scrap metal or casting grain in a small crucible held in a fixing arm. Add a pinch of powdered flux and, if possible, a pinch of fine-ground charcoal. **(A)**

2. Place an iron "ingot maker" level in the soldering area with a stop of sand or charcoal lump in place for the size of ingot required, then heat it with a large flame. If this is not warm enough when the molten metal is poured in, the metal will "freeze" on contact and not give a good cast. **(B)**

3. Move the flame onto the metal and hold it steady just where you see the metal look shiny. Keep it here until the metal collects and forms a spinning ball shape. Keep this ball spinning for at least 20 seconds to ensure every last bit of metal is completely melted. Then, while the flame remains on it, hold the crucible over the ingot mold, get the molten mass right to the edge, and pour it quickly into the mold. **(C)**

4. Tip the mold upside down to release the ingot and, when it has lost any redness, pickle, rinse, and dry. **(D)**

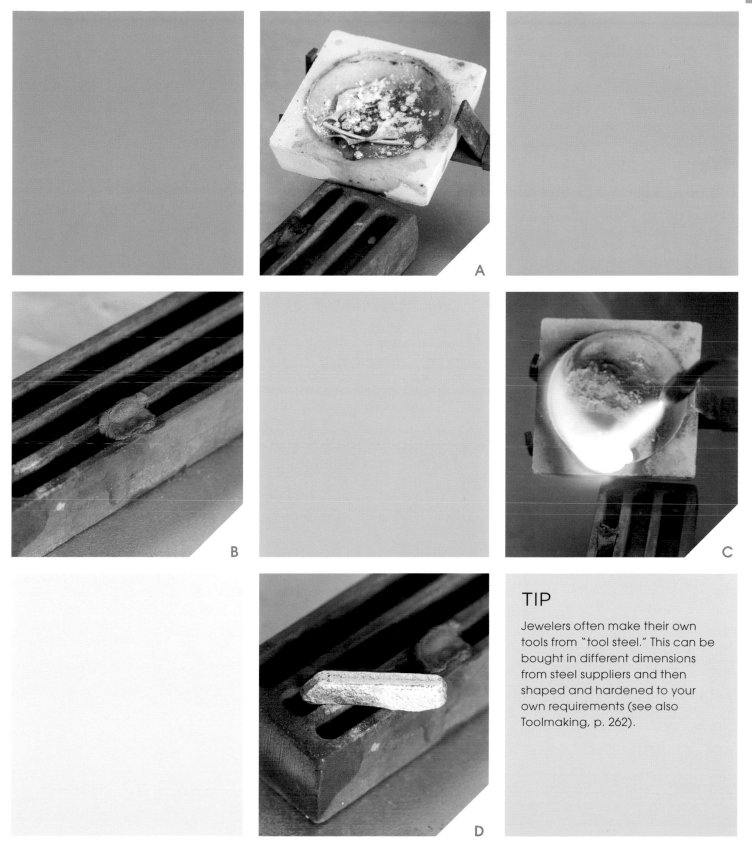

A

B

C

D

TIP

Jewelers often make their own tools from "tool steel." This can be bought in different dimensions from steel suppliers and then shaped and hardened to your own requirements (see also Toolmaking, p. 262).

FORGING A RING (CONT.)

The ingot or length of round wire is now lengthened to the size of the ring.

MAKING THE RING

1. Hold the metal at one end and place the other on the flat area of the anvil. Use the flat side of a heavy ball-peen hammer or a cross-peen raising hammer with straight but rounded ends, and work away from you along the surface of the metal (a cross-peen will achieve the length faster). Turn the metal through 90 degrees and work along in the same way, gradually working the end down so it becomes thinner. **(A)**

2. Now reverse the piece, lay the other end on the anvil, and strike it in the same way. Keep measuring the piece until it is the correct length. As the metal thins out toward the ends, the area in the middle should remain the same. **(B)**

3. At this stage you can decide what the final shape of the ring will be. If it is to have a rounded look, anneal the piece and place it back on the anvil. Use the ball-peen hammer to strike the metal while rolling it along the flat surface. This softens out the edges and gradually rounds them off.

4. Anneal the piece again and hold one end against the rounded nose of the anvil. Hammer around the nose until the curve is nearly halfway, then turn it around and work the other in the same way, until the two ends meet, or indeed overlap. **(C)**

5. Neaten the ends with a piercing saw or a file and solder them together. Place the ring on the mandrel and round it up with the ball-peen hammer. You can now file the ring smooth, then give it a high finish with flexifiles (or wet/dry papers). **(D)**

FORGING CURVES

To make interesting forged shapes, metal rods, wire, sheet, or cast pieces can be used. Cast pieces can be porous, so keep them annealed as they are being worked. Any large bends can be made over the anvil nose or around a mandrel first and then forged so that they will hold their shape.

In this example, a rod of $^3/_{16}$-in (4-mm) diameter is being forged to make a flat "S" shape for a pendant. A cross-peen hammer is used to lengthen the metal and a ball-peen hammer is used to broaden it.

1. Cut a 4-in (100-mm) length of 6-gauge (4-mm) round silver wire. Anneal it. Place either a wooden or metal former in the safe jaws of the vise and fasten one end of the rod with it. **(E)**

2. Pull the protruding end down toward you to make a bend of about 90 degrees. Lower the fastened end farther down the former and pull the end down again.

3. Remove that end from the vise and position the other end in the same way. Bend it over so that when it is removed you have a rough "S" shape. **(F)**

4. Anneal the shape again. Place it flat on the anvil. Strike the metal with a rounded cross-peen hammer, right at the top of the bend, then work it along the top to spread the width. **(G)**

5. Repeat this on the other bend. Now use the flat end of a ball-peen hammer to flatten out the rest of the rod, keeping the shape of the "S" by putting more emphasis on the outside curves.

6. Anneal the piece again and then flatten out the marks previously made in the curves, first with the ball-peen hammer, followed by a planishing hammer. **(H)**

7. The piece can now either be filed to a smooth finish or left with the smooth hammer marks.

A

B

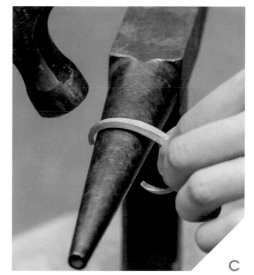

C

D

TIP

If a more gentle curve is required, there is no need to bend the metal first. The bend can be achieved by hammering on the outside of the curve. This spreads the metal, which causes the inside of the curve to draw in.

E

F

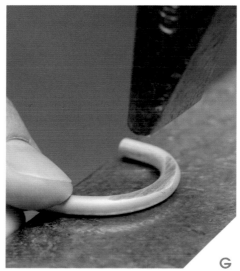

G

H

IMPRINTING

Imprinting involves passing a sheet of metal through a rolling mill in order to create an impression on it. You can create some really interesting patterns this way.

For the best impression the metal must be in a soft state. The stainless steel rollers on the mill are easily damaged by wet items and by materials that are harder than themselves. Do take care of your mill—it is a considerable investment and should be treated kindly. Ensure that everything is perfectly dry and that any hard materials (including those listed below) are covered by a softer one—e.g., if making an imprint of "binding wire" on a sheet of silver, place a copper sheet over the wire to protect the rollers. (The copper will not need to be annealed, but the silver will.) Various materials can then be used to make imprints. Here is a selection.

SOFT MATERIALS: Lace, old dish cloths, hessian, cotton wool, watercolor paper, paper towel, wrinkled tissue paper, muslin, and "skeleton leaves" (for creating leaf imprints) made from silk or man-made fibers.

HARDER ITEMS: Patterns cut out from stainless steel, steel wire, and steel (wire) wool.

USING THE ROLLING MILL

1. Take a sheet of silver, around 18 gauge (1 mm thick) and 3 in (80 mm) square. Anneal and pickle it three times, rinsing in water and drying it thoroughly between each anneal. Each time it is pickled, some of the silver's copper content is etched away, leaving a finer surface. This surface will be softer than the original sterling silver sheet, so it will take a deeper imprint.

2. Offer the silver up to the rollers to asses the gap through which it will pass. If the silver is 18 gauge (1 mm thick), the gap should be just less than that—find this by closing down the gap until it makes just a light impression on the metal. **(A)**

3. Place the imprinting material, pattern side down, on the surface of the metal. Hold these together in a straight line as they pass through the rollers. It should be quite hard to roll them through. **(B)**

4. If using a hard material, place a sheet of copper on top before passing it through.

5. After the silver has been rolled through, it will be curved and will need annealing before flattening it out again. You can do this either with your fingers or by placing it on a steel flat plate, covering it with some of the imprinting material as a protection and then placing a smaller flat plate on top and striking it with a wooden mallet. **(C)**

IMPRINTING BY HAND

Imprinting can also be achieved with the use of different materials and hammers. The results may be a little more haphazard than those achieved by passing the metal through the rolling mill, but they can still be effective.

1. Place the annealed piece on a flat plate and cover it with the imprinting material. (The material can be taped down to the flat plate to stop it from moving around as it is being hammered.)

2. Use a heavy, flat-headed hammer all over the piece or, for a softer appearance, a wooden mallet. The strikes need to be firm enough to leave an impression. **(D)**

3. The metal should bear the impression of the material. **(E)**

4. An interesting but subtle imprint can also be made simply by using an old hammer with a marked and pitted head. This will, of course, have the effect of moving and thinning the metal a little too, but you can compensate for this by starting with a slightly thicker metal. **(F)**

A

B

C

D

E

F

TIP

It is not worth using anything green from the garden for imprinting. It will simply get squashed, leave a mess on the rollers, and make them wet as well.

RAISING

Raising is generally used by silversmiths to make items such as vases, spoons, and bowls. However, it is also very useful in the jewelry workshop to own a few of the necessary tools and to know how to raise smaller items.

Raising is the basic technique of hammering metal against a solid form. Once you have practiced making a spoon or a bowl using this technique, you can use your imagination to find ways to apply it to your jewelry-making. The particular spoonmaking method shown here employs one piece of metal and no soldering. You will need a "mushroom" stake, which looks like it sounds, and a raising stake. You will also need a lead cake or a deep hollow in a tree trunk (see Doming, p. 192). The metal here is 19-gauge (0.9-mm) silver. The circle has a diameter of 5 in (13 cm). As this is a large piece, after annealing let it cool a little before pickling and/or quenching to prevent too much stress in the metal. (Raising requires much practice, so start with cheaper ones first, such as copper, gilding metal, or brass.) When raising any sort of vessel, it is best to first draw its outline on tracing paper, then draw a perpendicular line through the center point. Fold the paper in half along this line and check the outline for symmetry. Transfer the drawing to some card, cut it out, and offer this cutout to the metal as it is being formed to ensure the shape is adhered to.

MAKING A BOWL/TUMBLER

1. Set a pair of dividers at 3 in (75 mm) and cut a circle. Reinforce the center point. (A)
2. File the circle, then draw the area of the base with the dividers, set to around $9/16$ in (15 mm), drawing from the center point. Anneal, pickle, rinse, and dry. (B)
3. With the round end of a wooden bossing mallet or ball-peen hammer, block the metal into the tree-trunk hollow, ensuring the center point remains on the outside. Continue blocking until the base area is reached. Anneal, pickle, rinse, and dry.

4. Turn the piece over. Use a compass to draw a circle around $3/8$ in (10 mm) beyond the base line. Continue drawing circles at $3/8$-in (10-mm) intervals. This helps keep the circles true as hammering occurs. (C)
5. Fasten the mushroom stake into the vise. Place the base line on its edge. With a raising hammer strike the row above this down onto the stake. This is a hard strike, moving the metal obviously. Continue a circular motion, moving upward to $3/8$ in (10 mm) before the top. (D)
6. Anneal, etc. between each raising, redrawing the lines each time. Repeat Step 5 to shape the bowl, then place it over the mushroom stake and work all over it with a wooden mallet.
7. Fix a raising stake in the vise. The stake's flatter end will bring the sides up into a better shape. Hold the work on the stake's front edge; strike the sides down one at a time with a raising hammer. (E)
8. So far the top has not been hammered all the way up—this would make it thin and ragged. Place the piece on a sandbag and use a wedge-shaped hammer with a slightly curved edge to work around the top now. Work around it again with the flat side of the raising hammer to smooth out any marks. Any further raising is now done over the raising stake, and the top is hammered again before annealing. (F)
9. The top edge will have a little lip. Push it back into the wall with a planishing hammer, working over the raising stake. Once annealed, the piece can be planished—work gradually up and around with a well-polished planishing hammer to smooth out any marks. Then solder a ring to the bottom (see Tip). (G)

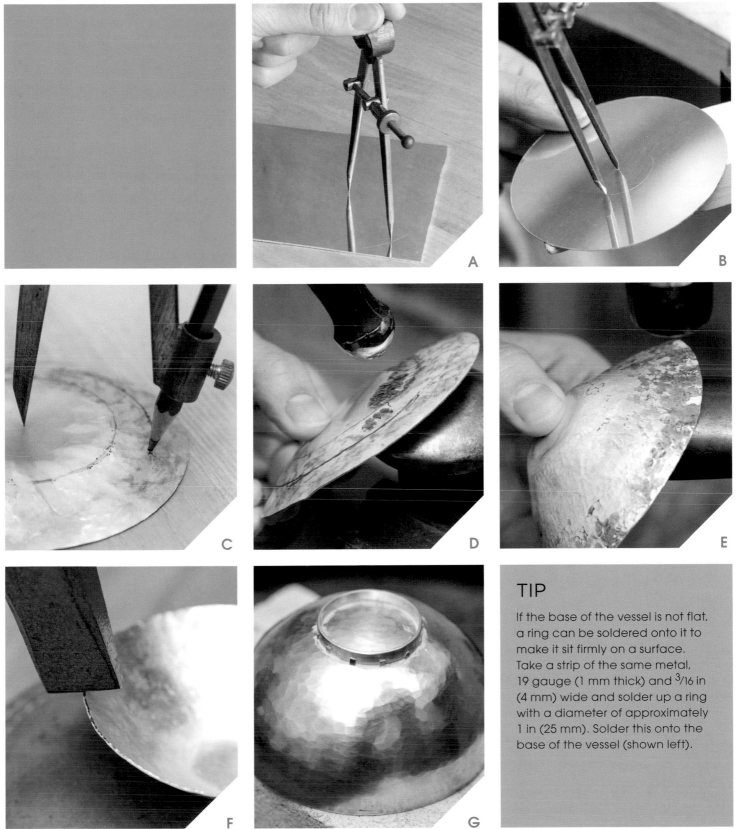

A

B

C

D

E

F

G

TIP

If the base of the vessel is not flat, a ring can be soldered onto it to make it sit firmly on a surface. Take a strip of the same metal, 19 gauge (1 mm thick) and 3/16 in (4 mm) wide and solder up a ring with a diameter of approximately 1 in (25 mm). Solder this onto the base of the vessel (shown left).

MAKING A JELLY SPOON

To start this you will need an ingot of silver weighing about 2 oz (60 g) or a section of $1/4$ in (6-mm) square rod.

1. After annealing, roll either of these through the rolling mill to even out and lengthen a little. **(A)**

2. The overall length of this spoon will be about $6^3/4$ in (170 mm). Starting about $1^5/8$ in (40 mm) in from one end, use the curved end of the raising hammer to strike the metal (placed flat down on the anvil) in consecutive steps right up to the other end. Turn it through 90 degrees and repeat from the start. **(B)**

3. Anneal between each pass. Keep working in this way until the handle is about 4 in (100 mm) long. **(C)**

4. Now take a wedge-shaped hammer and place the unworked end of the spoon on the anvil. Strike across this area to broaden it out until it becomes quite flat, then change to a heavy ball-peen hammer and, with the flat end, continue striking until it starts to become circular. **(D)**

5. Even the circle out with the planishing hammer; at this stage it should be about $1/16$ in (1.5 mm) thick. Draw a circle with a pencil to create the shape of the spoon. **(E)**

6. Cut around the circle with a piercing saw. File it smooth with a flat file and finish with wet/dry papers to remove all the hammer marks. After annealing, place the flat bowl of the spoon directly over a depression in either the lead cake or the tree trunk. Use a former that fits easily into the depression to force the bowl down into it. **(F)**

7. Now continue working along the handle, hammering it into the correct shape and graduating the thickness and width down from the bowl to the end of the handle.

8. File the handle to straighten out any bumps and to remove the hammer marks. File the area on the back too, where the handle meets the bowl, to remove any marks left from when the bowl was domed. **(G)**

9. Lay the spoon on a flat surface and gently bend it to shape. The end of the handle and the bottom of the bowl should sit in line on the surface.

A

B

C

D

E

F

G

RETICULATION

Reticulation—not to be confused with fusing—is a heating technique that brings the fine silver in a sheet of sterling silver to the surface, while the interior of the sheet remains as sterling silver.

Sterling silver is 925 parts pure silver and 75 parts copper. During annealing the copper content oxidizes, turning black. This oxidation is removed by "pickling" in either sulfuric acid, Sparex, safety pickle, or alum. With successive annealings and picklings, any copper remaining on the surface is removed, and the surface becomes whiter. After repeated annealing and pickling, heat is applied. This causes the inside of the silver sheet (which has remained as sterling silver) to melt and ripple up. This, in turn, pushes the fine silver (which does not melt as it has a higher melting point) into stunning patterns. This is an unpredictable art—the rippling may not happen, and the piece may even end up with large holes! A thickness of 22 to 15 gauge (0.7–1.5 mm) is suitable, but the thinner the piece, the greater the risk of holes. Some areas will be fragile, so after cleaning, cut out any usable areas, and scrap the rest. If it is robust enough, the piece can be shaped carefully (using a wooden mallet or, better, by hand) around a mandrel or former. The best surface can be achieved with an alloy of 80 parts fine silver and 20 parts copper ("800 silver"). However, this cannot be hallmarked as sterling silver (see p. 218). So a piece with this alloy should be set like a stone, with a collet, or attached without soldering.

MAKING A RETICULATED PIECE

1. Take a piece of 16-gauge (1.2 mm) silver measuring $2^3/8$ x $1^5/8$ in (60 x 40 mm) and anneal and pickle it at least seven times. The annealing, with a large, soft flame, should take the silver to a dull red, and it should be left in the pickle long enough for all the oxidation to disappear—say 4 or 5 minutes, depending on the speed of the pickle. **(A)**

As you work through the annealing and pickling you will see that the dull red color becomes more difficult to see. As you are heating you will see a pinkish glow starting to come under the white of the silver. If any black patches appear when heating, it means that the layer of fine silver has been broken and the layer below is exposed, so the annealing process must begin all over again.

2. The piece is now ready to be reticulated. Some people now clean the surface with a soft brass brush and liquid soap. I do not think it makes much difference either way, but see what works best for you. **(B)**

3. Lay the piece on a charcoal block (to reflect the heat). It should not hang over the end or have a gap in the middle, as the heat needed will cause it to slump. Heat it with a large, soft flame until it is bright red, at which point you can introduce a harder pointed flame and draw it somewhat like a paintbrush over the surface, all the while keeping the heat from the bigger flame steady. You should see the surface start to move, so keep drawing the hard flame along to allow the movement.

4. You may have to be patient for a few minutes while doing this and, at the first sign of a hole appearing, remove the flame. If you are lucky, the piece will perform beautifully and there will be no breakthrough on the surface. Even if there is breakthrough over the whole piece, do not get discouraged—once it has been pickled and cleaned it will still look great. **(C)**

5. A reticulated surface is quite porous, especially if there has been any breakthrough, so if you need to solder anything to the surface or edges, run some solder in first; otherwise it will just soak it up.

A

B

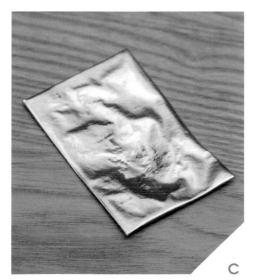

C

RETICULATING GOLD

I have not had great success reticulating gold, although 14- karat green gold (which has a higher content of silver than say a 14-karat red gold) is said to reticulate quite well. I have tried unsuccessfully with 18-karat gold—it seems to oxidize each time I heat it, so a fine gold layer never gets the chance to surface.

To get a gold surface reasonably similar to a reticulated surface, just heat it on a charcoal block until the surface starts to move (that is very near melting point, so caution is needed). The flame can be pushed along the piece, moving the surface until it has been completely covered. It will not be quite as effective as reticulation but will still look good when cleaned.

TIP

As the surface is so uneven, if a stone is going to be set on it, it is easier to remove the area for the setting with a piercing saw first. Then fit the setting to the area and solder it in, allowing for the depth of the receiving area when making the setting.

SWAGE BLOCK AND FOLDING

The swage block is a forming tool used to create smooth curves and semicircular lengths of metal. Folding is self-explanatory, although there are all sorts of different effects that can be produced by folding and unfolding metal.

When using the swage block, the shape is formed by a strip of metal being held over the concave curve and pushed down into it with another former, either wood or metal, that fits neatly into the curve.

As with so many metalworking techniques, when folding, the metal should be kept annealed to prevent any splits occurring as the folds are being created. It is worth folding a larger piece than is actually needed so that the best areas can be cut out and used on their own.

Folds in metal can be really effective when a raised selection of lines is required. These can be single lines, parallel, or crossed over each other. Areas where they meet can be drilled and then opened out, perhaps for a setting for a stone or to introduce a contrasting metal ball. The lines made by folding can be small enough to mimic soldered-on wires. Also, by folding along a length of metal and hammering along the outside edges, a lovely curve will appear and then these two sides can be hammered individually to produce flowing, wavy edges.

USING THE SWAGE BLOCK TO MAKE TUBING

This exercise demonstrates using the swage block to make a metal tube. Start by making a tube with an outside diameter of $3/16$ in (4 mm) and an inside diameter of $1/8$ in (3 mm).

1. Cut a length approximately $4^3/4$ x $5/8$ in (120 x 15 mm) of 25-gauge (0.5 mm) sheet. Starting about $3/4$ in (20 mm) from one end, cut it to form a taper. **(A)**
2. File the long edges so that they are nice and flat and parallel with each other. **(B)**

3. Anneal the strip, pickle, rinse, and dry. Now place it in the curve of the swage block that fits its width best. **(C)**
4. Choose a former that fits into the same curve of the block. Place it lengthwise on the strip of metal and, using a mallet, hammer it down evenly into the block. **(D)**
5. Remove the strip and place it into the next curve down, and use a former of the next size down to tighten up the curve. Continue in this way, decreasing the circumference each time. Anneal as necessary.
6. When it is no longer possible to complete the curve, use a $1/8$ in (3 mm)-diameter former on the inside of the curve. Place the piece on the metal flat plate, and use a mallet to tap down both sides to close up the tube. **(E)**
7. The two sides should fit really close together. If there are gaps along the seam, take a piercing saw and cut through it to straighten up the edges. **(F)**
8. Flux along the seam. Cut some small paillons of hard solder and place them at close intervals (every $1/4$ in or 7 mm or so) across the join. Solder carefully to close the join. File away any excess solder after pickling, rinsing, and drying. **(G)**
9. To make the tube completely round or to reduce the diameter further, place the tapered end through an appropriately sized hole in the round drawplate and pull it through. Continue pulling through the drawplate, working down through the different sizes until the correct size is achieved. **(H)**

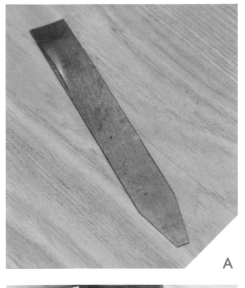

A

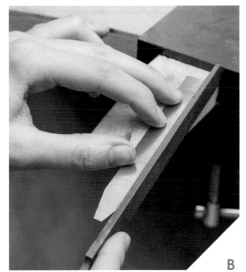

B

C

D

TIP

The strip of metal being curved should not be wider than the curve into which it is being hammered. If the edges go beyond that point, the edges of the metal will become quite deeply marked with the lines of the edge.

E

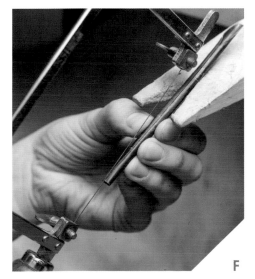

F

G

H

FOLDING

1. Cut a circle of copper with a diameter of around $2^3/_8$ in (60 mm) and a thickness of about $^1/_{64}$ in (0.5 mm). Anneal, quench, and dry. Mark a line down the middle with a pencil. **(A)**

2. Fold the metal in half along this line. You may need to hold one half in the safe jaws of the vise or in a vise that has smooth jaws, and then use a hammer or mallet to bend the protruding half over to 90 degrees. **(B)**

3. Now bend it over until it is in half and the two sides are nice and tight together. **(C)**

4. Anneal, quench, and dry again. You will need to anneal every time any hammering is done on this piece, as it will harden up very quickly. Place the folded edge into the jaws of the vise, keeping it parallel with the top edge and only a fraction of an inch down. Fasten up the vise tightly.

5. Open out the two edges of the metal. A thin metal ruler is a good tool to use for this; its length helps to give a little leverage. **(D)**

6. Once they are opened, push each side all the way down to touch the outer area of the vise jaws. Hammer them down with a ball-peen hammer. Then remove the piece from the vise and place on a flat plate. Hold the two outer edges down and hammer the top of the fold to flatten it a little. **(E)**

7. To make a line that crosses over the first line, repeat the above steps, but bend the metal first at right angles to the first fold. Do not worry about losing the first fold—it will take on the appearance of a woven line once the second line is completed.

MAKING A CURVE IN A FOLD

1. Cut a length of copper about $4^3/_4$ x $1^5/_8$ x $^1/_{64}$ in (120 x 40 x 0.5 mm). Anneal, quench, and dry.

2. Score a line right down the center where the fold will be.

3. Fold the metal strip in half along the line. If it is a little hard, place in the vise (safe jaws) with the scored line parallel with the top. Use a wooden mallet to hit the metal over, just past 90 degrees. **(F)**

4. Now make the fold complete, so that the two outer edges are touching, and use a mallet along the folded edge to tighten it.

5. After annealing again fasten about $^1/_8$ in (3 mm) of the fold into the vise and then open out both sides down onto the shoulders. **(G)**

6. Push those two outside edges right down so that they meet each other. Lay the piece on a flat plate and use a mallet to flatten the piece as much as possible.

7. After annealing, make sure the piece is completely dry and open up the rollers in the mill so that they just take the height of the folded area. Tighten them up a little and make the first pass through the rolling mill. **(H)**

8. Anneal again, dry, turn down the rollers again, and make another pass. This will ensure that the thickest part (the folded area) of the strip is thinned out, which causes it to stretch, which in turn causes it to make a lovely curve.

9. Anneal again before opening out the sides. To form a twist, instead of forging the folded side, open the outside edges and hammer all along their length. **(I)**

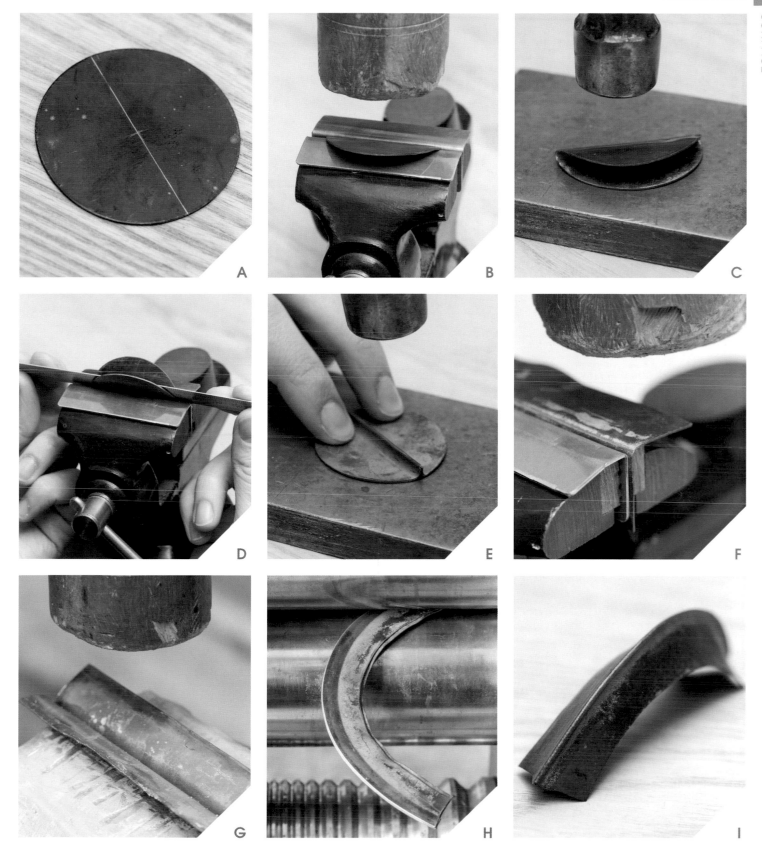

TAP AND DIE

Using the tap and die tool is basically another way of joining two pieces of metal together by making a screw and a "nut" for the screw to fix into.

The dies are small metal plates with holes in them, and the taps are small, tapered metal rods; both are numbered so that the die fits with a corresponding tap. The screw itself is made from round wire, the diameter of which is the final diameter of the screw.

The metal used to make the screws should not be annealed— the harder the better! Tubing can be used for the "nut," but the inside diameter must be slightly smaller than the diameter of the wire being used to make the screw. In other words, the wire should not fit into the tube but should come to about halfway across the walls.

USING THE TOOL

A typical tap and die tool is shown illustrated opposite. **(A)**

1. Cut a length of the wire needed for the screw. Make it longer than you need. Take the main handle for making the die and place in it the fitting that is the correct size for your wire. Push the wire into the hole, with a little protruding, and tighten it in. **(B)**
2. Hold the wire steady and then very gently move the handle in a circular motion all around the wire. This is now cutting the thread. Continue until you have the length required. **(C)**
3. Choose a tap that has the same outside diameter as the wire. Fix it into a handheld drill. **(D)**
4. Hold the tubing directly in line with the drill. The tap needs to enter the tube in a completely straight line. Start turning the tap, only making a quarter turn before turning in the opposite direction to release the tiny pieces of metal ("swarf") that have been cut to make the thread. Continue working down the tube one quarter-turn at a time and releasing the swarf until there is enough depth for the screw. **(E)**

5. The screw will need a little flat top on it to fasten it in. Cut a small piece of chenier that has an inside diameter the same as the outside diameter of the screw. Fit the end of the screw inside it and paint the flux, then put a very small paillon of solder on the top of the chenier and solder the two together. **(F)**
6. It is important to make sure that no solder runs down the thread of the screw, so only a very small paillon is needed. After cleaning, file the top of the chenier down to about $1/16$ in (1 mm) to form the "head." This can now have a little line filed across to screw it into the piece. **(G)**
7. The head of the screw can sit flush with the surface of the metal if it has been countersunk. Find a steel screw with the same diameter as the head just made, and turn it a few times to open out the receiving area. **(H)**

A

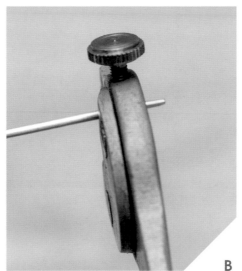

B

C

D

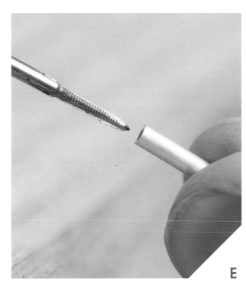

E

F

G

H

TIP

For most jewelry applications the screw is going to be quite small, and great care needs to be taken when using tap and die tools, as they can break quite easily if too much force is put on them.

PATINATIONS

A patination on the surface of a metal really means a change from its original appearance. When left exposed to the air, many metals change color and sometimes texture, which can either enhance them or be corrosive.

The color and texture of metals can be changed simply by leaving them exposed to air or burying them in earth. However, producing the desired change this way would take a very long time. Various chemicals can create similar effects to those that the natural environment will produce, so in the interests of saving time these are a practical choice.

If used and disposed of thoughtfully, these will not harm a wider area. Nevertheless, chemicals can be dangerous and, even when used with care, are quite noxious. Therefore, work in a well-ventilated area, wear rubber gloves, use protective eyewear, and, if possible, work near a sink so that you have quick access to cold running water.

Many different effects can be achieved with patination and oxidation. I have provided just a few recipes here, but it is always worth experimenting.

SIMPLE OXIDATION

When a metal is oxidized it becomes a shade of black. Copper, brass, silver, and most golds will oxidize when heat is applied. Lead will dull down naturally in air. Metals such as tin, aluminum, platinum, white gold, fine silver and fine gold, rhodium, and iridium do not oxidize naturally or when heat is applied. Palladium is mainly resistant to oxidation but may acquire a bluish hue when heated.

To oxidize any of the first group of metals, use potassium sulfide in either lump or liquid form. The piece itself should either be warm or the liquid should be very hot as it is applied (or both).

Chemical oxidizing takes place after a piece has been completed, except for stone or enamel setting. The surface of the metal should be clean and may be polished. Any excess solder should also be removed before oxidizing. After polishing, the surface should be cleaned with cloth dipped in acetone to remove any greasy deposits.

You can protect any areas that do not need oxidizing by painting them with a varnish, which can be removed later with acetone. Specific areas can be oxidized by dipping a paintbrush into the solution and painting it on the metal surface, although this can be messy and does not always give the desired results.

1. Attach a string or wire to the piece being oxidized. Pour boiling water on a small lump of potassium sulfide—just enough to dissolve it and cover the item. **(A)**
2. Hang the item in a cup of boiling water to heat it, remove it, then quickly dry it with some paper towel and immediately hang it in the potassium sulfide solution. **(B)**
3. Hold it immersed until it is completely black, then remove it and rinse it in cold water. Discard the potassium solution by running lots of cold water with it down the sink. It smells awful.
4. Areas that are to be highlighted can now be polished to reveal the metal underneath. **(C)**
5. If you do not like the result, simply remove the oxidation by annealing and pickling the piece. This will take you back to square one.

A

B

TIP

The same method can be used to get a blue/purple color, which works particularly well on silver. The item is dipped very quickly into the hot solution and then into cold water to stop the reaction. It may need a few goes to achieve the desired color.

C

MAKING COPPER AND BRASS GREEN

There are various ways of making these metals green. You will need some ammonia, vinegar, a small plastic box with a tight-fitting lid, a plastic spray container, and some rolling tobacco or garden soil.

The surface of the metals should be clean and grease-free. The patination should always take place after any shaping or soldering work.

METHOD 1

1. Put some soil or rolling tobacco in the plastic box (enough to cover the piece of metal). Pour in some vinegar and some ammonia. The precise amount of these two liquids depends on the amount of soil used, but it should be enough of each to make the soil or tobacco feel damp or slightly wet, not runny. The ammonia is very pungent, so pour it carefully. **(A)**
2. Mix everything up with a wooden stick and then tuck the piece of metal right into it. Leave it sealed up for a couple of days. **(B)**
3. Remove the piece, then rinse and dry. **(C)**

METHOD 2

Put a solution of 6 parts water, 2 parts ammonia, and 2 parts vinegar into a plastic spray container. Place the metal in bright sunlight and spray it with the solution. When it dries, spray it again; repeat this four or five times until the color is achieved.

MAKING COPPER RED

1. Take a piece of copper approximately $1^5/_8$ x$1^5/_8$ x $^1/_{16}$ in (40 x 40 x 1 mm) and remove any grease from the surface by annealing, pickling, and cleaning with either a brass brush and liquid soap, or some 240 wet/dry abrasive paper or a flexifile. **(D)**
2. Paint both sides of the copper with flux. Lay it on the soldering block and heat it until it is almost bright yellow. This looks a little alarming, but it needs to be really hot. Pick it up with a pair of insulated tweezers and turn it over to heat the other side to the same degree. **(E)**
3. Now quench it in water. The copper should have a lovely red and purple color. Any imprinting (see p. 198) can be done before this treatment, but any soldering should be done after the "red" treatment, and the piece should not be pickled, only quenched. **(F)**

MAKING SILVER PINK

1. Place some silver in your pickle with a piece of binding wire or some other steel object (not stainless steel). **(G)**
2. The binding wire will produce a copper oxide, making the silver turn pink. **(H)**
3. You may have already discovered that when binding wire is left on work that is then pickled, everything in the pickle will turn pink. If it has been there for a long time, you may need to completely replace the pickle as it will be contaminated. Otherwise, if you want to restore the metal to its true color, anneal and pickle it.

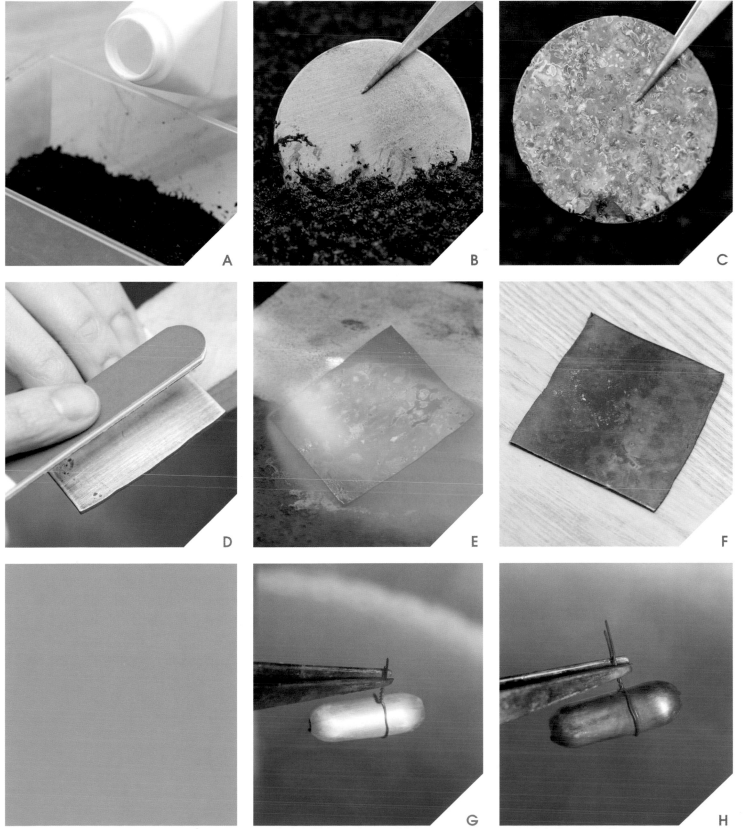

A

B

C

D

E

F

G

H

STAMPINGS

Stampings are usually employed when many identical pieces are required. Making the tools for commercial stamping is an expensive and precise business in order to be cost-effective, so numbers are important here.

This sort of stamping is always associated with a "die"— basically two parts, a male and female, which produce an intricate three-dimensional shape in metal. The stamp and die are cut, by a very skilled cutter, in steel blocks so that they replicate each other exactly, allowing for the thickness of metal being formed, in male and female form. These are then fixed in a press, with a metal sheet between them, and pressed down using considerable force to form the shape.

Punches with all the letters of the alphabet are available in different sizes from jewelry tool suppliers, and specific patterns for stamping can be cut and filed using steel tool stock in the workshop (see also Toolmaking, p. 262).

STAMPING WITH THE HYDRAULIC JACK

For a three-dimensional stamp in the workshop, a two-part pattern is made in acrylic, a sheet of metal is placed between them, and a hydraulic jack used to squeeze them together. You need a square of acrylic (3 x 3 x $^3/_{16}$ in [80 x 80 x 5 mm]), a square of metal (1$^3/_4$ x 1$^3/_4$ x $^1/_{32}$ in [45 x 45 x 0.6 mm]), and a rubber sheet (3 x 3 x $^3/_{16}$ in [80 x 80 x 5 mm]). The pattern to be stamped should fit into the middle area, leaving a little around the edge.

1. Mark the center point of the acrylic with the point of a scribe; draw a vertical then a horizontal line straight through it. **(A)**
2. Draw the desired shape on tracing paper, then place this over the 90 degree lines on the acrylic and copy them onto your tracing. Fasten the tracing down. **(B)**

3. With a small drill ($^1/_{16}$ in or 1 mm or less), drill a hole through the tracing and acrylic just inside your shape. **(C)**
4. Use a piercing saw to cut out the shape, keeping to the line drawn. From underneath, start to file the cutout shape into the shape desired. **(D)**
5. Use a medium-sized oval file on the inside area of the larger piece. It is helpful to draw a line using a pair of dividers about $^1/_{16}$ in (1 mm) around the outside edge, and then file at an angle up to that line. **(E)**
6. The separate shape can be made really smooth by filing and then using wet/dry paper. Curves should be nicely rounded, as any flats will show up once the metal has been pressed in. **(F)**
7. Check that the two pieces fit evenly together, leaving a small gap to allow for the thickness of the metal. Then place the annealed metal sheet on top of the larger piece of acrylic.
8. Place the small shaped acrylic piece on top of the metal, matching the lines on the two acrylic pieces. Use some masking tape to fasten the top piece in place. **(G)**
9. Place everything on the square metal plate for the hydraulic jack and put that on top of the jack arm. Place the rubber sheet on top of that and pump the arm up carefully so that it is touching the top plate. Keeping it steady, pump until you can see that the top acrylic piece has been pushed right down into the base piece. Now undo the jack and remove the metal. **(H)**
10. The flat area around the shape can now be pierced away.

A

B

C

D

TIP

This acrylic pattern can be used as many times as necessary, but just be careful not to put too much strain on either the metal or the pattern as this can cause cracking or too much folding.

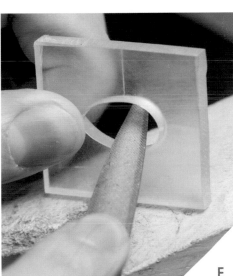

E

F

G

H

HALLMARKING

A hallmark is an official mark, or series of marks, that is used to verify the quality and fineness of a precious metal. Nonprecious metals do not need any such verification.

Rules and regulations of hallmarking differ greatly throughout the world. Many countries are self-regulating, which means that marks can be stamped on by the makers themselves. In 1972, the Hallmarking Convention established a mark that could be used by all its member countries. This is known as the CCM (Common Control Mark) and applies to silver, palladium, gold, and platinum. However, a truly international system remains difficult to establish.

HALLMARKING IN THE US

In the US, the quality and marking of metal used is regulated by jewelers themselves. Retailers and customers sometimes carry out their own assay (testing) on items that they are buying. If an item is made from a combination of different metals, then each seperate metal must be individually marked. The standard marks are as follows:

- Silver: 925, together with the word "silver," "solid silver," "sterling silver," or "sterl."
- Gold: 10k, 14k, 18k, 22k, together with the word "gold." Gold-plated items can also be marked with the number of microns of whatever karat gold is being used.
- Platinum: 950, 900, 850, together with "Pt" or "plat."

HALLMARKING IN THE UK

In the UK, hallmarking is a legal requirement. Pieces must be tested and marked by one of four official hallmarking centers, each with their own mark: a leopard's head (London), an anchor (Birmingham), a Tudor rose (Sheffield), and a castle (Edinburgh). There are three compulsory marks: the sponsor's mark (the maker or the company); the fineness mark (the type of precious metal and the parts per thousand of pure metal in the alloy); and the assay office mark. You can also apply to have your own unique sponsor's mark made.

SILVER

It is illegal to sell any item made with silver weighing more than 7.78 g ($\frac{1}{4}$ oz) without hallmarks. A seller must also display a board (supplied by the hallmark office), showing all the legal marks. The traditional fineness mark for sterling silver is a lion, and for Britannia silver, it is Britannia herself. There are four marks for the fineness of silver, with numbers marked within an oval—800, 925 (sterling), 958 (Britannia), and 999 (fine). All silver solders can qualify for the hallmark.

GOLD

An item made in any color of gold weighing 1 g ($\frac{1}{25}$ oz) or more must be assayed and marked. The traditional fineness symbol is a crown. There are five marks for gold, with numbers marked within an octagon—375 (9 karat), 585 (14 karat), 750 (18 karat), and 916 (22 karat).

PLATINUM

An item made of platinum weighing 0.5 g ($\frac{1}{50}$ oz) or more must be assayed and marked. The traditional fineness mark is an orb. There are four marks for platinum, with numbers marked within a pentagon; 850, 900, 950, and 999 (pure).

PALLADIUM

Any item made with palladium weighing 1 g ($\frac{1}{25}$ oz) or more must be assayed and marked. The optional traditional mark for palladium is the head of Pallas Athene, from whom palladium takes its name. There are three marks for palladium; the numbers are marked within three circles—500, 950, and 999 (pure).

COMPULSORY MARKS

THE SPONSOR'S MARK

THE STANDARD MARK

GOLD

(9 karat)   (14 karat)   (18 karat)   (22 karat)

SILVER

Sterling   Britannia

PLATINUM

PALLADUIM

2009   2010 Onwards

THE ASSAY OFFICE MARK

Birmingham   Edinburgh   London   Sheffield

Above: Images courtesy of the Assay Office.
Right: Hallmarked gold ring, by Neta Wolpe.

TIP

Assay offices now hallmark many pieces by laser. Previously, pieces that when soldered would have hollow areas, had to be sent in unassembled so they could be marked with punches without being damaged. They can now be sent in whole. Laser marking may not look as interesting, but it is a solution to a perennial problem.

TIP

In the US, the purity of gold is described in terms of "karat" (abbreviated to "k"). "Carat" (which in the UK means the same thing as "karat") is abbreviated to "ct" and is used as a unit of weight for gemstones in the US, equal to 200 mg.

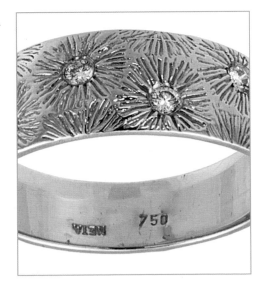

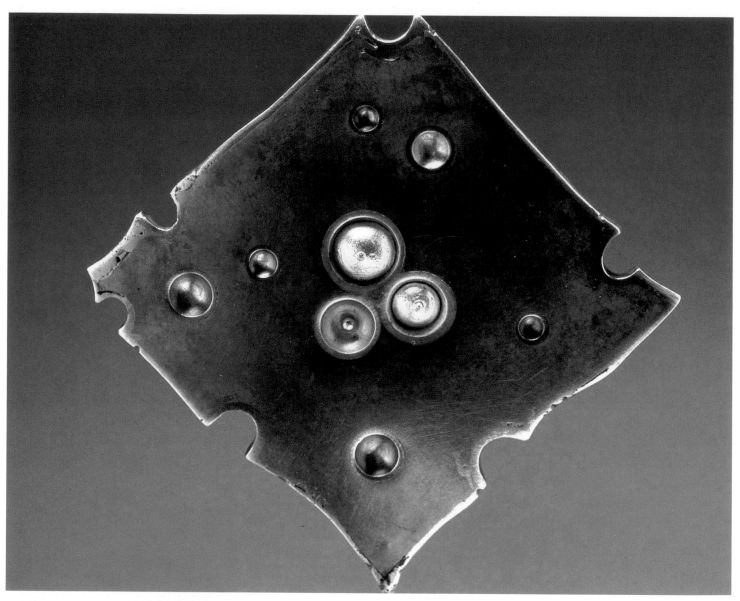

INTERVIEW: ANDY COOPERMAN

The work of Seattle-based artist Andy Cooperman is inspired by observations and encounters, and it encourages the viewer to engage with and examine the complex natural and industrial forms it represents.

Describe a typical work day for you.

I work alone so there are no set hours or even days. But there is always one constant: The morning is by far my most productive time. I'm excited and open, yet calm and thinking clearly. I'll work on finicky things like stone setting, or tackle something I've been avoiding. With the day stretching out in front of me I am also more likely to try something new. Play, in fact, is crucial: it's where new things come from and it is never a waste of time. But it's mostly a morning thing; as the day ages, its potential dims and the panic of not producing something begins to creep in.

How did you get started?

I discovered metalsmithing as a junior in college. A friend had made a little brass cube in a class called "Jewelry and Metalsmithing" and I was intrigued by it. I had walked past that classroom for months and was always curious about the sounds that rang through the door. So I signed up. That first day the teacher, Don Johnson, projected images of work that used reticulation, electroforming, photoetching, and mokume gane. Metal that looked like skin, wood, or a living thing. This blew me away. Don always had two maxims: "If you want to really learn how to do something, spend time with the people who are making a living doing it" and "Stop thinking about it and go do it." And that's what I did.

How would you characterize your approach to metalsmithing?

Curiosity is what really drives me. I want to know the "why" and "if" about almost anything. Sometimes I might push a material to see how far it will go, or build something from a quick sketch to see how it looks in three dimensions. Sometimes I find the only way to respond or to understand is to make. I am always on the lookout for new material. Something that resonates. I'm not always sure why something rings the bells, but I'm often drawn to materials that I characterize as somehow "vital."

How do you sell your work?

In lectures I often use the image of a pie cut into various slices to represent my career. Each wedge is labeled: one-of-a-kind work, production, commissions, repairs, teaching, etc. As my interests and abilities change, so do the relative sizes of the slices. I am not very good at production work, and that section of pie has become fingernail thin, while the commission slice has grown fat. My one-of-a-kind work has always been sold through galleries, but as I began to teach workshops and seminars I often found participants were interested in purchasing something. So selling has become associated with teaching—though I do have to remind myself of the boundary between classroom and marketplace.

Opposite
Top: Fused bronze and silver brooch.

Bottom left: Silver and copper forged ring.

Bottom center: Forged brooch made from silver, bronze, copper, and gold leaf.

Bottom right: Forged brooch made from silver, brass, copper, and gold leaf.

INTERVIEW: GRAHAM STEWART

Designer, goldsmith, and silversmith Graham Stewart has run his own workshop and gallery in Scotland since 1978. He specializes in innovative, sculptural pieces, using a range of traditional techniques.

How did you get started?

As I sit at my bench, I look across the garden to my late father's workshop. He was an industrial designer and also worked at his bench with silver. He taught silversmithing evening classes, and I often tagged along. He and my older brother were always making things at home, so I became very interested in how things were put together. So it's no wonder I do what I do. My brother now works with me, and I only wish my father was still here to see the pieces I now create. When I was at art school in the 1970s, it was relatively easy to get holiday jobs in various workshops in Scotland and London. So, I've been taught by some of the best.

Can you describe your usual design process?

The process sometimes starts with discussions with my wife, Elizabeth and the client; some research (including, on one occasion, a trip to the British Museum to look at Chinese ceramics); and lots of sketching and refining before the actual metalwork began. I am still very old-school about drawing with a pencil and watercolors. I don't do any design by CAD; I love the physicality of drawing. In fact, some of my earliest memories are of drawing. I clearly remember recycling Manila envelopes by carefully slitting them open to produce a larger surface to draw on.

My workshop today houses a gallery/shop, where I spend an average of 60 hours a week. Designing and making (two interdependent things for me) have a flow—I guess they call it being "in the zone." I'm not there alone, though. This work is only possible thanks to the outstanding skills of my small team. Everyone brings their own strengths to the workshop.

What forms the bulk of your work?

When I first started, I worked on a small scale —jewelry mainly—but it wasn't long before I was being asked to do larger-scale silversmithing work. This is what I'm most known for now. That and engraving. I still do a small range of jewelry, though, and people will often say there is something distinctly Scottish about it. A recurring theme is loosely based on a preening bird. I was shown a Pictish stone carving of a goose in a local field 30 years ago and it still influences my work to this day.

How do you sell your work?

Much of my work is designed and made to celebrate special occasions, commemorate events, or honor individuals. I have even had some remarkable jobs for palaces, cathedrals, governments, and embassies. However, just as important are the personal commissions for families and loved ones. I also make stock items for the gallery and the occasional exhibition. For 26 years I have shown my work at the Goldsmiths' Fair in London, which is always a highlight.

Opposite: Gold bracelet set with sapphires and diamonds.

GALLERY

1. Forged and heated silver and titanium earrings, by Marina Lampropoulou.

2. Oxidized silver hearts with fingerprint imprinting, by Kaleen Wolfe.

3. Forged and hammered gold cuff, by Doron Merav.

4. Folded gold-plated silver earrings, by Karola Torkos.

5. Domed silver ring, by Marina Lampropoulou.

6. Reticulated gold and diamond band, by Anna Bario and Page Neal.

1

2

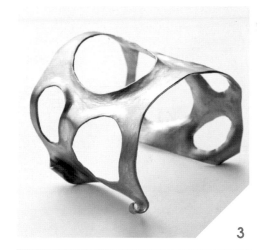

3

4

5

6

GALLERY

1. Anodized and textured titanium and silver bracelets, by Meghan O'Rourke.

2. Stamped silver and copper cuff, by Elan Lee-Vance.

3. Domed and printed pendant in patinated silver, by Lilia Nash.

4. Forged ring made from iron nails, by Janos Varga.

5. Chased white gold and diamond wedding bands, by Amy Tavern.

6. Hallmarked gold ring, by Neta Wolpe.

1

2

4

3

5

6

GALLERY

1. Stamped and engraved silver necklace with a vintage brass chain, by Helena Bogucki.

2. Domed silver earrings, by Marina Lampropoulou.

3. Patinated silver earrings, by Anna Siivonen.

4. Patinated silver earrings, by Anna Siivonen.

1

2

3

4

5. SPECIALIST TECHNIQUES

The techniques described in this section require quite a bit of practice to perfect. Most professional jewelers send out work that requires engraving, stonesetting, enameling, etc., to specialists who only practice particular trades or skills. For our purposes, understanding what is involved with these techniques and acquiring some of the necessary skills to do them is all worthwhile, and will help you decide whether or not your work needs to be sent to a specialist to be completed!

Opposite: Etched stainless steel brooch, by Nervous System.

Below: Silver rings set with a variety of stones, by Kirsten Muenster.

INLAY

This decorative technique involves setting one material into a recessed area of another contrasting material. There are several ways to achieve this, all producing different effects.

Inlay is a two-step process that requires the removal of material from the receiving metal before attaching the inlay metal or other material.

Whole areas of one metal can be soldered or pressed into another, then passed through the rolling mill. Alternatively, channels can be made through a sheet of metal with a fine chisel and a contrasting metal wire laid into it. This can either be soldered in, or, if the channel has a slight overlap at the top, it can just be pushed in. A traditional Spanish method of inlay is also described, right.

SOLDERING ONE METAL INTO ANOTHER

1. Draw two identical patterns on tracing paper—one will be the inlaid piece and the other will be the receiving metal. **(A)**
2. The inlay metal and the receiving metal should be the same thickness. Transfer your first pattern to the inlay metal. Use a piercing saw to cut accurately on the line. File any "over the line" edges back to the line. **(B)**
3. Transfer your second pattern to the receiving metal. Use a very small drill ($^1/_{32}$–$^1/_{64}$ in/0.5–0.7 mm) to make a hole just inside the line. Thread the saw blade through the hole and cut around the pattern, just to the inside of the line. **(C)**
4. Now offer up the inlay piece to see how it fits. If any filing is necessary, do this very carefully, offering it up each time to check that you have a really good fit. Once this is achieved, turn the piece over to the underside, flux where the two metals join, and lay several small paillons of hard solder (if using silver and gold, use silver solder) across the join line all the way around and solder them in. **(D)**
5. Finish by filing any excess solder away and rubbing the piece on wet/dry paper, held flat on a metal plate. The outside shape can then be cut. **(E)**

SPANISH INLAY

A few years ago in the old city of Toledo, I encountered a craftsman tapping down fine gold wires in a beautiful geometric design into a steel plate and asked him to describe his process. **(F–H)**

Francisco uses mild steel plate—about 14 gauge (2 mm thick), 4 x 4 in (100 x 100 mm)—and fine silver and gold wires, around 38 gauge (0.1 mm thick). He leaves the steel in a 50/50 solution of water/nitric acid until its surface becomes pitted, then he removes, rinses, and dries it.

The metal is then held in wax or pitch fastened in an engraver's block, to be turned while working. The sheet is divided into quarters, with squares marked with a sharp point, then turned 90 degrees, and marked again. A circle is drawn around the outsides.

All the lines are then accentuated by inlaying fine silver and gold wire. The wire is held in slight tension with stainless steel tweezers, pushed into the metal, then pressed firmly with a flat punch. For thicker lines or infilled areas, the wire is taken back on itself as many times as needed.

The piece is then placed in a hot solution of 66 percent caustic soda and 33 percent potassium nitrate to change the steel from dull gray to a beautiful blue/black. The piece is then rinsed and dried before a burnisher is used to brighten the silver and gold, which have been dulled by the solution.

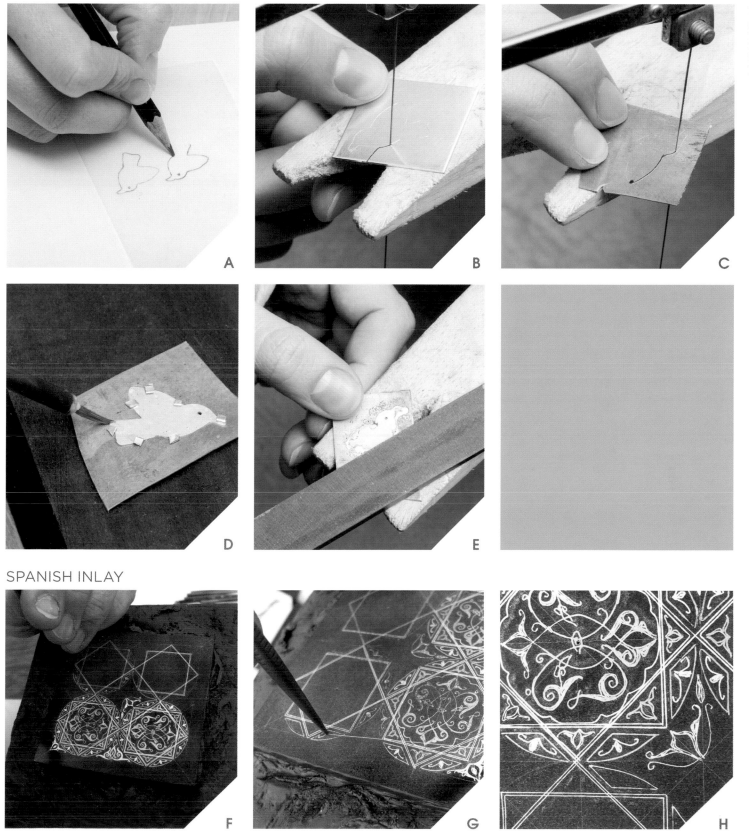

SPANISH INLAY

PRESSING ONE METAL INTO ANOTHER

In this method, the inlay metal is pushed through a pattern cut out from another sheet of contrasting metal. The inlay metal should be twice the thickness of the contrasting metal. The inlay metal should be annealed and cleaned with wet/dry paper.

1. The top sheet of silver should be no more than 24 gauge (0.5 mm thick). Pierce out a pattern that allows the inlay metal, when placed underneath it, to show through. **(A)**
2. Now sweat-solder the top piece to the bottom piece (see p. 124). **(B)**
3. When the piece has been soldered, pickled, rinsed, and dried, offer it up to the rolling mill and open the rollers to the same thickness as the two pieces of metal. Then close it down a fraction. **(C)**
4. Pass the piece through the mill, noting the direction, then turn it through 90 degrees, close down the rollers a fraction more, and make another pass through.
5. Continue rolling the piece through the mill in this way until the inlay metal has been pushed right through the pattern and is level with the top layer. It may need annealing after a few passes. Just make sure that it is completely dry before rolling it through again. **(D)**

MAKING A CHANNEL

In this exercise the areas to be channeled out of the receiving metal are marked out using a scribe or marker pen. The channel is cut using a sharp metal chisel, with a head size appropriate to the cut being made.

1. Place the metal in the pitch bowl. Hold it by turning down each corner and heating the pitch a little, just enough to hold the corners down (see p. 188).
2. Hold the chisel at 90 degrees to the line and hit it with a chasing hammer. This will start the cut. Now hold the chisel at about 45 degrees to the line and tap the end with the hammer to make a little curl of metal. As this curls up, whip it away to keep the line clear and continue the cutting to the end of the line. If it is uneven, level out the bottom of the cutout line with the chisel by just pushing it along without the hammer. **(E)**
3. Take some annealed, contrasting round or rectangular wire with the same diameter as the cut line and start to lay it down into the channel, lightly hammering it as you go. The top of the wire will be proud of the cut, so this can be hammered flat with a punch. **(F)**
4. Once in, the edges of the cut can be burnished or hammered to push them over onto the wire to hold it in.
5. Hammering the wire into the cutout groove can make it curl up and not do what you want it to! It may make life easier to solder the end in first and then hammer it down. If necessary, run more solder in to close any gaps.

A

B

C

D

E

F

ENGRAVING

A piece of work cut by a specialist engraver is an object of real beauty. Engraving can become the "raison d'être" of a piece, or it can be the hidden secret on the inside of a ring or locket. The art of engraving is to remove slithers of metal in such a way as to make it seem as if the cutting tool is as easy to use as a fountain pen.

The skilled engraver is a creative artist and can produce beautiful calligraphic images or wonderful, imaginative scenes. It takes time and lots of practice to become proficient with engraving tools, so giving yourself a few minutes every day to try engraving straight lines, curves, circles, and outlines of different thicknesses will help develop your control of the tools.

When using hand-engraving tools, access to a carborundum grinding wheel is desirable. These are available from most jewelry suppliers and should fit on an arm of the polishing wheel. It is essential to have a small, flat carborundum stone and a tin of oil for hand-sharpening the tools.

Engraving tools come in many shapes (see p. 36), each one having a slightly different purpose. For general workshop use, there are four or five really useful shapes that, with a little practice, will be in constant use as tools to help remove excess solder, open out the inside of settings, clean up messy joins, and add a minimum of decoration.

SELECTING AND PREPARING A TOOL

Buying engraving tools can be a bit confusing. You are shown a range of different shapes that all come in a length, mostly too long to be practical. The handles come separately, so which ones do you choose? Without any grinding and sharpening they do not work, so how are you supposed to start using them?

1. First, the handle should fit comfortably into the palm of the hand, with the tool protruding just long enough for the index finger to be able to touch the end area, which gives the control. If the point goes way beyond the finger, it is much more difficult to "steer." **(A)**

2. Having established the desired length of the tool, fasten it in a vise, with the jaws closing where the cutoff is to be and the superfluous end sticking straight up. If possible, hold this end in a cloth and give the tool a sharp blow with a mallet, which should immediately shear it off. **(B)**

3. Now place the tool the other way up in the vise so that the tang/handle area is protruding, and place a wooden handle centrally on it. Use a mallet to hammer the handle down as far as it will go into the tang. **(C)**

4. Some wooden handles have a flat side. This is to prevent them from rolling off the bench when not in use, so when these are hammered onto the prong area, check that the flat area is parallel with the bottom edge of the tool.

5. Precise lines can only be cut with a sharp tool. To test whether a tool is sharp enough to cut easily, hold the tip of the tool at an angle of 45 degrees on a thumbnail and push gently against it. If the tool slides off the nail it is not sharp; if it raises a tiny scrap, then it is! **(D)**

A

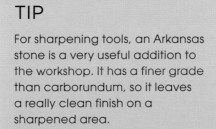

TIP

For sharpening tools, an Arkansas stone is a very useful addition to the workshop. It has a finer grade than carborundum, so it leaves a really clean finish on a sharpened area.

B

C

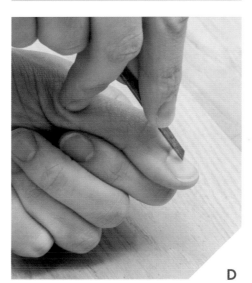

D

SHARPENING A TOOL

1. The top edge of a tool should be ground away in a curve to allow the cutting point to be visible as it is being worked. This can be done on the grinding wheel and up to about $3/4$ in (20 mm) away from the point.

2. When tools are being ground they will become warm. If they start to "color" they will lose the "tempered" state that is necessary for working. So keep a jar of water at the side of the grinder and dip the tool in it to keep it cool throughout the process.

3. By breaking it off in the vise to the correct length, the angle needed for cutting will have been lost. The initial angle can be ground on the wheel and then made accurate by hand-grinding it on a small carborundum stone. The face should be smooth and ground to an angle of between 30 and 45 degrees. The round, oval, and spitstick-shaped tools generally have a slightly higher angle—usually about 60 degrees.

4. Spread a little oil on the stone and place the tip at the correct angle on it. Use a slightly circular motion to grind the end smooth, all the time holding the graver steady and at the correct angle. **(A)**

5. The lozenge and square tools are given a more pointed end. The underneath of the very tip is slightly ground away on either side, and the sides leading up to the cutting face are also ground slightly away. **(B)**

USING A TOOL

1. Make sure the surface of the metal being engraved is clean and finished with wet/dry paper to a smooth, fine finish. Support the piece either held between the pins in an engraver's block or on a leather sandbag. It is really important that the piece does not slip around while it is being engraved. Draw the lines to follow clearly on the metal. **(C)**

2. To begin the cut, hold the graver at quite a high angle, with the handle neatly tucked into the palm of the hand. Once it is in the metal, lower the angle and push the tool carefully, raising a tiny slither (flick this away before continuing). Hold your middle finger down on the support to act as a sort of brake to stop the graver from slipping. Keep fingers and thumbs of the other hand holding the work, well out of the line of the tool. Cut a straight line using either a lozenge shape or a square. Cut a curve using an onglette, which is leaned over to follow a curve in one direction and then leaned over the other way to cut the other direction. **(D)**

3. To cut away a larger area, first cut the outside and inside lines with a lozenge, then use a flat graver to cut away the material in between. Flat engravers come with different cutting widths, so choose the one appropriate to the cutout area.

4. After all the lines are cut, rub the piece down with the papers to smooth away any ragged edges. **(E)**

ENGRAVING BY MACHINE

Small tools that fit into a pendant motor are suitable for making lines, but as the handles of these are quite large in the hand, have plenty of practice first on some copper or brass before starting on a special piece. There are machines especially designed for engraving, which can be used in conjuction with a computer. Some are hugely sophisticated and are priced accordingly; others, such as the pantograph engraver, are more basic and suitable for a small workshop. However, if engraving is not your thing, find a skilled hand engraver for beautiful work and use a machine engraver for more straightforward work.

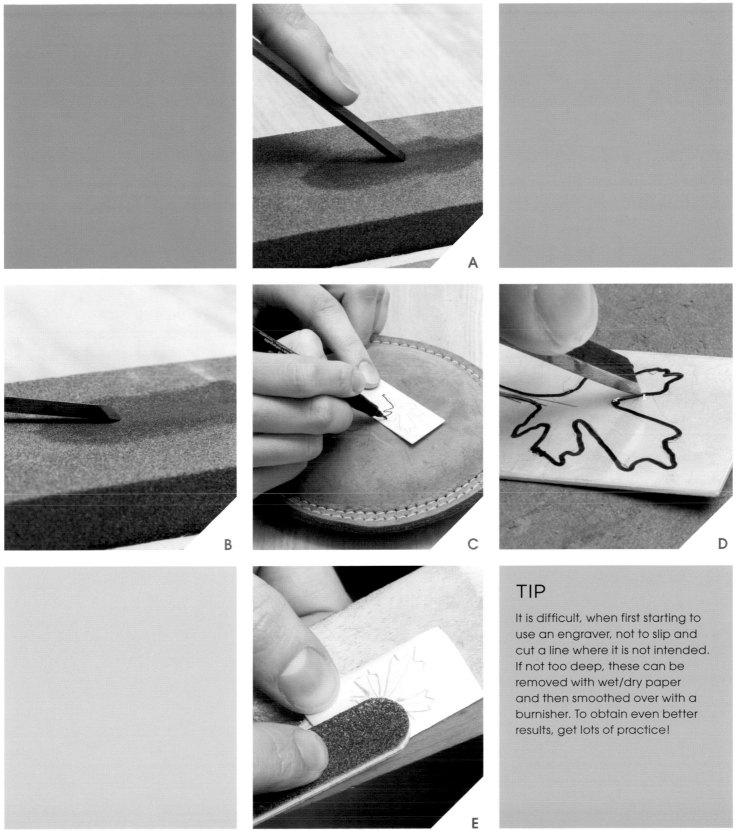

A

B

C

D

E

TIP

It is difficult, when first starting to use an engraver, not to slip and cut a line where it is not intended. If not too deep, these can be removed with wet/dry paper and then smoothed over with a burnisher. To obtain even better results, get lots of practice!

MOKUME GANE AND LAMINATION

Mokume gane ("woodgrained metal") originated in Japan, where it was used to make sword handles by combining different metals in very thin layers, laminating them, and then revealing those layers to resemble wood grain.

It is now possible to buy sheets of mokume gane which combine metals such as silver and copper, and palladium and white gold. The different sheets of metal are fastened closely together in a press and placed in a kiln. The surface on the sheets of metal starts to become liquid, causing them to fuse together. The challenge when making your own lies with the solder that must be applied between the sheets of metal to join them. With repeated solderings the solder tends to become brittle. Pockets of air also occur, causing the layers to raise slightly and the edges to become a little ragged. The fabrication for lamination is the same as for mokume gane, but each metal can be of a different thickness. Thinner sheets will show as thinner lines between contrasting metal. There are many variations possible using different thicknesses of metal and combining metals.

MAKING MOKUME GANE
This needs sheets of 20 gauge silver, copper, and brass or gilding metal, 2 x 2 in (0.8 x 50 x 50 mm).

1. Anneal, pickle, and rinse each sheet thoroughly, then rub it clean with 400-grade wet/dry paper. Each sheet should be completely flat so that there are no gaps between them later—the sheets should only be handled at the edges. **(A)**
2. Cut small paillons of hard solder and flux the back of two of the sheets. Place the paillons in rows to cover each sheet (see p. 124). **(B)**
3. Heat each sheet until all the solder runs. Pickle, rinse, and dry, then remove most of the solder with a flat file until just a fine layer remains. If any high points remain, adhesion will be more difficult later. **(C)**

4. Flux the soldered area of one sheet and lay it on an unsoldered piece, lining up the edges. If possible, solder them together by heating from underneath, bringing the flame to the top piece as the solder starts to run. (You can place a few paillons on a couple of edges so that you can see when it runs.) Cool, then quench in water.
5. Now solder the third piece to the other two in the same way. Make sure to flux the edges of the first two, and flux the third one all over the soldered base. Apply the flux as thinly but as evenly as possible. If too much is applied the sheets of metal will slide around when they are first heated, as the water dries out. **(D)**
6. When the three sheets are together the thickness should be around $1/8$ in (2.5 mm). **(E)**
7. Pass the sheets through the rolling mill, turning them through 90 degrees with each pass until the thickness is down to about $1/32$ in (0.8 mm), or less if desired. **(F)**
8. Now cut the sheet in half with a piercing saw and solder the two halves together in the same way as before by running solder on one piece first, filing, and soldering to the second.
9. By rolling, cutting, and soldering like this you can have as many layers as you choose. The more layers you can get, the more intricate the pattern will be. The last pass through the mill should leave the thickness at between $1/32$ and $1/16$ in (0.8 and 1 mm).

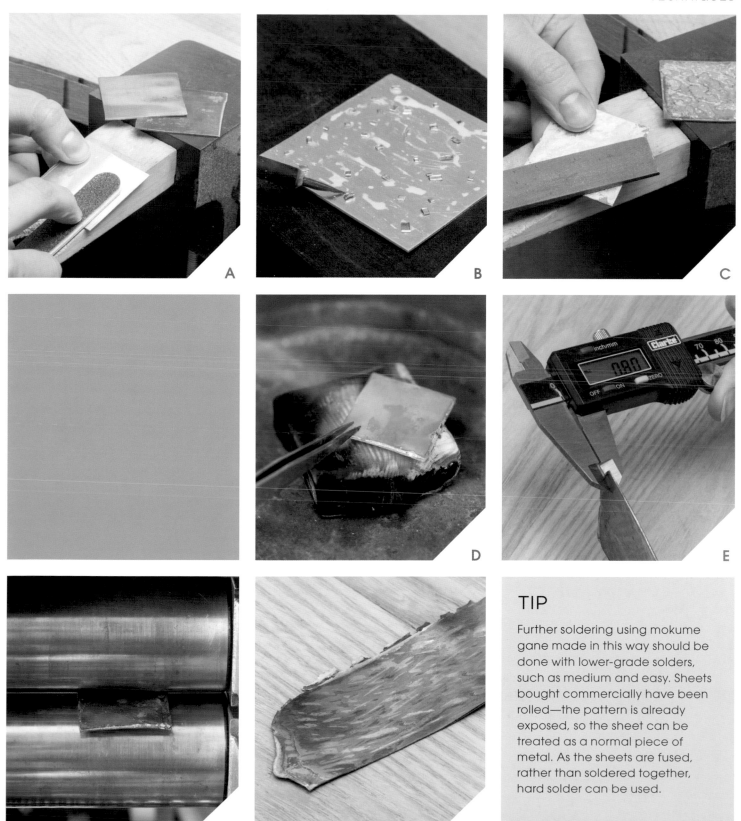

A

B

C

D

E

F

G

TIP

Further soldering using mokume gane made in this way should be done with lower-grade solders, such as medium and easy. Sheets bought commercially have been rolled—the pattern is already exposed, so the sheet can be treated as a normal piece of metal. As the sheets are fused, rather than soldered together, hard solder can be used.

USING THE MOKUME GANE

There are now two ways of exposing the layers of metal.
The first method is to use punches to make indents in the
metal. The second is to remove areas from the front.

METHOD 1

1. Lay the piece, right side down, on a bed of pitch.
2. Using an appropriately sized round-headed punch, make
   indents in the back of the metal. The indents should be no
   deeper than the thickness of the metal.
3. Now file away the bumps that have been created on the
   front of the metal. This should leave a flat sheet that is
   beautifully patterned. **(A)**

METHOD 2

1. Use a drill, or different-shaped diamond cutters held in
   the pendant motor, to remove the required areas. These
   obviously should not go right through the sheet.
2. Now pass the sheet through the rolling mill to flatten it
   out, when the pattern will appear. **(B)**

MAKING A LAMINATED RING

To make a ring with a stripe of a different metal, anneal,
pickle, rinse, and dry two rectangular strips of 18-gauge
silver that measures $3/16$ x $2^1/2$ in (0.7 x 5 x 65 mm). They
should be completely flat.

1. Solder a strip of 21-gauge copper measuring $3/16$ x $2^1/2$ in
   (1 x 5 x 65 mm) to one of the silver strips by running the
   solder on the back first, as for mokume gane. Then solder
   the second piece to the other side of the copper strip.
2. Cut the strip to length for the correct ring size (see
   Measuring, p. 112) and bend it up to be soldered. Bending
   the strip over a former, held in a vise, will make the
   bending easier. **(C)**
3. After the ring has been soldered, remove the edges with a
   large flat file so that the profile of the ring becomes a "D"
   section, with the flat side being the inside of the ring. As
   the filing takes place, the copper will reveal itself in a
   stripe all the way around. **(D)**

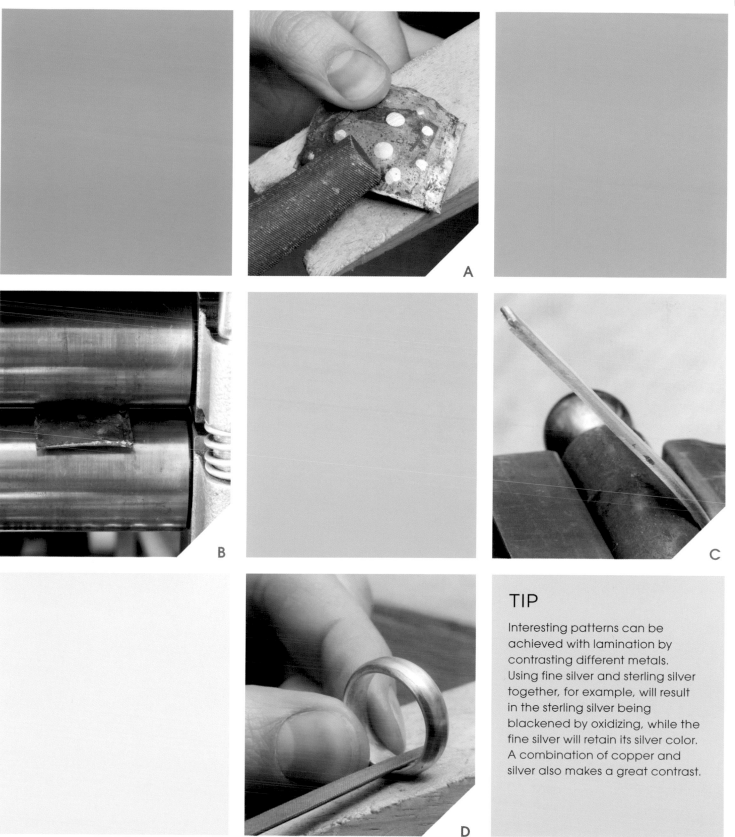

A

B

C

D

TIP

Interesting patterns can be achieved with lamination by contrasting different metals. Using fine silver and sterling silver together, for example, will result in the sterling silver being blackened by oxidizing, while the fine silver will retain its silver color. A combination of copper and silver also makes a great contrast.

STONESETTING

Beauty, color, texture, vibrancy, shape, and value are all factors to consider before deciding which stone, or combination of stones, to set, and in what setting.

Alongside my collection of precious stones I also keep a stash of pieces I find while out walking. In the right setting, ordinary stones can become glorious, and the settings can be any design you like, as long as they hold the stone secure.

Cabochon stones are usually held by a bezel, or collet—a metal collar. This is soldered to the metal base on which the stone will sit, and the top rim of the bezel is pushed down onto the stone, securing it. Faceted stones, to be held securely yet able to reflect the correct amount of light, need a more structured setting, depending on the shape and cut of the stone. Some cabochons may be slightly curved on the back and will rock back and forth on a flat metal back, so a little ledge in the setting (a bearer) will create space for the stone's curved base. Some faceted stones have a thicker "girdle" than others, so they need a higher bezel or claw. Stonesetting is an extensive subject, and only a few exercises are included here. However, some specialist books are listed on p. 300.

MAKING A SIMPLE SETTING

First make a rough estimate of the length of metal needed.

For a circle = diameter x 3.142 (pi)

For an oval = (length + width) x pi ÷ 2

For rectangles/squares: sum of all sides, allowing for corners

To this length add twice the thickness of the metal being used. Where necessary, round up rather than down; too long is better than too short. For an uneven stone, cut an overlong length using a rough measurement, but use the correct height.

For a cabochon stone, the height of the collet is assessed by measuring the height from the base to where the metal will turn over onto the slope to hold it in.

For a faceted stone, the height is assessed by the length from the top of the stone (the "table") down to the bottom of the stone (the "culet"). The distance from the girdle (the widest area of the stone) up to the top of the setting should be the minimum possible, but should allow the metal just to be rubbed over to hold the stone in place.

A SETTING FOR AN IRREGULAR STONE

1. Anneal the strip, pickle, rinse, and dry. Bend it around the stone. Mark where the ends meet; remove the extra length. **(A)**

2. Solder the two ends together and adjust the shape to fit the stone with half-round or round/flat pliers. Rub the bottom edge on a flat file so it is completely flat. **(B)**

3. Flux the underside of the bezel and place it on a base $1/16$ in (1 mm) thick and larger all around than the bezel. Cut small paillons of hard solder and place them evenly around the join, touching both bezel and base. **(C)**

4. Solder these together by heating around the base first and then moving on to the bezel too so that the solder runs evenly. If the bezel gets hot first, the solder will run onto its sides and not around the join.

5. After pickling, rinsing, and drying, cut around the bezel with a piercing saw, then file it so there is no visible line between bezel and base. **(D)**

6. Use a piece of tack to pick up the stone and offer it up to the setting to make sure it will fit. Do not push it in at this stage—it may get stuck! **(E)**

A

B

TIP

If a stone gets stuck in a setting when testing for fit, a small hole can be drilled at the back through the base, and the stone can be pushed out that way. The hole can be closed up by having a tiny piece of wire soldered into it.

C

D

E

MAKING A BEARER

To make a higher setting, or one for a stone with a curved back, or one soldered to fit the profile of a ring, increase the height of the bezel. Then make a smaller bezel ("bearer") to fit inside it. This will be the ledge upon which the stone will sit, so enough height of metal should be left on the outer bezel to set the stone. Solder the bearer in by placing solder around the bottom edge to avoid creating a solder "shoulder" on the ledge's edge. **(A)**

A STRAIGHT-SIDED SETTING FOR A FACETED STONE

1. Make the join halfway down one of the longer sides of the bezel. Hold the stone upside down on a little tack on a flat surface to keep it steady.
2. Cut a strip of metal longer than you need to go around all the sides of the stone. File one end straight. **(B)**
3. Lay it halfway along the straight edge and mark the metal where the first corner of the stone comes. **(C)**
4. Take a square needle file and file a groove along the mark to a depth just over half of the thickness of the metal. Hold a pair of flat-nose pliers close up to the groove and bend it to match the angle of the stone. **(D)**
5. Lay it against the stone and mark off the second corner. File a groove in the same way and check for fit.
6. Continue in this way until you are back to the first edge of the setting, mark this in line with the first edge, and then cut through the second end using a piercing saw. Check again that this now fits the stone, and make any adjustments if necessary.
7. Now solder the join, while soldering very small paillons of the same solder at each corner to make them more secure. Cut any bearers in the same way and tap them down into the outside bezel (collet) for a nice tight fit. **(E)**

A TRIANGULAR STONE

For a triangular stone I do the same thing, but the grooves have to be a little deeper if the angle is more than 90 degrees, and slightly less deep if the angle is greater. Start and finish the bezel halfway down one of the sides. A good alternative way to make a bezel with a good fit is to solder two pieces together, rather than work with just one.

A RECTANGULAR STONE

1. For a square or rectangle stone, measure two sides X + Y = Z and cut two identical pieces of metal a little longer than Z. Mark, with a pair of dividers, where the corner comes on each piece of metal.
2. File a groove along the mark and bend up to 90 degrees. Offer one right-angled piece up to the stone, and mark one end to come absolutely level with the stone. Now do the same with the other piece. **(F)**
3. Trim one end to the mark. The other end of each piece should remain overlong. Place the two pieces together so that they have a nice neat fit, then solder them together with soldering little paillons in each right angle. Then trim off the extra length on both sides. **(G)**
4. For a triangular stone, make a V shape first, then offer it up to the stone. Cut away the ends of the V extending past the stone, so they are level with it, then solder a flat strip across the top and trim after.

A MARQUISE OR PEAR-SHAPED STONE

1. Lay the stone on some tack on a flat surface and start the collet from halfway down one of its sides.
2. Make the initial curve with half-round pliers, then mark off the corner, filing the groove as deep as needed to get a nice, sharp bend that follows the shape of the stone.

FACETED STONES

Stones are faceted to create as much brilliance as their size will allow. Traditionally, therefore, they have been set with as little metal as possible in order for light to penetrate and be reflected at every angle. Today, faceted stones are often set using much more metal so the beauty and reflectiveness of both materials can be fully appreciated.

Any setting for a cabochon that has a bearer can be used for faceted stones, as long as the girdle of the stone sits comfortably on it. The top of the bearer can be filed down at an angle to accommodate the cone shape of the stone as it points toward the culet. However, a straight-sided setting is not always desirable, so cone shapes are also made that are suitable for ovals, round stones, rectangles, squares, and teardrops. Some cone shapes are made from sheet metal; others are made with wire.

After cutting out the shapes, the metal will need to be annealed, pickled, and so on. Bend up the sides using flat-nose pliers and solder them together, remembering to run some solder up the grooves. Offer up the stones to check the fit, then solder the setting to the piece using a softer solder than has been used already.

A CONE SHAPE FOR A PRONG SETTING USING WIRE

This construction, with small variations, can apply to a stone of any shape. The first thing to decide is how many prongs you want to set the stone. Here we will make a four-pronged setting. For more prongs, divide the outline of the stone in equal parts and make the prong framework accordingly.

1. Take two pieces of 16-gauge round wire (1.3-mm diameter), each approximately $2^3/_8$ in (60 mm) long, and use a round needle file to remove half the thickness at the center of each piece. **(A)**

2. Fit the pieces together and solder. As it is important to keep the right angles between the wires, place some pieces of charcoal or soldering blocks between them to hold them steady as they are being soldered. **(B)**

3. Make a frame with some thinner wire for the lower half of the stone that is being set so that it follows the shape. Lay it centrally over the wire prongs and mark each prong where they meet.

4. Using a round needle file, file a groove in each prong at the mark you have just made. Keeping the cross at the bottom as flat as possible, use a pair of half-round pliers to gently bend up each prong a tiny bit so that the frame can now sit into the grooves. Solder it in. **(C)**

5. Remove the central cross of wire with a piercing saw. **(D)**

6. Remove the curved edges of the inside of the cross with a file so that they are flat.

7. Make a second frame that fits neatly just under the girdle of the stone. File the inside of both frames at an angle so that the stone sits comfortably. Bring the prongs up farther until they sit neatly parallel with the bottom frame. Mark where they meet, and file another groove in each prong so that they are ready to receive the second frame. **(E)**

8. After soldering in the second frame, check that the stone sits comfortably and straight in the setting. This can now be soldered onto the ring or other piece. Once the stone is ready to be set, the prongs are cut down so that they are the same length and will be able to be bent over the girdle and down onto the stone. If necessary, a small groove can be filed in each prong at girdle level to ease the pushing down. The end of each prong can be filed to a round end and filed a little from the top edge to give a smoother appearance.

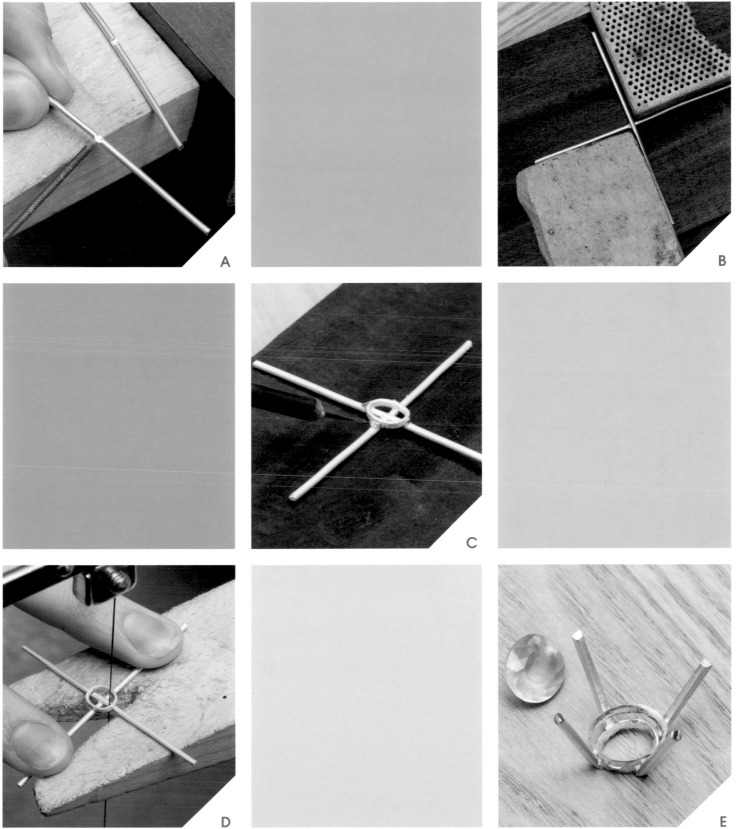

SECURING AN ITEM FOR STONESETTING

Before setting a stone you need to consider how the piece that will receive it is going to be held steady. Anything with a flat back can be held in jeweler's wax that has been melted onto a flat piece of wood, or tack can be placed on a flat surface and the piece placed firmly down onto it. If the stone has an open back, it is important not to allow either wax or tack to squeeze up into it, thus pushing the stone too high in the setting.

RINGS

Hold the ring in a ring holder so that the area with the stone is sitting flat on the top. The ring holder has protective leather at the top of the jaws, which will prevent the ring from becoming marked. **(A)**

EARRINGS

This is always a little more difficult, as the posts and clips have to be soldered on first. One way is to drill a hole in the wooden pin just long and wide enough to accommodate the whole post and then put a tack around the hole to help hold it in place. **(B)**

Another way is to heat up some wax on a "setting stick" (see Toolmaking, p. 262) and, when it is sufficiently soft, to press the earring down into it at the side so that the post cannot be bent by the wood.

SETTING A STONE

Once the piece is held steady, the setting can begin.

1. Check everything to see that the stone is sitting straight and that the bezel is not coming too high up around it. If necessary, file it down now so that you know it will not overpower the stone. With a faceted stone, the complete girdle should be sitting below the top of the bezel. File the top of the bezel with a flat needle file on the outside edge, at an angle of about 45 degrees. **(C)**

2. If the top is a little thinner it will help when pushing the metal over. If possible, hold one side of the setting against the pin as you start to push the opposite side with the pusher. Work from opposite sides so that the metal is being pushed equally all the way around. **(D)**

3. If the metal is too hard to push over, use a little punch. With the punch you will need both hands, so to prevent the stone from jumping out of its setting I place a fine sausage of tack over it. **(E)**

4. Initially the pusher or punch is held at an angle of 35–40 degrees to start pushing the bezel inward. After going around the setting at this angle, increase it to 60–70 degrees. Once all the edge is sitting comfortably down on the stone, raise the angle again so that it is almost vertical. This will give a nice-looking edge to the bezel.

5. Very carefully remove any marks made by the punch by using the cutting edge of the flat needle file. Hold your thumb right down over the stone as you use the file, because you do not want any scratches at this stage. **(F)**

6. Finish by rubbing around the setting with a burnisher.

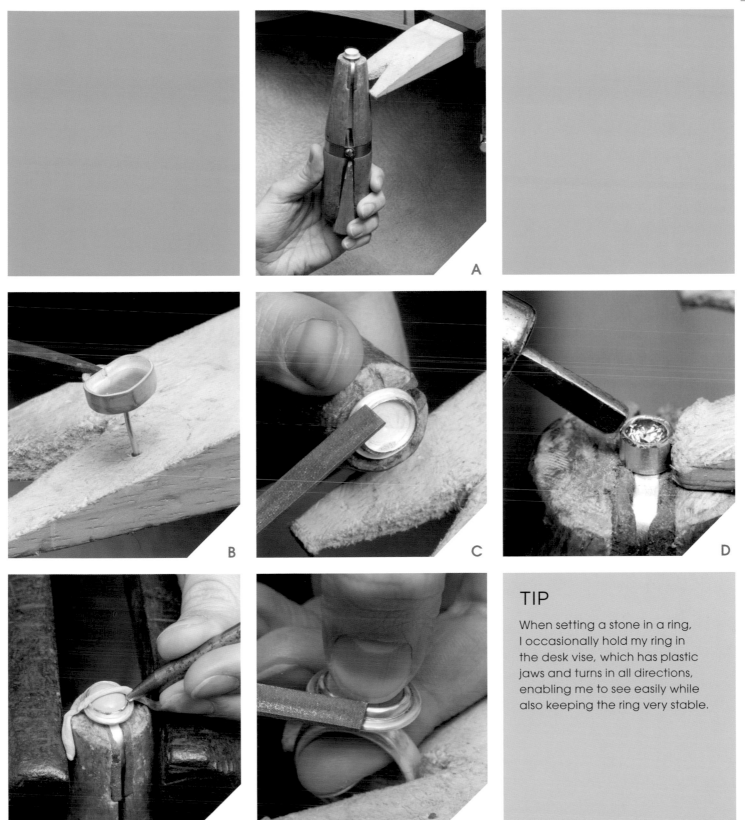

A

B

C

D

E

F

TIP

When setting a stone in a ring, I occasionally hold my ring in the desk vise, which has plastic jaws and turns in all directions, enabling me to see easily while also keeping the ring very stable.

GRANULATION

This involves fusing tiny balls of gold or silver to a metal surface. Granulation was, and often still is, a moment of fusing between a base sheet of precious metal and tiny beads of the same metal placed decoratively on top.

The fusion involved in granulation is made possible by a certain amount of copper compound being present, the quality of the alloys used, and the presence of an organic substance such as glue (gum tragacanth) and flux. The copper compound can be achieved by adding copper sulfate to the mixture of gum tragacanth and flux, or by grinding to a powder the black pieces of oxide that flutter off copper after it has been heated and mixing that with gum, flux, and water; or by placing the granules into the pickle with some binding wire (normally a real crime, but in this case the pink color that results is exactly what we are looking for) and placing them onto a paste of gum, flux, and water. Use high-karat gold wire or fine silver wire to make the balls. Sterling silver wire can be used to make the balls but it is better to solder them to the base rather than fusing them.

MAKING THE BALLS

1. To make a few balls, make a row of small indents in a new charcoal block with a small drill. Cut several same-sized little pieces of thin wire (say, 24 gauge/0.5 mm) and use fine tweezers to place them in the indents. Use a hot flame to melt each piece, which will then form into a ball. Place these in a small container and pickle them. **(A)**

2. For a greater number of balls, you will need a small container that will fit into a kiln and withstand temperatures up to the melting point of gold or silver, whichever is being used. A crucible would be suitable. Sprinkle a layer of fine powdered charcoal in the bottom of the container.

3. Space the little cut pieces of wire evenly on top and then sprinkle another layer of charcoal over them. Continue with these layers, finishing with a layer of charcoal. **(B)**

4. Place the crucible in the kiln, heated to 1650°F (900°C) for silver and 2010°F (1100°C) for gold. The wire pieces should become little balls. Remove the container from the kiln, cool, and sieve to retrieve the little balls.

FUSING THE BALLS

Clean, pickle, rinse, and dry the surface the balls will be fused to. Then paint a tiny bit of the flux/glue/copper sulfate paste where each ball will go.

METHOD 1

1. Remove the balls from the pickle, rinse, and dry. Pick them up with a fine paintbrush dipped in the paste and position them on the piece. Leave to dry thoroughly, preferably under a lamp. **(C)**

2. When dry, introduce a reducing flame around the whole piece, concentrating a little more on the base, until it is evenly heated and near soldering temperature. As the heat increases and the paste turns black, there will be a little flash as fusing takes place. Cool, then pickle. Any balls that have not adhered can be fixed again.

METHOD 2

1. Mix flux and gum tragacanth together. **(D)**

2. If necessary, make small indents where the balls are to be placed, using a hand drill. Paint these areas with flux, then place the balls. File some solder to make very fine pieces. Sprinkle over the area containing the balls, and solder in the usual way. **(E)**

A

B

C

D

E

ENAMELING

Essentially, enameling is the process of fusing layers of "glass" onto a metal surface, similar to firing glazes on ceramics. Enamels themselves consist of a mixture of silica (the largest part of the makeup), soda ash, and a metallic oxide; the choice of oxide determines the color.

SIFTED ENAMEL: Washed and dried enamel is shaken through a sieve onto a metal surface that has a layer of organic glue painted on it. **(A)**

EN RONDE BOSSE: "In the round." The enamel is applied all around a shaped surface. It is applied wet but is held in place by a fine layer of organic glue and the water drawn off at regular intervals with the edge of a paper towel. **(B)**

WET-PACK ENAMEL: The enamel is ground and washed and kept under water in a palette. It is placed evenly, with a small tool, on the metal and spread until it covers the whole surface. It is then dried before firing. **(C)**

CHAMPLEVÉ: "Raised field." The enamel is laid in an area of the metal that has been hollowed and leveled out by etching or engraving (see p. 260, p. 236). This can also refer to enamel that has been laid inside a raised framework. **(D)**

CLOISONNÉ: "Small cells." The cells are formed with fine flat wire, bent and shaped to a pattern, laid on edge, and then fired onto the metal or a base coat of enamel to form little cells that are then filled with colored enamel. **(E)**

PAINTED ENAMEL: The enamel is very finely ground and mixed to a fine paste with a pure oil. It can be painted, either behind a transparent color or on top of a light opaque color. The oil should evaporate before firing. **(F)**

SCRAFFITO: After the enamel has been laid on the piece and dried, lines are drawn through it with a fine point. After firing, another color can be placed in the lines, or the piece can be left with the underneath color exposed. **(G)**

BASSE-TAILLE: "Low cut." The metal surface is engraved with a pattern, before any enameling. The difference in the levels of the surface of the metal shows through the enamel, and where the lines are deepest the enamel is darker. **(H)**

GRISAILLE: From *gris*, meaning "gray." One color is used to make a picture on a contrasting background. This is usually a black background onto which is painted a white enamel, which sinks down into the background to become gray. **(I)**

MILLEFIORI AND STICKS: Premanufactured shapes and sticks of enamel that can be fired on top of a smooth coat of previously fired enamel. They usually have patterns with different colors running all the way through them. **(J)**

PLIQUÉ-À-JOUR: "Letting daylight through." There is no back for the enamel to adhere to, so it adheres to the sides of the metal instead. The pattern is pieced out from a sheet of metal, and the wet enamel is held in the cells by means of a capillary action. It must be dry before being fired. **(K)**

In order, from A to K
Sifted enamel copper brooch, by L. Sue Szabo; en ronde bosse enamel on silver pendants, by Ruth Ball; silver metal clay pendant with wet pack enamel, by Alison Lesniack; champlevé caddy spoons, by Ruth Ball; gold cloisonné brooch with pink tormalines, by Alexandra Raphael; pendant with acrylic paint enamels, by L. Sue Szabo; scraffito enamel pendant, by L. Sue Szabo; silver engraved ring with baisse-taille enameling, by Rachel Emmerson; grisaille portrait of Admiral Nelson, by Gillie Hoyte Byrom; mosaic necklace made with millefiori and seed beads, by Liz Tonkin; pliqué-à-jour brooch, by Nicole Barr.

A

B

C

D

E

F

G

H

I

J

K

TIP

Enamelling can be a very time consuming process. It is recommended that you double the amount of time needed to make your piece if you plan on enamelling it.

METALS THAT CAN BE ENAMELED

For jewelry purposes, the best metals to enamel are:
- high-karat golds (9/10 karat will enamel but can be problematic)
- fine, Britannia, and sterling silver
- copper
- gilding metal with a low zinc content
- steel (stainless steel or the precoated steel used to make wall panels and decorative tiles)
- precious metal clay

PREPARING THE METAL

Before enameling, metals must be scrupulously clean. Enamel will not adhere to metal that is greasy, oxidized, or has fingermarks all over it.

1. Clean the metal by heating and then pickling it in the appropriate pickle. For steels this can be hydrochloric or sulfuric acid, and for copper, silver, golds, and gilding metals this can be a safety pickle, alum, or sulfuric acid.
2. After pickling and rinsing, handle the piece at the edges only and hold it under cold running water. The water should run smoothly across the surface and not run up into balls or leave clear patches. If this happens, the piece should be heated and pickled again.
3. To give the metal a shinier surface for the enamel, use a brush with a liquid soap across the whole surface. **(A)**

DEALING WITH OXIDATION OR FIRESCALE

Nothing spoils enameling on silver more than if firescale (see p. 61) comes through after the piece is fired. This can and does happen. It will turn a transparent enamel cloudy and an unexpectedly nasty color. To prevent this, anneal and pickle the piece no fewer than three times to build up a layer of fine silver that will not oxidize unless it becomes overheated. You can also use the following procedure:

1. Use a solution of 4 parts water and 1 part nitric acid. Hold the piece using plastic tweezers and dip it into the acid solution; it will turn a gray/black color. **(B)**
2. Remove it quickly and scrub it with a brass brush and liquid soap until clean. Dip and rinse it again until the black/gray color completely disappears. **(C)**

Care must be taken with this second method as nitric acid will dissolve silver if left long enough. A quick dip in and out is what is required. Solder joins are particularly vulnerable, so take extra care of these. Sometimes, while firing, however well it has been cleaned, areas of copper will oxidize.

PREPARING THE ENAMEL

Enamel supplied in lump form will keep a little longer than powdered but will need grinding each time it is used. All types of enamel should be kept in an airtight container. Powdered enamels can be kept for a few weeks after they have been washed by covering them with distilled water in an airtight container. The color of the enamel in its powdered or lump form may be different once it is fired.

1. Perform a test before firing enamels onto a piece. Besides indicating whether the enamel is hard or soft, this will indicate the temperature for firing. **(D)**
2. Use a mortar and pestle to wash and grind both types of enamel (apart from powdered painting enamel). Cover the enamel with distilled water in the mortar. **(E)**
3. Grind it until it becomes really fine, then pour away the water and replace it with fresh. **(F)**
4. Tap the bowl on the side with the pestle to settle the enamel and mix it around to wash it before pouring the water away again. Continue doing this until the water is quite clear—it is surprising how many washes it takes.
5. Once the water is clear, pour most of it away, leaving just enough to cover the enamel. **(G)**
6. Transfer this to a palette. The mortar is rinsed out, before grinding and washing another color. **(H)**

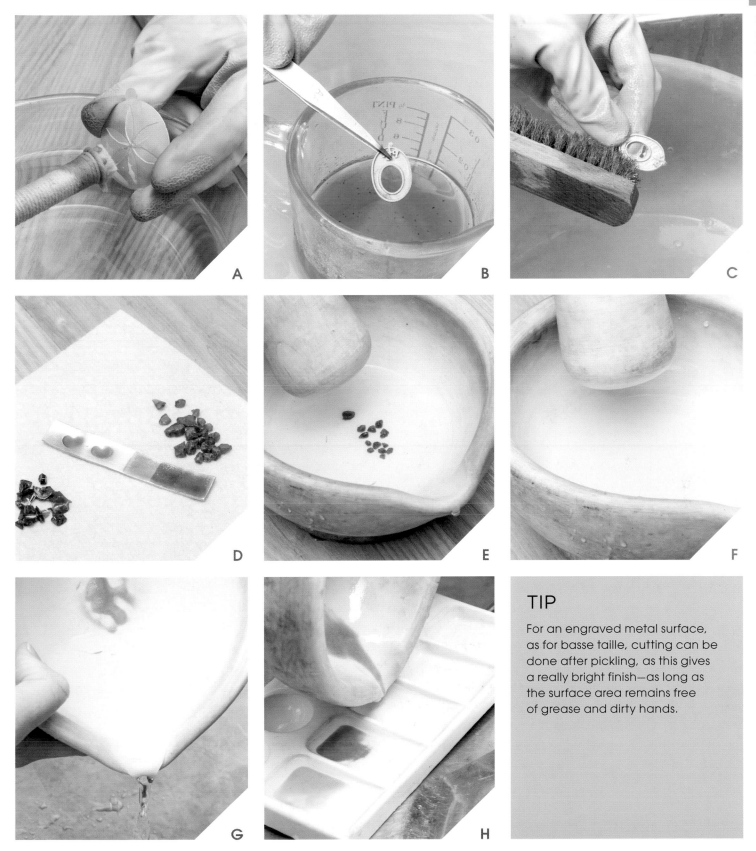

A

B

C

D

E

F

G

H

TIP

For an engraved metal surface, as for basse taille, cutting can be done after pickling, as this gives a really bright finish—as long as the surface area remains free of grease and dirty hands.

APPLYING DRY ENAMEL

1. Place the piece on a support suitable for high temperatures, then place everything on a sheet of clean paper. Paint the surface of the metal with a little organic glue. **(A)**

2. Place the dry enamel in a fine sieve and tap it gently to spread it as evenly as possible across the whole surface. If there is not enough powder, the result will be very thin and need to be done again; too much and it will be a little lumpy and will probably crack off. The piece and support are now ready to be fired as for wet enamel. **(B)**

3. The sifted enamel that has not fallen onto the metal can be poured back into the sieve (providing it is clean) from the sheet of paper.

APPLYING WET ENAMEL

1. Take the enamel from the palette in very small amounts using the end of a "quill" or a little spatula, which can be made by forging the ends of a small round piece of brass or copper wire. **(C)**

2. Hold the piece in the other hand. This allows greater flexibility than placing it straight down on a rack. **(D)**

3. Place the enamel in the cells or on the champlevé area, and spread it evenly, tapping the sides of the metal with the spatula to even it out. When an area is full, draw off the water by using the edge of some absorbent paper.

4. When all the enamel has been laid, place on a rack to dry.

5. The firing should only take place once the enamel is dry. Lift the piece into the kiln with a long fork and set it down gently on the kiln floor. **(E)**

6. Due to constant exposure to high temperatures, soldered fittings become a little vulnerable in the kiln. Minimize the risk of them dropping off during firing by placing the piece on a mica sheet through which holes have been made to accomodate the fittings. **(F)**

7. For most enamels the kiln needs to be at around 1530°F (830°C). Hard enamels require a higher temperature, and there are a few red and orange colors that will produce a better color if fired at a slightly lower temperature. The time taken for the enamel to adhere to the metal depends on the size of the metal—a 2 x 2 in 22 gauge (50 x 50 x 0.75 mm) piece may only need a minute; a larger, heavier one will need longer. When the enamel is ready to take out of the kiln, its surface will have become shiny (as opposed to looking a little like salt when it went in) and the metal will be similar to its annealing color. Let the piece cool before the next enamel coat is applied.

8. As it is fired the enamel will sink, so several firings are needed. Ideally, each layer should be as thin as possible.

9. When the top of the enamel is slightly higher than the surrounding metal or cloisonné wires, grind it back to a flat, smooth surface. This can be done by keeping it wet under running water, using a carborundum stone, coarse wet/dry papers, or a diamond-impregnated cloth. After the initial coarse application, use finer stones or papers until the surface is smooth and scratch-free. **(G)**

10. Now dry and refire it to give a high shine finish or, if refiring is not possible, polish it with a felt mop charged with water and pumice powder.

11. After the final firing, oxidation often occurs on the surrounding metal, as any fine silver surface has usually been removed in the rubbing-down stage. This can be removed with pumice and water either by hand or on a felt mop or, if the test for the piece has been immersed in pickle for a few minutes without any detrimental effects, it can be placed in the pickle to clean it. Never leave an enameled piece in the pickle for too long, as it may start to attack the surface of the enamel.

12. If soldering is necessary after enameling, the piece should be laid face down, balanced between two soldering blocks so that the metal edge is the only part that is touching anything. Use easy solder to rejoin the fitting, and then, leave it in that position until it is completely cool. **(H)**

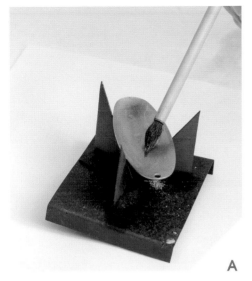

A

B

C

D

TIP

To protect fittings, annealing and pickling several times before starting to enamel will build up a fine surface around a solder area, which should not oxidize in the kiln. A paste around the fitting that stops the heat penetrating can be applied, but be careful—it tends to flake a little and can get into the enamel surface.

E

F

G

H

ETCHING

For most etching, a metal is covered with a stop-out and the desired lines are drawn through it. Alternatively the pattern is outlined on the metal and the stop-out painted up to these lines. Immersion in an acid bath then attacks exposed areas, removing them to the required depth.

As etching requires the use of acids, it is crucial that you work in a well-ventilated area, wearing rubber gloves and a face mask. **Make sure the acid is always added to water, not the other way around.**

SOLUTIONS FOR ETCHING

Copper, brass, and aluminum: 1 part ferric chloride + 4 parts water

Silver, copper, and pewter: 1 part nitric acid + 4 parts water

Copper and brass: 1 part sulfuric acid + 2 parts water

Gold: 4 parts aqua regia (nitro-hydrochloric acid); 40 parts water OR 1 part nitric acid + 3 parts hydrochloric acid + 40 parts water

Steel and iron: 1 part hydrochloric acid + 1 part water

Enamel: 2 parts hydrofluoric acid + 2 parts water

Etching can be done on a small scale in the workshop but it can be a little unpredictable. Larger, more repetitive work can be outsourced for "photoetching," which produces very accurate results (see p. 281).

ETCHING SILVER FOR ENAMELING

This piece will have an area etched out from the main piece, leaving a raised metal edge. It should measure around $1/100$ in (0.3 mm) less in the etched area than the outside area.

PAINTING THE STOP-OUT

1. Draw your outline on a piece of paper. Transfer this to the piece of silver. Go over this line with a scribe, making a single, deeper line. **(A)**
2. Anneal and pickle the piece, rinse it, and, if the water runs into droplets, clean both sides with a glass brush to get rid of any grease. Dry with a clean paper towel. **(B)**

3. Holding the piece by the edges only, place it on two supports so that the underside is not touching anything. Dip a fine paintbrush into the stop-out varnish and paint carefully up to the scribed line. Cover the rest of the surface and all the edges that are not to be etched. **(C)**
4. When the varnish is touch-dry (this can be speeded up if the piece is placed under a lamp), turn it over carefully and paint varnish all over this side. Allow it to dry.

PREPARING THE ACID

Pour $8^1/_2$ fl oz (250 ml) water into a glass pitcher. Slowly and very carefully add 2 fl oz (60 ml) nitric acid to make a solution of 4 parts water and 1 part acid. This can be made weaker with more water for a slower etch. Allow any fumes to evaporate, then transfer the solution to a plastic container with a close-fitting lid. Put it in a plastic tray and keep it secure. **(D)**

ETCHING

1. Hold the metal with plastic, stainless steel, or brass tweezers and slide it into the solution. **(E)**
2. Rinse the tweezers in water immediately. Agitate the solution occasionally by rocking the tray slightly. This helps clear the etched metal away from the surface.
3. Remove the piece from the acid with the tweezers and rinse both under running water, before using the vernier to check the depth of the etch. **(F)**
4. The etch will take 20 minutes to an hour, depending on the solution strength. Swill it every 10 minutes. Then anneal with a soft flame and pickle. **(G)**

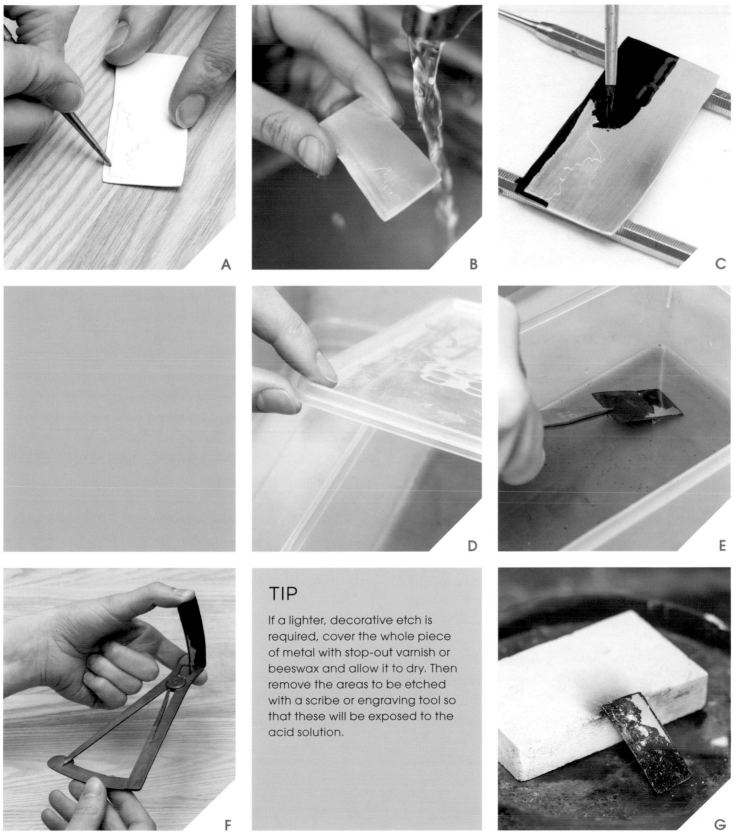

A

B

C

D

E

F

TIP

If a lighter, decorative etch is required, cover the whole piece of metal with stop-out varnish or beeswax and allow it to dry. Then remove the areas to be etched with a scribe or engraving tool so that these will be exposed to the acid solution.

G

TOOLMAKING

There are many times in the small jewelry workshop when it is impossible to find exactly the right-sized tool for the job. For this reason, it is useful to be able to make your own.

One of the most useful tools that I have in my workshop is a little steel punch that I use for nearly all my settings. Another one is a little pusher with a short, shaped piece of brass held in a wooden handle. I use it to push down the tops of small collets onto stones (see p. 244). When making repetitive wire links for a necklace or bracelet, it is useful to make a "jig" so that each one will be the same as the last.

Most engraving tools are supplied too long and not always in the shape you need, so it is important to know how to shape the ends of these to meet your requirements (see Engraving, p. 236). Another useful tool that you can make yourself and that you cannot buy ready-made is a setting stick. This is a piece of wooden dowel or a small, flat piece of wood, with setter's wax melted on top of it and shaped so that small items can be held steady in order to set stones.

MAKING A STEEL PUNCH

Smaller steel punches can be made with tool steel of various diameters.

1. Take a $^3/_{16}$ in (4 mm)-diameter rod and use a hacksaw to cut a 3 in (8 cm) length. **(A)**
2. Secure one end in the chuck of a small lathe and use a flat file at an angle to produce the shape of a sharp pencil. Do not make a sharp point; just file until you have a little flat end measuring around $^1/_{16}$ in (1.5 mm) in diameter. **(B)**
3. Use coarse wet/dry paper to smooth off the point. There should be no lip on the little $^1/_{16}$-in (1.5-mm) end. Polish it until smooth and shiny. Lay the punch on a soldering block and heat the area that is to be hardened to a dull cherry red. Pick it up with a pair of tongs and quench in water or oil, agitating it. Remove and dry. **(C)**

4. Place the tool on the soldering block. It must now be tempered so that the working end is softened just enough to ensure there is no risk of it shattering as it is worked. Use a soft flame back and forth along the sharpened area and watch to see colors appear in this order: yellow, brown, purple or blue, dark blue, then gray/black. For this punch purple/blue is correct. Quench immediately in water or oil. If too high a temperature is reached, the whole process must be repeated. **(D)**

MAKING A PUSHER

This little tool is invaluable. Pushers are available to purchase from jewelry suppliers, but these little ones are easy to make yourself. The idea is to have the handle tucked into the palm of your hand, with the brass rod just protruding about $^3/_8$–$^9/_{16}$ in (10–15 mm) beyond.

1. Take some brass stock, approximately $^1/_8$ in (3 mm) round and 1 in (25 mm) long. Taper one end with a file. **(E)**
2. Drill a hole in a handle that has one straight side.
3. Hold the untapered end of the brass rod in the safe jaws of the vise, place the hole in the handle over the taper, and use a mallet to bring down the handle into position on the rod. **(F)**
4. Now file the protruding end of the rod into a rectangle, so that the face measures about $^1/_8$ in (3 mm) across and $^9/_{16}$–$^1/_{16}$ in (1.5–2 mm) down. Polish the end so that there are no burrs or rough edges. **(G)**

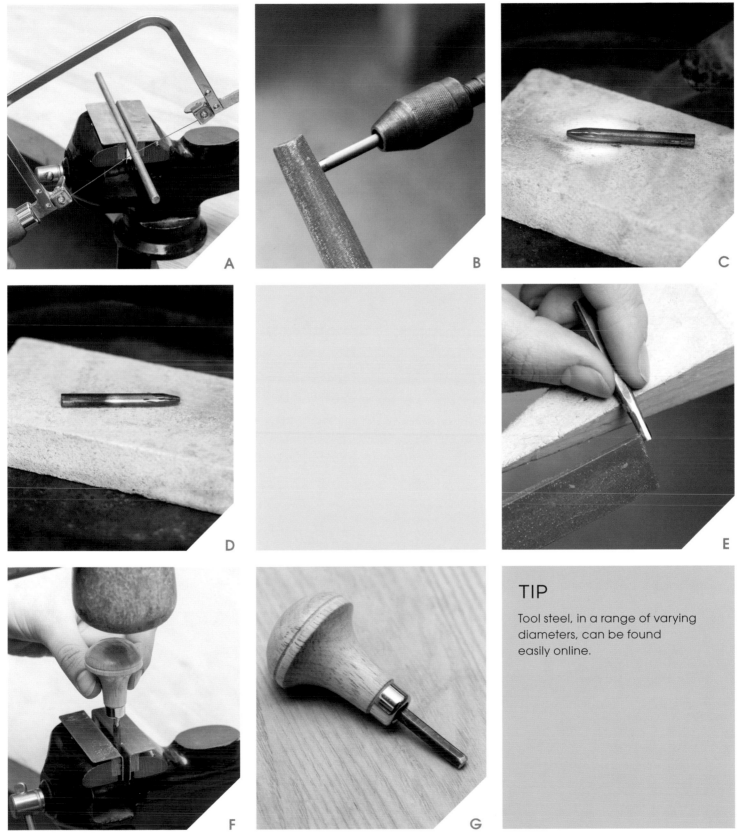

A

B

C

D

E

F

G

TIP

Tool steel, in a range of varying diameters, can be found easily online.

MAKING A JIG

1. On some tracing paper, draw the pattern that you will be making with wire. Take a flat piece of wood and glue the paper to it. **(A)**

2. Use galvanized nails, carpet tacks, or pins, depending on the size of wire being used. Remove the heads and then tap them in along the lines of the pattern at intervals of about $^3/_8$–$^9/_{16}$ in (10–15 mm), depending how many tight corners there are. You should have a few more to make a tight curve. **(B)**

3. Anneal the wire and, holding the short end with a pair of serrated-edge pliers (for grip), start winding the wire around the jig. Do this as many times as the height of the pins will allow, then cut it off and start again. **(C)**

4. The wire can now be cut through to produce individual pieces. **(D)**

MAKING A SETTING STICK

You will need some wooden dowel with a diameter of about $^9/_{16}$ in (15 mm), and a flat piece of wood, approximately 4 x 6 in (10 x 15 cm). You will also need a slab of jeweler's wax. If you find the wax a little too brittle at any point, add a little beeswax to make it softer.

1. Place a piece of the jeweler's wax on a flat metal surface and place a small soft flame over the top of it. Try not to burn the wax, but as it starts to melt push the top of the wooden dowel down into it until it sticks well enough to lift it slightly away from the metal surface. **(E)**

2. Keep playing the flame gently around the wax so that the edges start to soften. As they do so, start to push it slightly down the stick while turning it on the metal. Keep doing this until all the wax has taken on the shape of the dowel but is wider at the top than the bottom. **(F)**

3. Your setting stick is now ready for use. **(G)**

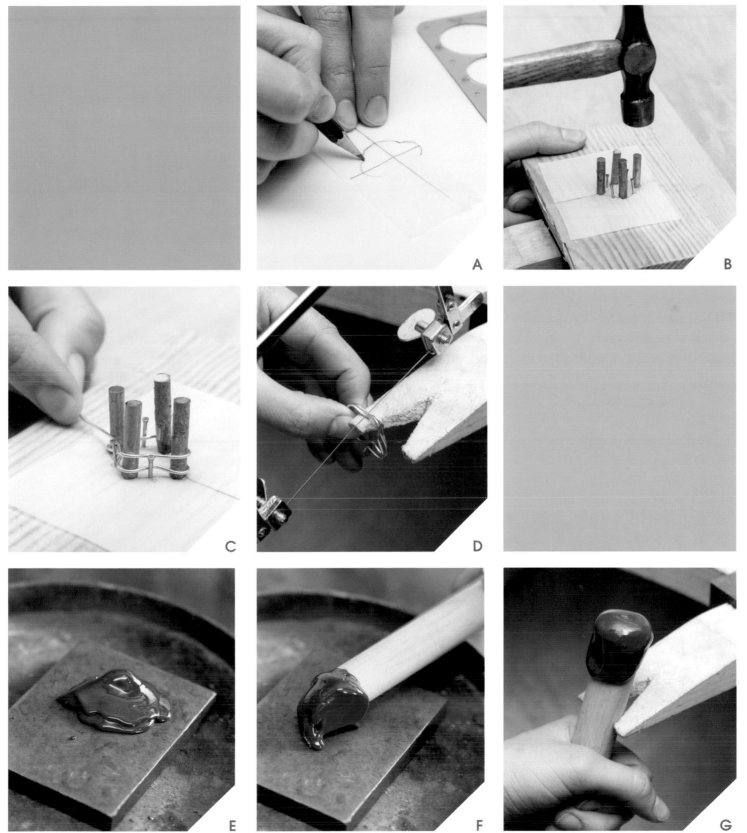

A

B

C

D

E

F

G

REPAIRS AND RESIZING

Sooner or later a friend or customer will ask you to repair a favorite piece. It is nice to be able to help, but think carefully before doing so! Always point out all connotations of repair, and check that they are still happy to proceed.

A PIECE HAS BEEN BADLY BASHED AROUND AND THERE IS CRACKING ALONG A SEAM
This sort of repair should be taken to a professional. If the metal is very thin and indented it may not be repairable.

A CHAIN HAS BROKEN
Very fine chains are hard to mend with a normal soldering torch, so consult a professional repairer. On a larger chain a new link can be made of the right size and held with tweezers while soldering with easy solder.

A BROOCH HAS LOST ITS PIN
Relatively easy if the hinge and closing hook are still intact. It is preferable to make a hard wire, maybe stainless steel, pin, but if a precious metal is to be used, make sure it is hardened after shaping. A new fixing pin will have to be made to keep the pin in place.

SOMEONE WOULD LIKE A BROOCH TO WORK AS A PENDANT AS WELL
As with all repairs, check that any soldering is safe to do. A bail could be made (described on p. 140), and a jump ring soldered to the base of the bail through a drilled hole in the pendant.

AN ENAMELED PIECE HAS BEEN CHIPPED
Best done by a specialist enameler. Their time is expensive, though, so the customer may be willing to have a "cold enamel" repair, which just involves matching up the color as well as possible and painting it in.

AN EARRING FITTING HAS COME OFF
Check for hallmarks to identify the metal. If there are none, file away a tiny area on the back with a fine needle file. If the piece is plated there will be a difference in the color of the metal—this will be very hard to repair. If you are sure that it is silver, gold, platinum, or palladium, then file off the small area of previous solder used for the fitting until it is clean, flux the area, and use easy solder to attach a new fitting.

SOMEONE WANTS TO CHANGE THEIR EARRINGS FROM CLIP-ONS TO STUDS
Check them all for metal quality—if in doubt, do not do it! Any stones should be removed, which takes time, so is the cost justified? It is possible to isolate stones to protect them while a piece is being heated—a very hot flame is needed for the soldering—but great care must be taken. Hang the piece on a steel wire so that the stone is immersed in water (held in a heatproof container). Or hide the area with the stone in some dense sand (see p. 269).

A CUFF LINK FITTING HAS COME OFF
Always check for metal quality and do not touch it if it appears to have been previously repaired with a lead or tin solder. Sometimes a replacement fitting can be glued on using a strong adhesive, but this is rarely the answer on a precious metal piece. Glues become discolored and tend not to last.

THE BAND OF A RING HAS BECOME VERY THIN AND BROKEN IN THE MIDDLE

This is usually because it has been worn for a long time, probably close to another. If set with stones such as diamonds, this is best done by a professional. If it is a simple band, you can do it yourself. Make sure, though, that you know what metal you are dealing with. Check for any previous soldering. If it looks clean, then the thin area can be cut away and a newer, thicker piece soldered in to replace it. If the ring is thin all the way around it might be better to sell the metal as scrap and offset it against the cost of making a new one.

A PIECE IS VERY DIRTY

If silver is very oxidized, dip it in a deoxidizing liquid for no more than a minute, then rinse it thoroughly in soapy water and then under running water. Impregnated cloths are very useful for shining up a piece without having to immerse it in a liquid. Care should be taken with any stones and liquids, and the softer and more vulnerable ones should not be placed in them. Ultrasonic cleaners are excellent for cleaning out dirt from behind open set stones, but check that the stones are secure, as the soundwaves can dislodge them. Do not put softer stones in the ultrasonic. Softer stones include: opal, fluorite, turquoise, amber, lapis, and emerald.

ENLARGING A RING OR BRACELET

To add a size into a ring, fasten a piece of binding wire around a lettered ring mandrel at the current size. Remove it and cut it in half opposite the twist (see Measurements for a Ring, p. 112). Then, fasten a second piece of binding wire around the new size that is required to make it larger. Remove it and cut it in half. Straighten out both pieces of wire and measure the difference in length between the two pieces. This is the amount of extra metal to be soldered into the ring.

1. First make sure you know what the metal is that is going to be enlarged. Once it is safe to do so, anneal the piece and quench it in water. The line of the original solder will show up. Cut through this with a piercing saw and then pickle to clean it.

2. Cut a piece, a little longer than you need, of either wire or sheet that has a larger dimension than the piece. It can be straight at this stage. **(A)**

3. Place the ring on a soldering block with the extra piece sitting straight in line with one side of the join. Flux the join, place some hard solder across it, and solder it up. **(B)**

4. Open up a pair of dividers to the extra length required and mark this on the extra piece just soldered on. Cut through the line with a piercing saw and bring it into line with the unsoldered half of the ring. Flux this new join and use medium or easy solder to join it. Do not worry about the shape yet; after it is soldered it will be shaped on the mandrel. **(C)**

5. File the inserted piece so that it is the same shape and dimensions of the ring. Shape around the mandrel, clean, and polish. **(D)**

DECREASING THE SIZE OF A RING

First make sure you have identified the metal that is to be made smaller. Once it is safe to do so, anneal the piece and quench it in water. The line of the original solder will show up. Cut through this with the piercing saw and then pickle to clean it.

1. Assess the amount of metal that needs removing in order to decrease the size of the ring—the difference between the size it currently is and the smaller size required.

2. Cut open the join. Open the dividers by the length to be removed and place one side of them on one side of the join and draw a line down the metal with the other point. **(E)**

3. Cut along this line. Bring the join together so that the sides are sitting really closely together. If there are no other visible joins in the ring, solder it up with hard solder; if there are, use easy solder.

4. If the ring has a stone set in it, bring the join together and push the whole stone area down into some casting sand. This will protect the stone while the soldering takes place. A small piece of charcoal is useful at the back of the ring to reflect the heat. **(F)**

5. Reshape on the mandrel. **(G)**

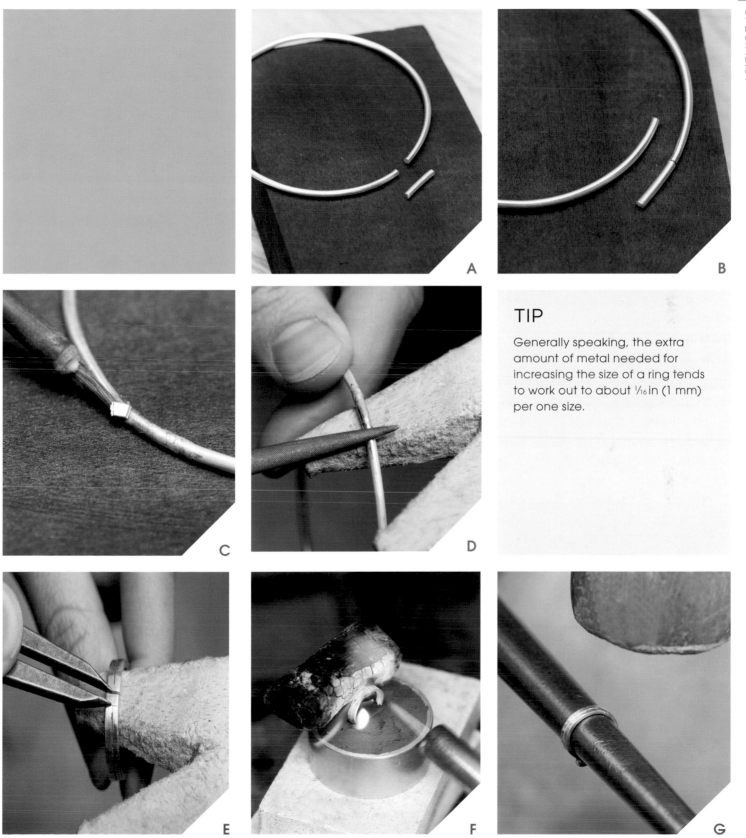

A

B

C

D

TIP

Generally speaking, the extra amount of metal needed for increasing the size of a ring tends to work out to about $1/16$ in (1 mm) per one size.

E

F

G

GALLERY

1. Hand-engraved silver pendants
   with champlevé enameling,
   by Rachel Emmerson.

2. Oxidized and polished silver earrings
   with soldered silver granulation,
   by Beth Pohlman.

3. Stamped and engraved silver plate on leather
   coin purse, by Helena Bogucki.

4. Etched zinc earrings, by Malou Paul.

5. Gold earrings with clusters of gold and silver
   granules, by Hannah Bedford.

1

2

3

4

5

GALLERY

1. Mokume gane pendant,
   by Sabine Amtsberg.

2. Silver rings with fused gold, set with rough-cut lapis lazuli and Afghan turquoise, by Jinks McGrath.

3. Silver rings set with a Mexican fire opal and an aquamarine, by Regine Schwarzer.

4. Gold-plated silver earrings with enameling, by Karola Torkos.

5. Cast gold bracelet with enameling, by Anna Bario and Page Neal.

1

2

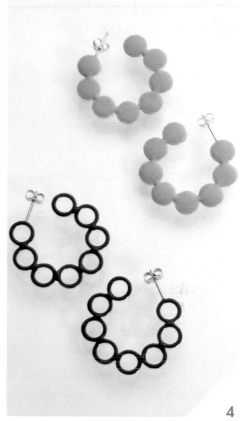

3

4

5

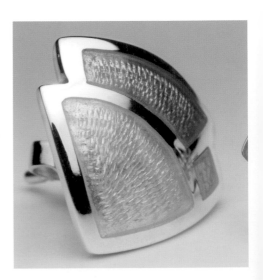

SECTION 3
GOING PRO AND RESOURCES

6. TAKING IT FURTHER

This section aims to give some advice to those of you who are thinking of making a living from jewelry making, or at least selling your work and not making it all just to give away as presents!

In addition, all the basic resources you will need are covered here, from temperature and measurement charts through to listings of trade fairs, colleges offering jewelry training, and suppliers and services, as well as suggestions for further reading.

Previous page, from left to right:

Silver clay earrings, by Esmeralda Woestenenk.

Moissanite and palladium white gold ring and recycled gold ring, by Tamara McFarland.

Champlevé enameled and hand-engraved ring, by Rachel Emmerson.

Silver clay, keum boo pendant, by Esmeralda Woestenenk.

Silver and diamond pendant, by Cynthia Nge.

Silver clay pendant with gold detail, by Esmeralda Woestenenk.

Opposite: Oxidized silver necklace with granulated detail, by Beth Pohlman.

Right: Anodized titanium necklace, by Meghan O'Rourke.

STARTING OUT

If you have just finished, or are still attending a college or university, you will probably be thinking about jewelry making, designing, teaching, or selling, as a career. It is not always easy to know how to get started, or what level of commitment it will require. It is a good idea to talk with fellow students to see if there is any future in pooling resources and working together, but at the same time making your own original work.

There are two basic directions to go in. The first one is: Do I want to be a "designer/jeweler," selling mainly through exhibitions, galleries (where mostly they deal on a sale or return basis) and commissions, making one-off pieces or collections, and possibly doing some teaching? Or: Do I want to design and produce jewelry on a more commercial basis, where I either have my own store or I sell through trade shows or agents, designing items on a commercial scale?

At the beginning, it is not necessary to have every conceivable tool in the workshop. It is more important to have a few simple ideas and start making! Add to your tool collection when and if you need to. Years ago I made a rule that I only bought a new tool (unless it was very reasonable) when I had really wanted it and knew I needed it for one year!

Lots of young designer jewelers have part-time jobs, which helps to finance their jewelry work. I think it is important to make sure that the hours worked at jewelry are always more than the hours worked at the part-time job, otherwise it can quickly become the other way around and get more difficult to reverse the situation.

To start selling, tell all of your friends and relatives what you are doing; they will love supporting your enterprise and they will have friends who, in turn, will tell more friends. These days, of course, there are many different grants available to apply for, but as not everyone can be successful in this, just make as beautifully as you can with what you have.

Once you have a few sales under your belt, do some research to see if there is a nearby guild or association that you can join (some of these are listed on p. 302). They arrange for shows and exhibitions in various venues within a given region where it does not cost a fortune to take a stand to show your work. Being a designer/jeweler means that you will be dealing with the public and clients of all different types, and I know most of us find it quite difficult to "sell" our own work at first, but this comes with practice! These exhibitions give you a chance to talk about your work, the materials and techniques you use, and how you design.

It is also beneficial to go to as many exhibitions and museums as you can fit into your schedule. See what influences your thought processes and find a way of putting your own creativity into new work. But please do not think about copying. It is not a good idea and you will not gain any gold stars! Having a website is a must, but I do not think that there is any need to rush into it. You will need to produce a coherent collection first, however small, and be prepared to make to order and know exactly how much everything costs. You may also need to be registered with one of the four assay offices, who will make a stamp with your initials and then mark your pieces, with a date, the metal quality, their own mark, and yours (see p. 218).

Opposite: Applying wet enamel.

TECHNOLOGY

Although not covered in detail in this book, you may want to explore the ways in which the latest technology can aid you in your work. CAD/CAM is a fast-growing area, as is the use of lasers to perform a variety of tasks. Training programs in both subjects are now offered at many institutions.

CAD/CAM

CAD/CAM (computer-aided design/computer-aided manufacture) is the use of software programs to both design and then output a 3-D version of a product. This technology is being used increasingly in the jewelry-making world. A software program, such as Adobe Illustrator or Rhinoceros, is used to create a 3-D design on screen. This information is used to generate a wax model, which in turn is used to cast the final piece (see Casting, p. 168). Output devices can be divided into two main categories—milling machines or rapid prototyping (RP) machines. A CNC (computer numerical controlled) milling machine is the least expensive and can be used to mill about 80 percent of all designs. It usually mills wax, although more expensive models can do metal, too. This machine mills away the wax (i.e., takes away from a solid), leaving you with the design only. An RP machine is more complex, and more expensive. It builds up the design by adding a layer of resin or wax during each pass. Both are equally accurate, producing results that can be measured to the nearest micron. A CNC milling machine is usually faster.

ADVANTAGES

1. Although working out a design using CAD can take a long time, hand-carving a wax model requires great skill, and it can be difficult to ensure that all surfaces are worked to the same dimensions. When handling a piece for carving, fine particles of dust are also easily transferred onto the model, which can be hard to remove—the smoother the model is, the better the casting will be.

2. CAD/CAM also allows you to build a model with incredible accuracy. If designing a dragonfly, for example, with two pairs of wings and a body, you can build these as three separate components, knowing they will fit together perfectly. When designing pliqué-à-jour (see p. 254), you can be sure the width and depth of the wires are all the same. You can also be sure that a design has the same depth throughout—something that can be tricky when making a model by hand, especially if the surface is uneven. Amazingly fine lines can be cut too, from $1/16$ in down to $1/8$ in (1–0.3 mm).

3. Most CAD programs can calculate the weight of metal in the finished piece. This can be very important in reckoning the final cost of the piece you are making.

4. Adjustments to metal thickness can be made accurately. This is particularly useful when creating models for enameling because of the need to consider the ratio of enamel thickness to metal thickness. (The risk of cracking problems with the enamel goes up as the thickness of the metal goes down.) Whatever thickness adjustments you make, though, must be made in light of a good understanding of the casting parameters of the metal you intend to use.

5. CAD offers the opportunity to go back and make adjustments to the design. Various versions can be saved under different file names so that you can experiment with different approaches or fine-tune your design, thus ensuring a design that comes out looking "just right," with no increase in manufacturing time.

6. You also have the option to build up a virtual library of designs on your computer—but do not forget to make regular and safe off-site backups.

LASER WELDING

For a busy workshop with several jewelers, a laser welder is a must; as prices have come down, the popularity of these machines has increased, and lasers are now used in almost every commercial workshop. For the smaller workshop, a laser is an expensive tool, which can be difficult to justify. However, it is still worth understanding the process if you are going to be outsourcing work to specialist firms.

The material used for laser welding is a rod of the same material as the subject piece. The two sides to be welded are held together so they are touching but with no pressure, and the laser beam produces the contact. As with soldering, just the right amount of weld is required.

For enameling, laser technology provides a breakthrough. Traditionally, almost all soldering must be done before enameling and any component must go through repeated pickling and firing (problematic for delicate pieces). Now this task can be performed using a laser after the enameling process. Platinum, which needs very high temperatures to be soldered, can be laser-welded very successfully at many different points. When resizing a platinum ring, any set stones do not need to be removed, and the laser weld can be performed close to the stone—almost impossible with a flame. Tiny holes in the finished surface of castings, caused by porosity (usually due to poor casting techniques) can also be filled with the use of a laser. Very intricate repairs—to a necklace with tiny stones or the jump rings in a charm bracelet—can also be performed much more efficiently than with conventional methods of soldering.

PRACTICAL TIPS

1. Laser uses intense, virtually instant heat in a tiny area. Small joins can be made with just a few "shots," fusing the existing metal from both parts together. Often, though, a join will require more shots and some supplemental fill or weld metal—usually a thin length of solder wire.

2. If a join requires more than a few seconds of laser impulses, the heat buildup will be significant. If the join is near any enamel, precious stones, or pearls, this can do damage, so it is best to weld the join by short stages followed by cooling-down time to let the heat dissipate.

3. As laser welding is generally done through a microscope, first-time users may feel dizzy or get tired eyes. It can take time before operators can work for longer periods.

4. Since silver is one of the most highly reflective metals, and laser is a form of light, there can be problems as the laser energy tends to be reflected away. Therefore, a darker, perhaps more tarnished surface responds better than a bright surface. But since we must often work with bright, nearly finished pieces, using a dark magic marker at the join can help to make silver more absorptive.

PHOTOETCHING

A hand-drawn or electronic copy of a design (between two and four times larger than actual size, to allow for greater accuracy) is used to produce a transparency, which is placed on top of a metal sheet with a photosensitive film between them. When exposed, certain areas are covered with a resist coating, while exposed areas are left ready to be etched.

The minimum size of sheet that is commercially viable is around 12 x 22 in (300 x 550 mm); thickness can range from 31 down to 17 gauge (0.25–1.2 mm). The photoetching process can cut right through a metal sheet up to this thickness, so any areas to be cut out should be drawn on the hard copy in black. Areas to be cut to a specific depth, i.e. less than the thickness of the metal, should be drawn in red for the front surface and blue for the reverse.

The fineness of a line to be cut through is dictated by the thickness of the metal—i.e., if a line is $1/64$ in (0.5 mm) wide, the sheet itself should be that thickness. After photoetching, the pattern is pierced out.

WORKSHOP LAYOUT

A jewelry workshop can be made to fit into a very small space, and when first set up, it is very often made in the small corner of a bedroom or an area at the back of a garage. Here are a few key considerations when deciding on the layout of your working area, whatever the size. A fuller summary of the tools you will need is given in Chapter 1, Tools.

THE BENCH

A bench can be bought ready-made from a jewelry tool supplier, handmade, or even adapted from an old workbench. The main thing is that it should sit firmly on the floor and be at the right height for you to sit. A purpose-built jeweler's bench will have a curved cutout section at the front, and a piece of leather (apron) strung horizontally underneath. This will catch any dust and filings. Make sure, too, that you have adequate lighting while you work.

THE FLOOR

It is beneficial for the workshop floor to be smooth, this way a piece of metal or stone that is dropped can be found easily.

PLIERS

On, or very close to your bench, make a rack for your pliers to hang on so that they are available when you need them.

PENDANT MOTOR

If you have a pendant motor it should be hung within easy reaching distance, with the drill end clear of the bench.

SMALL TOOLS

Small tools such as needle files and engraving tools can be kept on the bench in separate compartments.

POLISHING MACHINE

The polishing machine should ideally be kept away from your working area as, even with an extractor fan, it creates a lot of black dust that will get everywhere if it can!

CHEMICALS

All chemicals should be kept in a locked cabinet and only mixed in a well-ventilated area (see also Safety, p. 284).

SOLDERING

Your soldering torch should be kept immediately on hand, with the stand containing the soldering blocks just above it on the bench. Make sure you protect the bench using a heatproof mat or something similar. Any large soldering should be done in a darker designated area.

PICKLES

Pickles can be kept on the bench but make sure they are kept away from any metal tools.

WATER

Access to running water is desirable, but if it is not possible, simply keep a metal container full of water handy, along with a plastic bowl of water, some liquid soap, and a bristle brush.

VISE

It is useful to have a fairly heavy-duty vise fixed solidly to the wall or floor, with enough space around it to be able to draw down lengths of wire through the drawplate.

HEATING

For keeping warm in your workshop, an electric heater is much better than a gas one, as the gas will cause condensation, which will inevitably rust your tools.

Opposite: A collection of pliers from the author's workshop.

SAFETY

Safety in the workshop involves common sense. It is a case of always being aware of the tools, the flame, or the noxious substances that are being used. Awareness is essential for avoiding both minor and major injuries.

CLOTHING

Wear an apron or some other type of protective clothing in the workshop. Dangly bracelets are best avoided as they catch very easily; I usually remove my rings as well so that they do not get damaged as I am filing or using chemicals. Tie up long hair so that there is no chance that it can become entangled in an electric motor, and avoid wearing loose sleeves and scarves. Always concentrate—a moment's distraction can lead to serious mishaps.

SITTING AT THE BENCH

The top of your bench should be at about the same height as your elbows when held out to just under shoulder height. So your pin should be a little below eye level. This position will help keep your back straight and prevent your neck from having to be lowered too much. Avoid repetitive strain injury by getting up and walking around at regular intervals.

PIERCING SAW

Be aware of the direction that you are cutting in, and keep your fingers out of the way. A little cut from the blade is surprisingly painful.

PENDANT DRILL

Always hang up the pendant drill after using it. If it hangs down and is accidentally activated it can get caught in clothing or work.

SOLDERING

When you are doing a lot of soldering it is fine to keep the torch on with the pilot light, but if you do something else, or leave the room, turn it off. Turn off the gas and/or oxygen for the torch at source every night. When replacing a cylinder, always paint the new fittings with some liquid soap. Any bubbling will indicate a leakage. Do not lean over a pilot light—it will singe hair and clothing from quite a distance.

THE ULTRASONIC

Do not place your hand in the liquid while the machine is on—the ultrasonic beam and/or the cleaning liquid can cause skin and bone damage.

GOGGLES

If you are using a lathe, electric drill, or polishing motor, then wear clear goggles. If platinum is being heated/soldered, special dark goggles should be worn.

MASKS

A simple mask will prevent inhalation when carrying out any work that creates dust.

CHEMICALS

After the polishing motor, chemicals are the worst hazard in the workshop, so be careful when using them. Read the instructions on the label. Here are some general rules:

1. Always add acid to water, never the other way around.
2. Always wear rubber gloves, protective clothing, and light goggles, and work in a well-ventilated area.
3. Make sure that there is a supply of water on hand to wash off any spilled drops.
4. When adding acid to water, place the water container in a rubber bowl in a sink to catch any drips. Very small amounts of acid can be disposed of by diluting them in a very large quantity of water.
5. Acids should always be kept in a locked cabinet and marked as hazardous.
6. Any accidental spills on a person should be immediately diluted with running water and then attended by a doctor if necessary.
7. Cover any large spills on a surface with sodium bicarbonate (an acid neutralizer). This should be readily available in the workshop as it is often used with hot water to neutralize any remaining pickle in soldered items. Allow the bicarbonate to slightly harden and soak up the acid before picking it up with a dustpan and brush, wrapping it in a large quantity of newspaper in a plastic bag, and disposing of it through a local waste disposal company.

Right: Patinated copper clay necklace, by Anna Siivonen.

MEASUREMENTS

RINGS

To make a ring to a specific size you will need to know the exact length of metal that has to be cut. The size of a finger is measured with a ring sizer. When the ring size is known, a ring stick is used to get the correct length for the metal.

See the opposite page for a standard chart with the different measurements, letters, and numbers that apply to ring sticks in various countries.

I find a simpler, and even more accurate, way to measure for a ring, is as described on p. 112, where a length of binding is wrapped and tightened around the appropriate letter or number on the ring stick, snipped in half, straightened out, and then measured against a steel rule. Do not forget that this is the measurement for the inside diameter of the ring, and that just under twice the thickness of the metal used must be added to that measurement.

BRACELETS AND BANGLES

For a bracelet with a hinge, which will fit neatly around the wrist, the measurement can be taken with a tape measure or strip of paper, which you can then hold against a tape measure for a reading. Place this just above the wrist bone going up the arm. It will need to be a little larger for comfort. For a bangle, the measurement should be taken with the thumb tucked into the palm of the hand and the little finger tucked in as much as possible. Twice the thickness of the metal used should be added to this length.

An average measurement for a bracelet is between $6^1/_2$ and 8 inches (16–20 cm). The average measurement for a bangle is between 8 and 10 inches (20–25 cm).

NECKLACES

Manufactured chains are usually supplied in lengths of 16, 18, or 22 inches (40, 46, or 56 cm). Obviously chains and necklaces can be made to any length you like. Chokers, which usually keep their round shape, should have a diameter of at least 5 inches (13 cm).

Above: Gold rings, by Niessing.

CONVERSION CHART FOR RING SIZES

Inside diameter		Inside circumference		Sizes			
(in)	(mm)	(in)	(mm)	US, Canada	UK, Ireland, Australia, New Zealand	India, China, Japan, South America	Italy, Spain, Netherlands, Switzerland
0.522	13.26	1.64	41.7	2	D	2	1.75
0.53	13.46	1.67	42.3	2 1/4	D 1/2		2.25
0.538	13.67	1.69	42.9	2 1/2	E	3	3
0.546	13.87	1.72	43.6	2 3/4	E 1/2		3.5
0.554	14.07	1.74	44.2	3	F	4	4.25
0.562	14.27	1.77	44.8	3 1/4	F 1/2	5	4.75
0.57	14.48	1.79	45.5	3 1/2	G		5.5
0.578	14.68	1.82	46.1	3 3/4	G 1/2	6	6
0.586	14.88	1.84	46.8	4	H	7	6.75
0.594	15.09	1.87	47.4	4 1/4	H 1/2		7.5
0.602	15.29	1.89	48	4 1/2	I	8	8
0.61	15.49	1.92	48.7	4 3/4	J		8.75
0.618	15.7	1.94	49.3	5	J 1/2	9	9.25
0.626	15.9	1.97	50	5 1/4	K		10
0.634	16.1	1.99	50.6	5 1/2	K 1/2	10	10.5
0.642	16.31	2.02	51.2	5 3/4	L		11.25
0.65	16.51	2.04	51.9	6	L 1/2	11	11.75
0.658	16.71	2.07	52.5	6 1/4	M	12	12.5
0.666	16.92	2.09	53.1	6 1/2	M 1/2	13	13.25
0.674	17.12	2.12	53.8	6 3/4	N		13.75
0.682	17.32	2.14	54.4	7	N 1/2	14	14.5
0.69	17.53	2.17	55.1	7 1/4	O		15
0.698	17.73	2.19	55.7	7 1/2	O 1/2	15	15.75
0.706	17.93	2.22	56.3	7 3/4	P		16.25
0.714	18.14	2.24	57	8	P 1/2	16	17
0.722	18.34	2.27	57.6	8 1/4	Q		17.5
0.73	18.54	2.29	58.3	8 1/2	Q 1/2	17	18.25
0.738	18.75	2.32	58.9	8 3/4	R		19
0.746	18.95	2.34	59.5	9	R 1/2	18	19.5
0.754	19.15	2.37	60.2	9 1/4	S		20.25
0.762	19.35	2.39	60.8	9 1/2	S 1/2	19	20.75
0.77	19.56	2.42	61.4	9 3/4	T		21.5
0.778	19.76	2.44	62.1	10	T 1/2	20	22
0.786	19.96	2.47	62.7	10 1/4	U	21	22.75
0.794	20.17	2.49	63.4	10 1/2	U 1/2	22	23.25
0.802	20.37	2.52	64	10 3/4	V		24
0.81	20.57	2.54	64.6	11	V 1/2	23	24.75
0.818	20.78	2.57	65.3	11 1/4	W		25.25
0.826	20.98	2.59	65.9	11 1/2	W 1/2	24	26
0.834	21.18	2.62	66.6	11 3/4	X		26.5
0.842	21.39	2.65	67.2	12	X 1/2	25	27.25
0.85	21.59	2.67	67.8	12 1/4	Y		27.75
0.858	21.79	2.7	68.5	12 1/2	Z	26	28.5
0.866	22	2.72	69.1	12 3/4	Z 1/2		29

CALCULATIONS

CALCULATIONS

The circumference of a circle: diameter x pi (3.142)

The circumference of an oval: width + length, divided by 2, x pi (3.142) (+ twice the thickness of metal being used)

The carat weight of a stone: weight of the stone in grams x 5

Therefore a stone that weighs 0.75 g is 3.75 carats, and a stone that weighs 0.02 g will be a 10 pointer. Stones are measured by carat and up to one-hundredth of a carat.

Before ordering a supply of any metal, it is useful to know approximately how much it is going to cost. To calculate this, you will need a chart providing the specific gravity of different metals. Below is a chart showing the metals that are most commonly used.

SPECIFIC GRAVITY

Platinum	21.5	9-karat gold	11.5
Palladium	12.02	Silver 999	10.5
24-karat gold	19.32	Silver 925	10.4
22-karat gold	17.7	Copper	8.94
18-karat gold	16.5	Water	1.00
14-karat gold	14.5	Plexiglas	1.20

To find the weight, and therefore the cost, of a sheet of silver, 100 x 150 x 1.25 mm:

Multiply 100 x 150 x 1.25 = 18750

18750 x specific gravity of 925 silver (10.4) = 195000

Now divide by 1000 because we have done the calculation in millimeters. The weight of the silver is 195 g. If the price of silver is, for example $1.04 per gram, the piece will cost $202.80.

To find the weight, and therefore the cost, of a sheet of 18-karat gold, 60 x 7 x 1 mm:

Multiply 60 x 7 x 1 = 420

420 x specific gravity of 18-karat gold (16.5) = 6783

Divide by 1000 because we have done the calculation in millimeters. The weight of gold is 6.78 g. If the cost of 18-karat gold is, for example, $35.00 per gram, this will cost $237.30.

To find the cost of a length of wire 100 x 2 mm diameter:

Volume = pi x diameter x length

3.142 x 2 x 100 = 628.4

Volume x specific gravity = weight

628.4 x 10.4 = 6535.36

Divide by 1000 as we have worked in millimeters. The weight of gold is 6.53g. If the cost of the wire is $1.04 per gram, the cost will be 6.53 x $1.04 = $6.79.

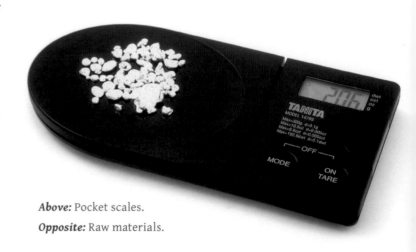

Above: Pocket scales.

Opposite: Raw materials.

15/32=11.90625

17/32=13.49375
19/32=15.08125
21/32=16.66875
23/32=18.25625
25/32=19.84375
27/32=21.43125
29/32=23.01875
31/32=24.60625

TEMPERATURE TABLES

ANNEALING TEMPERATURES

	Fahrenheit	Centigrade
Copper	700–1200	370–650
Brass	800–1380	430–750
Silver	1120–1300	600–700
Gold	1200–1380	650–750
Palladium	1470	800

Platinum:
to relieve stress 1100°F (600°C);
to soften 1830°F (1000°C)

SOLDER MELTING TEMPERATURES

	Hard	Medium	Easy
Silver	1370–1450°F (745–790°C)	1330–1410 (720–765)	1300–1340 (705–725)
9k gold	1390–1465 (755–795)	1355–1390 (735–755)	1200–1330 (650–720)
14k gold	1380–1445 (750–785)	1360–1390 (757–774)	1310–1350 (710–730)
18k gold	1450–1525 (790–830)	1415–1430 (765–781)	1290–1320 (700–715)

MELTING TEMPERATURES

	Fahrenheit	Centigrade
Aluminum	1215	655
Brass	1660	900
Copper	1981	1083
Pure gold	1945	1063
Iron	2797	1536
Lead	621	328
Nickel	2647	1453
Palladium	2826	1552
Platinum	3217	1769
Silver	1760	960
Tin	449	232
Titanium	3272	1800
Zinc	786	419

Opposite: Soldering.

COSTS

Ah, costs! This is always one of the most difficult tasks to get right. The information given here is very much a guide only, but includes a list of actual costs that must be accounted for when figuring out prices. There are two different structures for pricing: wholesale and retail.

WORKSHOP RUNNING EXPENSES

First, you will need to figure out your monthly expenses. When first setting up, it really does make sense, if at all possible, to find a small space at home where you can work. This will save you from paying rent each month. On the other hand, working from home can be quite isolating, so finding a workshop where others are also working can be very stimulating. Typical overheads may include:

• Rent for workshop
• Proportion of utilities
• Proportion of property taxes
• Insurance*

* It is also worth investing in a safe. There are only a few insurance companies that will deal with jewelers, and the costs can be astronomical. If you are careful, and everything is locked away at night, the affordable insurance will just cover the building, and possibly tools. Shop around to see what coverage you can get, but it is always a good idea to lock away precious materials and stones when not in use.

OTHER COSTS

• Advertising
• Hallmarking
• Metals
• Phone
• Postage
• Stationery
• Stones
• Subcontractors
• Tools
• Travel

WHAT SHOULD YOU CHARGE?

Find a realistic amount that you can charge per hour. The main thing is not to charge too much and then gradually increase the amount. Find out what others are charging per hour and try to stay competitive! As a rough guide, somewhere between $150 and $200 per day is average.

To make a profit, if you are selling wholesale you will need to add up all your costs and then add a small percentage, or whatever you think your wholesale buyer can bear. Also, add up to 40 percent to your metal costs to allow for wastage.

To start with, you may only be charging for your time and covering your costs. Remember, a buyer will add 100 percent to the prices you charge, so you have to know that the final retail price is realistic. Check out jewelry shows, stores, and galleries and see what pieces sell for. "Sale or return," whereby a sales agent pays for sold goods only, should be worked out at a slightly higher rate as the seller should not really be adding 100 percent to your price. But check first!

When selling directly into the retail market, making a profit is a little easier—but of course you will only be selling one piece at a time rather than in batches of 10 or 20. Your selling price should be comparable with your wholesaler's prices. If it is much cheaper, you will soon lose your wholesale buyer. Commissions should be priced slightly higher to allow for the extra time taken for discussing the commission with clients, as well as creating the designs.

Opposite: Silver metal clay pendant, by Esmeralda Woestenenk.

SELLING

WHOLESALE

To get your work seen by as many potential outlets as possible, it is a good idea to prepare a collection to sell at a trade show (see overleaf). Even the smallest stand will cost a great deal by the time the electricity, screens, and any extras are paid for, so it is worth making a really good display for your work. If the outlay is too much, then think about sharing a stand with a colleague. Before committing to a show it is advisable to visit it—probably a year in advance so that there are no big surprises when you eventually participate. Here are some considerations:

1. Make your stand as flexible as possible. Stands usually come in a "shell" scheme and can be different sizes.
2. Do not make any cabinets or shelves, etc., heavier than you can carry—or make sure you have a suitable way to transport them.
3. Try to make your stand as welcoming as possible. Visitors often welcome a chance to sit down and have somewhere to put down their bags while talking to exhibitors and choosing what to buy.
4. Have plenty of catalogs to give out. These should show photos of everything, along with a short description of the materials and stones used. All of your work should be given codes, so that ordering is straightfoward. It is better if the price list is a separate item as this may need amending sooner than the catalog. Terms and conditions should also be included. To ask for payment within 30 days is fair, although if you are lucky enough to sell to a large outlet, you may have to wait at least three months for payment. Name, address, phone number, website, and e-mail address should all be nicely visible too.
5. You should have a website. You may want to have two different means of entry—one for wholesale customers and the other for retail. Payment online costs more to set up, and since an electronic bank transfer is so easy these days, I would recommend that to start with.

6. Make sure you have order forms printed up so that both you and your customer have a copy.
7. Be realistic about delivery dates and think about postage costs. Are they going to be added onto the price or will you include postage in the price?
8. It is usual, if you have not dealt with a customer beforehand, to ask for pro forma payment. This means that you send the bill before sending the goods, and do not release the goods until it has been paid. Once customers start to make repeat orders, the 30-day payment can be made.
9. Trade customers are a demanding group and will keep you on your toes! They expect to see new things every time they see you at a show. So, if you are bursting with ideas, hold some back to introduce at decent intervals!
10. Even if you are having a bad day, SMILE! It will get better.
11. Make phone calls to follow up with customers who have been interested but have not yet placed an order.

SALE OR RETURN

Most small outlets, such as specialist galleries, will ask you to do sale or return, and in many cases it is better to have work out there in a good gallery, rather than it sitting in the safe in the workshop. However, it is often very slow getting payment for anything that has sold, and after six months or so, when your unsold work is returned, it can be quite grubby (having been handled) and quite possibly have firescale owing to the bright lights used for display. The best advice I can give is to keep well abreast of all your sale or return galleries and be prepared to have to size rings, make slight alterations, set a different stone etc., which you must charge for! Some of the most prestigious galleries only work on SOR, so if you are invited to display your work it is wonderful for your reputation. Just make sure you know, and are happy with, what sort of percentage they will be adding to your work before you agree to supply them.

COMMISSIONS

The most important thing about a commission is that both you and the client are perfectly clear about everything. That includes the materials, the stone or stones, the size, the length, the design, and the cost. If a client is unsure about what they want, find out a little about what they do and do not like and then sketch a few designs with materials indicated and an estimated cost for each. Once a design has been decided upon, the estimate can be made into a definite cost, with a possible proviso made for fluctuation in metal prices. Once this is agreed, a deposit should be paid and any ring size or other fitting should be confirmed before any stones are set.

RETAIL SHOWS

Much of what has been said about trade shows applies to retail shows, although catalogs and price lists are not so crucial. These shows require a more personal approach—getting to know your customers and having them build up trust in your work. Stand fees can be quite hefty, so if you are considering generally doing retail shows, join a guild (see p. 302), as stands are less expensive and venues can be quite varied. A few pointers:

1. You will need to design your stand because shell schemes are not always available. Allocated space may vary, so make your stand flexible.
2. Lighting is important, so take extension cables with you. Figure out how you are going to display your work before you go, as set-up time is often quite short.
3. Business cards are a must. These can be postcard size with a good picture of your work on the front, or just a well-designed card to hand out.

4. Take a price list and, where necessary, use neat tags to either number your work with a code or price pieces individually.
5. At the end of the day you will need to remove all of your work, then set it up again the next day. Handle your pieces carefully and wear a pair of cotton gloves so that no fingerprints are left on the metal.
6. Many retail shows are held in marquees. These sometimes will have uneven floors, so take some wooden wedges with you to keep your stands upright. Marquees can also get cold, so be prepared. Remember, too, to take an electric fan with you in the summer—you and your customers will appreciate it.
7. Invest in a machine that takes credit card payments. Most customers do not carry check books—or wads of cash.
8. Have a supply of presentation boxes, to fit rings, earrings, bangles, necklaces, etc. Suppliers will usually print your logo free of charge, but make sure to order them in time.
9. It is useful to have a helper at your stand. If that is not possible, when you need to leave your stand ask your neighbor to keep an eye on it for you and then offer to do the same for them. Eat away from your stand if possible—apart from looking strange, it is a nightmare trying to show a potential customer a ring when you have mayonnaise on your fingers!

TRADE SHOWS

To do well in the wholesale market you will need to start with some interesting and original ideas. It is not necessary to start "big"—you can try out your ideas on a fairly small scale, being confident that you can reproduce what you are selling in a reasonable time.

Customers, which generally means stores, do not like waiting more than six to eight weeks for their order. It is really important when selling wholesale to have a good website—one that is easily navigated and where the products are clear. When you start, it is not necessary to have online payment facilities, as most companies will require at least a month after receiving the goods to submit payment. Consider, too, whether you can afford to give small discounts for very prompt payments and for orders over a certain amount.

Trade shows usually last between three and five days and you will need a day to set up beforehand.

About J
Vicenza, Italy
www.aboutj.it

Australian Jewellery Fair
Melbourne, Australia
www.jewelleryfair.com.au

Autumn Fair International
Birmingham, UK
www.autumnfair.com

Baselworld
Basel, Switzerland
www.baselworld.com

China International Gold, Jewellery & Gem Fair
Shanghai & Shenzhen, China
exhibitions.jewellerynetasia.com

Collect: International Art Fair for Contemporary Objects
London, UK
www.craftscouncil.org.uk/collect

Left: Silver eardrops with rough-cut lapis lazuli and Afghan turquoise, by Jinks McGrath.

The Couture Show
Las Vegas, USA
www.nationaljeweler.com

Expo Prestige
Montreal, Canada
www.cbq.qc.ca/QJC.html

Goldsmiths' Fair
London, UK
www.thegoldsmiths.co.uk

Home and Gift Show
Harrogate, UK
www.homeandgift.co.uk

Iberjoya
Madrid, Spain
www.ifema.es

Inhorgenta
Munich, Germany
www.inhorgenta.com

Intergem Messe
Idar-Oberstein, Germany
www.intergem-messe.de

**The International Gem
and Jewelry Show**
Various cities, USA
www.intergem.com

International Jewellery Fair
Sydney, Australia
www.internationaljewelleryfair.com.au

International Jewellery London
London, UK
www.jewellerylondon.com

International Jewellery Tokyo
Tokyo, Japan
www.ijt.jp

JA New York
New York, USA
www.nationaljeweler.com

Japan Jewellery Fair
Tokyo, Japan
www.japanjewelleryfair.com

JCK Las Vegas
Las Vegas, USA
lasvegas.jckonline.com

The Jewellery Show London
London, UK
www.thejewelleryshowlondon.com

Jewellery Week
London, UK
www.jewelleryweek.com

JOGS Tuscon Gem and Jewelry Show
Tuscon, USA
jogsshow.com

Mumbai Jewellery & Gem Fair
Mumbai, India
www.jewelleryfair.in

Origin at Somerset House
London, UK
www.somersethouse.org.uk

**SIERRAD International Jewellery
Art Fair**
Amsterdam, the Netherlands
www.sieraadartfair.com

SOFA Art & Design Fairs
Chicago and New York, USA
www.sofaexpo.com

Spring Fair International
Birmingham, UK
www.springfair.com

Top Drawer
London, UK
www.topdrawer.co.uk

EDUCATION

I guess if you are reading this, you may have already started, or have an interest in, making jewelry. There are many different opportunities for pursuing your interest and it is sometimes a bit of a minefield to find the right one for you. Some of the possibilities are given here, although there are many other options, too.

DEGREE COURSES

A degree course will usually take about four years to complete. It is good to take a foundation course first, as this helps to steer you in the right direction and helps you choose the right college. Degree courses often take a more intellectual approach to designing and making than other courses, but in the end, you do receive a Batchelor of Arts degree and, if you are so inclined, you can then follow up with further study by completing an MA. Some colleges also offer part-time courses, which will take a bit longer.

APPRENTICESHIPS

Hopefully, apprenticeships are on the increase, although, talking to friends and collegues, it seems as if they are still few and far between for those wishing to start a career in jewelry making. If you can get on an apprenticeship track, it is a marvelous way of learning—with practical experience at the bench from skilled makers, and then going to college perhaps one day a week. This is also a great way to build up a good list of suppliers and contacts, and to learn how the jewelry business works.

DAYTIME AND EVENING CLASSES

Many boutique jewelry stores and galleries now offer day, evening, and weekend classes on a weekly basis. These can be really helpful. Apart from learning all the techniques used for making jewelry, you get to use equipment that you may not have in your own workshop. This is also a good way to be inspired by others taking the same course but doing something completely different. Keep a look out in your local newspapers to see where you can take such a course, or pop into your nearest jewelry store—they will usually know where such classes are being offered.

ADULT EDUCATION COURSES

Some of these courses can be great, but I would advise checking out the premises and what sort of equipment there is before signing up. I was once asked to run one of these courses, and the room allocated for the class turned out to be a kitchen—hardly conducive for bench work! There can also be a large number of students in these courses, so with just one very hard-pushed instructor, getting enough attention can be a challenge.

COLLEGES

Alberta College of Art + Design
Alberta, Canada
www.acad.ca

Alchimia Contemporary Jewellery School
Florence, Italy
www.alchimia.it

American Jewelers Institute
Portland, USA
www.jewelersacademy.com

American School of Jewelry
Fort Lauderdale, USA
www.jewelryschool.net

Le Arti Orafe Contemporary Jewellery School & Academy
Florence, Italy
www.artiorafe.it

Australian National University
Canberra, Australia
www.anu.edu.au

Birmimgham City University
Birmingham, UK
www.bcu.acu.uk

California College of the Arts
San Francisco and Oakland, USA
www.cca.edu

Central St Martins College of Arts and Design
London, UK
www.csm.arts.ac.uk

Cranbrook Academy
Bloomfield Hills, Michigan, USA
www.cranbrookart.edu

Edinburgh College of Art
Edinburgh, UK
www.ed.ac.uk

Fashion Institute of Technology
New York, USA
www.fitnyc.edu

Glasgow School of Art
Glasgow, UK
www.gsa.ac.uk

Goldsmiths College
London, UK
www.gold.ac.uk

Hiko Mizuno College of Jewelry
Tokyo and Osaka, Japan
www.hikohiko.jp

Hochschule Trier
Trier, Germany
www.hochschule-trier.de

London Jewellery School
London, UK
www.londonjewelleryschool.co.uk

London Metropolitan University
London, UK
www.londonmet.ac.uk

Maastricht Academy of Fine Arts and Design
Maastricht, the Netherlands
www.abkmaastricht.nl

Rhode Island School of Design
Providence, USA
www.risd.edu

Royal College of Art
London, UK
www.rca.ac.uk

Rochester Institute of Technology
Rochester, USA
www.rit.edu

Sint Lucas Antwerpen
Antwerp, Belgium
www.sintlucasantwerpen.be

University of the Arts
London, UK
www.arts.ac.uk

University for the Creative Arts
Farnham, UK
www.ucreative.ac.uk

University of Lincoln
Lincoln, UK
www.lincoln.ac.uk

FURTHER READING

BOOKS

Following is a list of good reading. Some of these books you will just want to dip in and out of, and some of the bigger ones are pretty expensive, but all are worthwhile!

PRACTICAL BOOKS

The Art of Enameling
Linda Darty. Lark Books, 2005.

Centrifugal or Lost Wax Jewelry Casting
Murray Bovin. Grobet File, 1973.

Classical Loop-in-Loop Chains
Jean Reist Stark and Josephine Reist Smith. Brynmorgen Press, 1999.

The Complete Metalsmith
Tim McCreight. Davis Publishing Co., 1991.

Creative Gold and Silversmithing
Sharr Choate. Crown Publishers, 1988.

Creative Stonesetting
John Cogswell. Brynmorgen Press, 2008.

Curious Lore of Precious Stones
George Kunz. Kessinger, 2003.

Enamelling
Ruth Ball. A & C Black, 2006.

Enameling on Metal
Oppi Untracht. Gazelle, 1983.

Engraving on Precious Metals
A. Brittain and P. Morton. NAG Press, 1993.

Form Emphasis for Metalsmiths
Heikki Seppa. Kent State University Press, 1992.

First Steps in Enameling
Jinks McGrath. Book Sales Inc., 1994.

The Jeweler's Directory of Decorative Finishes: From Enameling and Engraving to Inlay and Granulation
Jinks McGrath. Krause, 2005.

The Jeweler's Directory of Gemstones
Judith Crowe. Firefly Books, 2012.

Jewelry: Concepts and Technology
Oppi Untracht. Robert Hale, 1985.

Metalwork and Enamelling
Herbert Maryon. Dover, 2011.

The New Encyclopedia Of Jewelry-Making Techniques: A Comprehensive Visual Guide to Traditional and Contemporary Techniques
Jinks McGrath. Running Press, 2010.

The Platinum Bench
Jurgen Maerz. MJSA/AJM Press, 2002.

Silversmithing for Jewelry Makers
Elizabeth Bone. Interweave, 2012

Silverwork and Jewellery
H. Wilson. BibiloBazaar, 2010.

Stonesetting for Contemporary Jewelry Makers
Melissa Hunt. St. Martin's Griffin, 2012

The Theory & Practice of Goldsmithing
Erhard Brepohl, Tim McCreight, Charles Lewton-Brain. Brynmorgen Press, 2001.

BOOKS FOR INSPIRATION!

Lark Jewelry Books: 500 Bracelets, 500 Brooches, 500 Earrings, 500 Necklaces, 1000 Rings
Lark Books, 2005; 2005; 2007; 2008; 2004.

Traditional Jewellery of India
Oppi Untracht. Thames and Hudson, 2008.

MAGAZINES

Art Jewelry Magazine
www.artjewelrymag.com

Craft & Design
www.craftanddesign.net

Crafts Magazine
www.craftscouncil.org.uk/crafts-magazine

Findings
www.acj.org.uk/index.php/findings

Lapidary Journal Jewelry Artist
*www.jewelrymakingdaily.com/blogs/
jewelryartistmagazine/default.aspx*

Metalsmith
*www.snagmetalsmith.org/metalsmith-
magazine/about-metalsmith*

Professional Jeweller
www.professionaljeweller.com

Retail Jeweller
www.retail-jeweller.com

Schmuck Magazin
www.schmuckmagazin.de

WEBSITES

The best online site I have found is the Ganoskin Project—practicing jewelers and authors give good advice about many different aspects of jewelry making. Other good sites for technical information are the Goldsmiths' Company, and for information on working with platinum and palladium, Johnson Matthey.

The Aspiring Metalsmiths
aspiringmetalsmiths.blogspot.co.uk

Ethical Metalsmiths
ethicalmetalsmiths.org

The Ganoksin Project
www.ganoksin.com

The Goldsmiths' Company
www.thegoldsmiths.co.uk

Jewelry Making Daily
www.jewelrymakingdaily.com

Johnson Matthey
www.johnsonmattheyny.com

Klimt 02 International Art Jewellery Online
www.klimt02.net

Metalcyberspace
www.metalcyberspace.com

Metalsmiths Unite
metalsmithsunite.blogspot.com

GUILDS AND ASSOCIATIONS

In addition to the following selection of guilds and associations, most regional areas will also have their own local guilds.

AFRICA

Jewellery Council of South Africa
www.jewellery.org.za

ASIA & FAR EAST

Delhi Jewellers Association
delhijewellersassociation.com

Federation of Goldsmith and Jewellers Association of Malaysia
fgjam.org.my

Gem & Jewellery Export Promotion Council
www.gjepc.org

Gemmological Association of Hong Kong
www.gahk.org

Hong Kong Jewelry Manufacturers' Association Limited
www.jewelry.org.hk

International Colored Gemstone Association (Hong Kong)
www.gemstone.org

Japan Jewellery Association
www.jja.ne.jp

Japan Jewellery Designers Association
www.jjda.or.jp

Singapore Jewellers Association
www.sja.org.sg

Sri Lanka Gem & Jewellery Association
www.slgja.org

Thai Gem and Jewelry Traders' Association
www.thaigemjewelry.or.th

AUSTRALIA

Gold and Silversmiths Guild of Australia
www.gsga.org.au

Gemmological Association of Australia
www.gem.org.au

Jewellers Association of Australia
www.jaa.com.au

Jewellers and Metalsmiths Group of Australia
www.jmgansw.org.au

Jewellers & Metalsmiths Group of Queensland
www.visualartist.info

Silver Society of Australia
www.silversociety.com.au

BELGIUM

Antwerp Diamond Jewellers Association
www.adja.be

Societe Belge de Gemmologie A.S.B.L.
www.gemmology.be

CANADA

Canadian Gemmological Association
www.canadiangemmological.com

Canadian Jewellers Association
www.canadianjewellers.com

Canadian Jewellery Group
canadianjewellerygroup.ca

Metal Arts Guild of Canada
www.metalartsguild.ca

Responsible Jewellery Council
www.responsiblejewellery.com

Silver Society of Canada
www.silversocietyofcanada.ca

FINLAND

Finnish Goldsmith Association
www.suomenkultaseppienliitto.fi

Finnish Silversmiths Association
www.suomenhopeasepat.fi

FRANCE

Ateliers d'Art de France
www.ateliersdart.com

Institut National des Métiers d'Art
www.institut-metiersdart.org

GERMANY

Association for Goldsmiths' Art
www.gfg-hanau.de

German Crafts Association
www.bundesverband-kunsthandwerk.de

IRELAND

Crafts Council of Ireland
www.ccoi.ie

CraftinIreland
www.craftinireland.com

Federation of Jewellery Manufacturers of Ireland
www.fjmi.com

Irish Jewellers' Association
www.irish-jewellers-association.com

Retail Jewellers of Ireland
www.rji.ie

ISRAEL

Israel Jewelry Manufacturers' Association
www.ijma.org.il

ITALY

Assogemme (Italian Association of Gem and Precious Stone Companies)
www.assogemme.it

NEPAL

Nepal Gem and Jewellery Association
www.negja.org.np

NEW ZEALAND

Nga Taonga a Hine-te-iwa-iwa
craftinfo.org.nz

Jewellers Association of New Zealand
www.retail.org.nz

POLAND

Goldsmithing Artists' Association
www.zlotnictwo.info

SPAIN

Spanish Association of Jewelers
www.iberjoya.es

SEBIME: Spanish Fashion Jewellery Manufacturers Association
www.sebime.org

SWITZERLAND

CIBJO—The World Jewellery Confederation
www.cibjo.org

UK

Association for Contemporary Jewellery
www.acj.org.uk

British Jewellers' Association
www.bja.org.uk

Crafts Council
www.craftscouncil.org.uk

Design Nation
www.designnation.co.uk

Designer Jewellers Group
www.designerjewellersgroup.co.uk

Gemmological Association of Great Britain
www.gem-a.com

Goldsmiths' Company
www.thegoldsmiths.co.uk

Guild of Jewellery Designers
www.guildofjewellerydesigners.co.uk

Institute of Professional Goldsmiths
www.ipgoldsmiths.co.uk

National Association of Goldsmiths of Great Britain and Ireland
www.jewellers-online.org

Platinum Guild International
www.platinumguild.co.uk

Scottish Gemmological Association
www.scotgem.com

Silver Society
www.thesilversociety.org

Silver Trust
www.silvertrust.co.uk

World Gold Council
www.gold.org

GUILDS AND ASSOCIATIONS (CONT.)

USA

American Gem Society
www.americangemsociety.org

American Gem Trade Association
www.agta.org

American Jewelry Design Council
www.ajdc.org

American Society of Jewelry Historians
jewelryhistorians.org

Art Jewelry Forum
www.artjewelryforum.org

Chicago Metal Arts Guild
chicagometalartsguild.com

Colorado Metalsmithing Association
www.coloradometalsmiths.org

Contemporary Jewelry Design Group
www.cjdgjewelers.org

Ethical Metalsmiths
www.ethicalmetalsmiths.org

Fashion Jewelry and Accessories Trade Association
fjata.org

Florida Society of Goldsmiths
www.fsg4u.com

Ganoksin Project
www.ganoksin.com

Gemological Institute of America
www.gia.edu

Indian Arts & Crafts Association
www.iaca.com

International Fine Jewelers Guild
www.internationalfinejewelersguild.com

Jewelers of America
www.jewelers.org

Jewelry Design Professionals' Network
www.jdpn.org

Manufacturing Jewelers & Suppliers of America
www.mjsa.org

Metal Arts Guild San Francisco
metalartsguildsf.org

Mid-America Jewelers Association
www.midamericajewelers.org

Mineralogical Society of America
www.minsocam.org

New England Jewelers Association
newenglandjewelers.net

New Jersey Metal Arts Guild
www.njmag.org

New York State Jewelers Association
www.newyorkjewelers.org

North Carolina Society of Goldsmiths
ncsg.net

Pennsylvania Society of Goldsmiths
www.pagoldsmiths.org

Seattle Metals Guild
www.seattlemetalsguild.org

Silver Institute
www.silverinstitute.org

Silver Users Association
www.silverusersassociation.org

Society of American Silversmiths
www.silversmithing.com

Society for Midwest Metalsmiths
www.midwest-metalsmiths.org

Society of North American Goldsmiths
www.snagmetalsmith.org

Southwestern Association For Indian Arts
swaia.org

GALLERIES AND MUSEUMS

Alternatives
Rome, Italy
www.alternatives.it

British Museum
London, UK
www.britishmuseum.org

CODA
Apeldoorn, the Netherlands
www.coda-apeldoorn.nl

Contemporary Applied Arts
London, UK
www.caa.org.uk

Danner Rotunda, Die Neue Sammlung
Munich, Germany
die-neue-sammlung.de

Deux Poissons
Tokyo, Japan
www.deuxpoissons.com

e.g.etal
Melbourne, Australia
egetal.com.au

Galerie Marzee
Nijmegen, the Netherlands
www.marzee.nl/galerie

Galerie Rob Koudjis
Amsterdam, the Netherlands
www.galerierobkoudijs.nl

Houston Center for Contemporary Craft
Houston, USA
www.crafthouston.org

Lesley Craze Gallery
London, UK
www.lesleycrazegallery.co.uk

LOD
Stockholm, Sweden
www.lod.nu

MMKA
Arnhem, the Netherlands
www.mmkarnhem.nl

MUDAC
Lausanne, Switzerland
www.mudac.ch

Musée des Arts décoratifs
Paris, France
www.lesartsdecoratifs.fr

Museum of Arts and Design
New York, USA
madmuseum.org

Museum of Contemporary Craft
Portland, USA
mocc.pnca.edu

Museum of Fine Arts
Boston, USA
www.mfa.org

The National Ornamental Metal Museum
Memphis, USA
www.metalmuseum.org

OONA
Berlin, Germany
www.oona-galerie.de

Ornamentum
Hudson, USA
www.ornamentumgallery.com

Schmuckmuseum
Pforzheim, Germany
www.schmuckmuseum.de

Velvet Da Vinci
San Francisco, USA
www.velvetdavinci.com

Victoria and Albert Museum
London, UK
www.vam.ac.uk

World Jewellery Museum
Seoul, Korea
www.wjmuseum.com

SUPPLIERS

Although some are more specialty suppliers, many suppliers listed below provide a full range of products, from tools through to chemicals, metals, and books. All offer an online ordering service; some offer a next-day service.

TOOLS

Allcraft Tool and Supply
www.allcraftusa.com

Bloomsteins of Brighton
bloomsteins.co.uk

Buck and Ryan
www.buckandryan.co.uk

Cooksons
www.cooksongold.com

Durston Rolling Mills
www.durston.co.uk

Gesswein
www.gesswein.com

H.S. Walsh
www.hswalsh.com

J. Schmalz
J-schmalz.de

Jewelry Supply
www.jewelrysupply.com

Karl Fischer GmbH
goldschmiedebedarf.de

Lacy & Company Ltd.
lacytools.ca

Lacy West Supplies Ltd.
lacywest.com

Metalliferous
www.metalliferous.com

Myron Toback
www.myrontoback.com

Otto Frei
www.ottofrei.com

Rio Grande
www.riogrande.com

Schöne Edelmetaal B.V.
Schone.nl

Shesto
www.shesto.co.uk

Sutton Tools
www.suttontools.co.uk

ENAMELING

Thompson Enamel
www.thompsonenamel.com

Vitrum Signum
v1.vitrumsignum.com

WG Ball
www.wgball.co.uk

GEMS

Capital Gems
www.capitalgems.com

Fire Mountain Gems
www.firemountaingems.com

Holts
www.holtsgems.com

Ward Gemstones
www.aewgems.co.uk

METALS

C. Hafner GmbH & Co.
c-hafner.com

C. R. Hill Company
www.crhill.com

David H. Fell & Company
www.dhfco.com

Hauser & Miller
www.hauserandmiller.com

Johnson Matthey
www.jewellery.noble.matthey.com

Rashbel

www.rashbel.com

Rudgwick Metals

www.rudgwickmetals.co.uk

T. B. Hagstoz & Son

hagstoz.com

Umicore Precious Metals Canada & USA

www.umicorepreciousmetals.com

Alec Tiranti

www.tiranti.co.uk

Kassoy

www.kassoy.com

Noble

www.noblepack.com

Potters

www.pottersuk.com

Above: Enamel stored in air-tight jars.

FURTHER TECHNIQUES

While we have discussed metalsmithing in some detail in this book, here are a few more techniques you might want to learn more about.

ENAMEL

Although a few enameling exercises appear on pp. 254-59, enameling is a big enough discipline to warrant a book of its own, and there are several very good ones that you can refer to (see p. 300).

An enamel finish can be opaque, translucent, or transparent, and it can provide a piece with a variety of colors that would be difficult to achieve any other way. It does takes time, though—count on doubling your time on a piece if you are enameling it. The scope for design opens up hugely when enameling is added to your repertoire—it sits well with both faceted and cabochon stones; it can be used on castings; and it can be used like a stained-glass window, placed in open cells so that the light shines through. Transparent enamels allow the metal behind them to reflect through. Translucent enamels, which depend on firing temperature for their translucency, allow a metal to be seen through them, but in a less obvious way.

Suppliers will provide color charts for their enamels. Enamel can be purchased either already finely ground or in "frit" form, consisting of lumps of all shapes and sizes, which need to be ground down with a mortar and pestle before use. Enamels come as hard, medium, or soft, and this dictates the temperature at which they are fired—generally the hard ones have the highest firing and the soft ones the lowest.

FILIGREE

Although a highly specialized artform in itself, carried out by expert craftsmen, filigree employs many of the basic wireworking processes described in this book.

This detailed technique, popular in West Africa and India, employs fine twisted silver wire, worked within a framework of slightly larger plain or twisted wire. It requires patience and a steady hand! The fineness of the wires enables jewelry to be made larger than usual, yet light to wear.

The framework is made of 18–24-gauge wire (1–0.5 mm), while the inside filigree work uses 22–28 gauge (0.3–0.6 mm). The wire is usually silver, gold, or platinum, and is annealed before twisting. Lengths up to 10 feet (3 meters) of the finer wires are straightened, stretched, then bent in half, with the ends held in a vise, and the other end looped over a hook fastened into a drill. The drill handle is then turned to create a tight, even twist all the way up the wire.

The wire is then flattened, and lengths are cut off, spiraled, and shaped to fit the desired pattern, then placed in the frame before soldering. The entire piece is then soldered, pickled, rinsed, and dried. Filigree can be polished in a barrel polisher or, after pickling, the top edges can be brightened with a burnisher, providing a lovely contrast with the matte finish of the inside wires.

Opposite: Silver filigree earrings, by Jinks McGrath.

GLOSSARY

ALLOY

A substance composed of two or more metals or of one metal and one nonmetal, which have been fused together when molten.

ANNEALING

The process of heating a metal to reduce the stresses that have built up as the metal has been worked.

ATOMIC WEIGHT

The weight of one atom of a metal compared with one atom of water.

BASE METALS

A group of metals that are less resistant to corrosion than noble metals. They occur more commonly than noble metals.

CABOCHON STONE

A stone that has been shaped and polished, usually with a convex top and a flat bottom. This type of cut is usually applied to opaque stones.

CARAT

The unit of mass used for measuring gemstones and pearls. One carat is 200 mg and stones are measured to the nearest hundredth of a carat.

CONDUCTIVITY

The capacity of a metal to conduct heat.

DOMING

A technique used for creating a concave or convex surface in a circular or oval-shaped piece of metal using a doming block and round or oval-ended punches.

DUCTILITY

The ability of a metal to be drawn out into a wire or stretched through a rolling mill.

ENAMELING

The process of fusing layers of glass onto a metallic surface.

ENGRAVING

A surface technique where slivers of metal are removed with a cutting tool.

FACETED STONE

A stone that is cut with flat faces on its surface. This style of cut is usually applied to transparent stones.

FORGING

A process of creating a shape and texture by hammering metal.

FIRESCALE

A layer of oxide that forms on the surface of silver when it is worked at high temperatures. It is caused by oxygen mixing with the copper content in silver.

FUSING

A technique for joining one piece of metal to another by heating the surface of the metal until it starts to melt and move. No solder is used for fusing.

GRANULATION

A decorative technique where tiny balls of gold or silver are fused to a metal's surface.

IMPRINTING

A surface decoration technique where a sheet of metal is passed through a rolling mill to create an impression on it.

INLAY

The decorative technique of setting one material into the recessed area of another, contrasting material.

KARAT

The unit of purity for gold, equal to $1/24$. Pure gold is 24 karat.

MALLEABILITY

The measure of how easily a metal can be worked.

MOKUME GANE

A technique where very thin layers of metal are combined, then compressed so that the different layers are revealed.

NOBLE METALS

A group of metals that are highly resistant to chemical reaction and corrosion. They occur more rarely than base metals.

NONFERROUS METALS

Any kind of metal that does not contain iron. A nonferrous metal is not prone to rusting.

NONPRECIOUS METALS

See Base Metals.

PATINATION

A change in the original appearance of the surface of a metal, which can be done for decorative purposes.

PICKLING

A treatment applied to a metal's surface to remove impurities.

PRECIOUS METALS

See Noble Metals.

QUENCHING

The process of rapidly cooling a piece of metal before working on it further.

RAISING

The technique of hammering metal against a solid form to shape it; often used to make bowls and spoons.

REPOUSSÉ AND CHASING

A technique used to make a three-dimensional piece where the design is pushed up from the back of a metal sheet. Lines are then drawn on the front of a metal sheet, defining the areas raised by repoussé.

RETICULATION

A heating technique that brings the fine silver in a sheet of sterling silver to the surface, while the interior of the sheet remains as sterling silver.

SOLDERING

The process of joining one piece of metal to another by applying pieces of solder and heat.

SPECIFIC GRAVITY

The ratio of the weight/mass of a given volume of metal to that of a given volume of water.

INDEX

INDEX

INDEX

CONTRIBUTORS

Gordon Aatlo Designs
www.gordonaatlo.com
Photos by Kelly Allen/Gordon Aatlo
Designs and Lee-Carraher Photography

Dauvit Alexander
www.justified-sinner.com

Sabine Amtsberg
www.sabinea.com

Maria Apostolou
www.createjewelry.gr
Photos by Ioannis Tissizis

Ruth Ball
ruthball.weebly.com

Anna Bario
www.bario-neal.com
Photos by Alyssa Robb

Nicole Barr
www.nicolebarr.com

Hannah Bedford
www.hannahbedford.co.uk
Photos by Jeremy Johns and Keith
Leighton

Helena Bogucki
www.helenabogucki.com
Photos by Bewley Shaylor

Heather Braun
www.dalkullanjewelry.etsy.com

Gillie Hoyte Byrom
www.enamelportraitminiatures.co.uk

Michelle Chang
www.michellechang.com

Barbara Christie
www.barbarachristie.com

Andy Cooperman
www.andycooperman.com

Giovanni Corvaja
www.giovanni-corvaja.com

Carrie Crocker
www.carolyncrocker.com

Rachel Emmerson
www.rachelemmerson.com

Fish Enterprises
www.fineenamels.com

Mabel Hassell
www.mabelhasell.com
Photos by Emily Hassell

Elena Howell
www.tomtomjewelry.com

Marina Lampropoulou
www.tothemetal.com

Elan Lee-Vance
www.hapagirls.etsy.com

Alison Lesniack
www.copperheartdesigns.com

Emmanuelle Le Fur

Stephanie Maslow-Blackman
www.metalicious.com

Tamara McFarland
www.mcfarlanddesigns.com

Melissa McGraw Petrusch
www.woowooworkshop.com

Betsy Menson Sio
www.eaststreettins.etsy.com

Doron Merav
www.doronmerav.com
Photos by Anat Merav

Christine Mighion
www.christinemighion.com

Kirsten Muenster
www.kirstenmuensterjewelry.com
Photos by Hap Sakwa

Lilia Nash
www.liliandesigns.co.uk
Photos by Steven Nash

Page Neal
www.bario-neal.com
Photos by Alyssa Robb

Cynthia Nge
www.minicyn.etsy.com

Niessing
www.niessing.com

Shauna O'Brien
www.vivileejewelry.etsy.com

Delia O'Farrell
www.fiorejewellery.etsy.com

Meghan O'Rourke
www.meghanorourkejewellery.com
Photos by Tom Roschi

Malou Paul
www.maloupaul.nl

Felicity Peters
www.felicitypeters.com
Photos by Victor France

Beth Pohlman
www.bethpohlman.com
Photos by Joseph Hyde

Alexandra Raphael
www.araphael.co.uk
Photos by Richard Valence

Meghan Riley
www.meghanpatriceriley.com
Photos by Toky Photography

Iris Saar Isaacs
www.nsyncdesign.com.au
Photos by Ben Hermans

Regine Schwarzer
www.regineschwarzer.com
Photos by Grant Hancock, Simon Hill,
Michael Haines, and Steve Wilson

Sakurako Shimizu
www.sakurakoshimizu.com
Photos by Takateru Yamada

Anna Siivonen
www.silverlera.nu

Graham Stewart
www.grahamstewartsilversmith.co.uk
Photos by Shannon Tofts

L. Sue Szabo
www.lsueszabo.com
Photos by L. Sue Szabo and Ericka
Crissman (painted enamel)

Amy Tavern
www.amytavern.com
Photos by Hank Drew

Liz Tonkin
www.etsy.com/people/liztonkin

Karola Torkos
www.karakola.com

Janos Varga
www.blindspotjewellery.carbonmade.com

Mary Walke
www.marymaryhandmade.etsy.com
Photos by Alan Walke

Vanessa Williams
www.vrwjewellery.wix.com/vrw
Photos by Grant Hancock, Kara
Growden, and Craig Arnold

Esmeralda Woestenenk
www.silverblueberry.etsy.com

Kaleen Wolfe
www.flirtandflutter.etsy.com

Neta Wolpe
www.netawolpe.co.il
Photos by Taron Tsezana

OTHER CONTRIBUTORS

Cookson Precious Metals
www.cooksongold.com

Durston Rolling Mills
www.durston.co.uk

Rofin-Baasel UK Ltd
www.rofin.co.uk

Sutton Tools
www.suttontools.co.uk

ACKNOWLEDGMENTS

My warm thanks go to those who have provided interviews and very useful information for inclusion in the book.

Nick Castleden, Andy Cooperman, Marcus Cornish, Giovanni Corvaja, Fleur Grenier, Felicity Peters, Erica Sharpe, Graham Stewart, and Penny Warren. Thanks also to everyone who provided photos of work.

Many thanks to Sam le Prevost for his help in the workshop, and Jen and Michael for keeping the stress levels down during the workbench photo sessions.

Many thanks also to Myron Kliewer at Fish Enterprises Thailand, for sharing his knowledge of lasers and CAD/CAM.

My main thanks go to Barbara Christie, for her truly inspirational work, which has been a source of delight and intrigue all my working life. She was one of a kind.